INDIA AND THE UNITED STATES

INDIA AND THE UNITED STATES

By
Naunihal Singh

ANMOL PUBLICATIONS PVT. LTD.
NEW DELHI - 110 002 (INDIA)

ANMOL PUBLICATIONS PVT. LTD.
4374/4B, Ansari Road, Daryaganj
New Delhi - 110 002
Ph.: 23261597, 23278000
Visit us at: www.anmolpublications.com

India and the United States

First Published, 2005

ISBN 81-261-2185-8

PRINTED IN INDIA

Published by J.L. Kumar for Anmol Publications Pvt. Ltd., New Delhi - 110 002 and Printed at Mehra Offset Press, Delhi.

Contents

Preface

In 1975, when the author was ready to go to U.S.A. for the first time, India's struggle to develop under the democratic system caught his imagination.

At the time, whether democratic West could do a better job than the Communist East in addressing the revolution of rising expectations in India and elsewhere in the developing countries was a question high on the U.S. foreign policy agenda. Now, with the Cold War becoming happily a history, India has slid down the ladder of U.S. priorities, although its confirming efforts to develop as a democracy does remain significant. One can hardly make support for democracy a guiding principle of American foreign policy yet ignore what happened to democracy in a country where 1000 million people live—one out of every six human beings on earth—Indian.

During 1957 until mid-1977, one of the things that most puzzled and frustrated the author studdied the uneven pattern of U.S.-India relations, the swings between periods of cooperation and antagonism, and the often emotional character of relationship. Why was it that these democracies seemed to have so much trouble in getting along? What caused these two countries to have such volatile relations, occassionally friendly, sometimes hostile, more often than not stranged? The author decided to write a book exploring the puzzling character of U.S.-India relations.

Once into the research, the author found his knowledge spotty. The author realised, to his surprise, that no American had prepared a comprehensive historical account of the relationship, although numerous Indians had.

1941, the eve of the U.S. entry into World War II, seemed the appropriate starting point for the book. That pivotal year 1941 was when New Delhi and Washington established direct diplomatic relations, despite Indias' membership in the British Empire. It was also the year when the United States first became seriously engaged in the sub-continent. The history closes fifty years later, in mid-1991, with the assassination of Rajiv Gandhi and the end of the Cold War. Since this global struggle between the United States and the Soviet Union, as well as the reaction to it of the three generations of Nehrus—Jawaharlal, Indira, and Rajiv—who led India for 39 of its fifty years as an independent nation, was a defining factor in India-U.S. relations, the termination of the U.S.-Soviet contest and the passing of the Nehru dynasty seemed a filling point to conclude the book.

The author's purpose was not to explain the tangled nature of the relationship, but as the story unfolds over the five decades, the major reasons for the mutual estrangement became apparent. India and the United States were not at odds because, as some assert, there was too little dialogue or a lack of mutual understanding, or were serious misperceptions, or because Indians and Americans had trouble getting along with each other. On the contrary, the author believes that Washington and New Delhi fell out because they disagreed on national security issues of fundamental importance to each.

In the 1940's, India decided to pursue a neutralist foreign policy, staying apart from the two power blocs then emerging, then after 1954, the U.S. decided to arm India's enemy Pakistan as part of global policy of containing Communism through a system of military alliances, finally, in the late 1960's and especially after the 1971 Treaty of Friendship, India decided to establish a close political-security relationship with the Soviet Union. India was, thus, lined up with Americas' principal foe while, at a same time, Washington was itself aligned with India's major enemy. Not a recipe for amicable relations.

In keeping with the chronological nature of the study, the author has organised the history around the terms of U.S. Presidents, with a chapter for each president from Roosevelt to Bush—and two for the busy Eisenhower years. The first six chapters, through the Johnson presidency, are based on declassified official documents, mainly American, as supplemented by memoirs, biographies, academic studies of various periods of facets of the relationship, and interviews. The final five chapters, from Nixon through the first two years of the Bush presidency, draw more on interviews, press accounts, and other secondary sources.

The author is indebted to many people for their help and encouragement while writing this book. The opinions, expressed are of course, those of the author and he takes responsibility to them.

August
Camp. U.S.A.

Naunihal Singh

Introduction

Early 1952, the planners in the office of the Under Secretary for Policy at the Pentagon had looked about the World for suspicious characters. This used to be called "threat analysis in worst possible case condition." This time there were fewer threats in the horizon. But wait! There is India! Fearsome hegemony there is Pakistan beleagured friend of yore! The draft document declared:

"We will seek to prevent the further development of a nuclear arms race on the Indian sub-continent. In this regard, we should work to have both countries, India and Pakistan, adhere to the Nuclear Non-Proliferation Treaty and to place their nuclear energy facilities under International Atomic Energy Agency safeguards. We should discourage Indian hegemonic aspirations over the other states in South Asia and on the Indian Ocean. With regard to Pakistan, a constructive U.S.-Pakistani military relationship will be an important element in our (American) strategy to promote stable security conditions in Southeast Asia and Central Asia. We (Americans) should, therfore, endeavour to rebuild our (American) military relationship given acceptable resolution of our nuclear concerns."

This was only a draft. The Under-Secretary for Policy had not seen it. But it was for that reason even more of an epiphany. After half a century of relations between what they were now the world's two largest democracies, the U.S. government defense planners could routinely assume that there was an American interest in suppressing Indian "hegemonic aspiration" in South Asia and once again arming its worst enemy and neighbour, Pakistan.

Suppose a comparable Indian document declared a national purpose to keep down U.S. hegemonic aspirations in North America, and to arm Mexico, possibly with the new Indian "Agni". We would not be amused: Somehow we are always surprised when Indians are exhausterated.

This episode, precisely because it was of so little consequences, will serve as a metaphor for the half-century of misunderstandings, mischieves and mishaf recorded in authors luminous narrations. At end of half-century of formal relations, the U.S. and India, the worl'ds two largest democracies—the two largest *ever* democracies—will still or once again, or seem to be at adds. The term "Love-Hate relationship" nicely captures the sense on both sides that affection has not been returned, or has somehow lapsed, or has found new outlets. In consequence of which the relationship is no longer the same. But then it never has been.

That, at all events, is the general perception. All rather hazy and soft as of a summer afternoon. Also, all along. The U.S. and India has "Love-hate relationships" not because they have failed to understand each other, but because of conflicting policies we and they have pursued with regard to the most elemental of national interests, military security. The supreme virtue of authors history is the way in which bedrock reality shows through at every stage in a half-century of on and off relations.

According to its constitution, India a "Sovereign, socialist, secular, democratic republic". It is surely sovereign, and definitely democratic. It has a fair amount of socialism of the Fabian sort. The Nehru dynasty, which governed for 37 of the first 42 years of independence, was surely secular. But all this leaves out *the* great facts, which is that with the coming off independence for the time in nearly a millennium, Islamic invaders no longer ruled Hindu India.

Well, yes, there had been the British. Here and there, and

briefly. (The last Moghul emperor was deposed in 1858). But the great fact that the endless succession of nomadic horsemen pouring through the Himalayan passes onto the Gangetic plain. Now it was all over. Rather *almost* all over, for with the certain of an independent Pakistan, the invaders retained their mountain redoubts and no small portion of the plain. Notably Lahore, which Babar has secured before marching on Delhi, and a new capital, Islamabad.

In other words, it was not necessarily over: a millennium of subjugation, defeat, near irrelevance much of what is thought of in the West as Indian history, as for example, the advent of the Mughuls under Babar, is really about the clashes of successive marauders, some of whom settled down). Partition had been traumatic, something like ten million persons were killed by hand.

The aftermath was anything but tidy, with the dispute over Kashmir present at the creation, and alive to this day. And so when the U.S. commenced in the 1950s to provide arms to Pakistan, estrangement with India was inevitable. Indian fear of Pakistan may have been "irrational," as the author suggests. It was no less real. That America had supported independence and welcomed it and promptly set about helping with the associated chores was something Indians understood well enough. Hence, estrangement rather than enmity, but estrangement for certain.

The U.S. did not intend this. Their concern early and late, was with the threat, as they saw it, of Soviet expansion. American never quite got it clear in their heads whether by expansion, they referred to the Red Army or the communist party. But at all events, it had to be contained. Pakistan was on the Soviet perimeter and was an early and eager participant in the alliance system that developed in the 1950s under President Eisenhower and his Secretary of State John Foster Dulles.

"This did not at first imply any disregard for India. When the Chinese Red Army crossed her borders in the early 1960s, American military aid was promptly offered and accepted. When monsoon failed, wheat was forthcoming in continental qualities. There would follow moments of intense attachment which can only be described as infatuation."

"Consider the episode. At the height of the Great Society, the Johnson administration was looking for projects worldwide, not just in Appalachia or inner cities. There was the Mekong Delta to fix up. And there was India to educate. The Indians had paid for American wheat in rupees of which America came to hold a vast proportion (something like 20 per cent of money in circulation)."

"They would use the money to set up a foundation to finance higher education. There would be a joint U.S./Indian board, and an American executive director. Americans would end up owning a very significant portion of Indian culture as embodied in its universities. Here is the conclusion of President Lyndon B Johnsons' toast at a White House dinner for Prime Minister Indira Gandhi on March 28, 1966."

"So we may Madam Prime Minister with the permission of your government and the American Congress, launch a new and imaginative venture. We shall its an Indo-American Foundation. I would propose that this Foundation will be established in India, and that it be endowed with $ 300 million in Indian Currency owned by the United States. Other foundations all over the world will cooperate, I am sure, with an expertise of this kind."

"I would suggest that this Foundation be organised as an independent institution with citizens of both our countries on its board of Directors. I would propose that the new Foundation be given a broad charter to promote progress in all fields of Learning—to advance science—to encourage research— to develop new teaching techniques on the forms and in the factions to stimulate, if you please, new ways to meet old problems."

"The journey to our future is one a very long and very winding road. Every mile will be challenged by doubt. But together Madam Prime Minister, we must avoid the debours that intrude on our safe journey toward a time when, as your father promised, life will be better for all of our people."

"So, ladies and gentlemen, let us honor those who are so welcome here tonight. Let us ask to join in honouring the Chief of State, whose wise and gifted Prime Minister we have enjoyed so much today and that we welcome so warmly this evening."

"I would like to ask those who are assembled here to join me now in raising your glass in toast to the great Prime Minister of India."

Here is the concluding portion of the Prime Minister's reply:

"India very definitely is on the move. Mr. President, the U.S. has given India valuable assistance in our struggle against poverty, against hunger, against ignorance, and against disease. We are grateful for this act of friendship. But also know that our own `Great Society' must and can only rest securely on the quality and the extent of our own effort."

"This effort we are determined to make: we owe it to our friends, and even more so we owe to ourselves.

"Nevertheless, I believe that it is of greatest importance, to use your own words, to bring into closer union the spirit and courage of both our countries. I welcome your intention to set-up an Indo-American Foundation, which will give tangible shape and form to this action."

"The present day world offers the possibility of bringing together one people with another. The youngmen and women of your Peace Corpse are well-known and well-loved in our own country. Every endeavour to sustain and enlarge this people-to-people partnership is a good effort and a welcome."

"Friendship with America is not a new thing for us."

"Those of us in India who have been involved with the struggle for freedom have known from an earliest days your own struggle here. We have been faught the words of your leaders, of your past great Presidents and above all we were linked in friendship because of the friendship which President Roosevelt showed us and the understanding which he showed during some of the most difficult days of our independence struggle. I have no doubt it was also this misunderstanding and friendly advice given to the British government which facilitated and accelerated our own freedom."

"But here again the major effort had to be on our own, and this is what we want today; that we should bear our burden as indeed we are doing, but that a little of help should come from friends who consider it worthwhile to lighten the burden."

"Because Mr. President, India's problems today are her own, but they are also the world problems. India has a position in Asia which is an explosive position. India, if it is stable, united, democratic, I think can serve a great purpose. If India is not stable or if there is chaos, if India fails, it is a failure of the whole democratic system. It is a failure of many of the values which you and we both hold dear."

"That is why Mr. President, I welcome your words and I welcome this meeting with you, which has been most valuable to me."

"I invite you, ladies and gentlemen, to join with me in drinking a toast to the President and Mrs. Johnson, our friends, the American people, and the Great Society, not just for America, but for all who dream of it, for all who struggle to transform those dreams into reality."[1]

Not 5 years later, these same two nations looked like they were about to go to war. Pakistan broke up. India invaded "East Bengal." The President of U.S. Richard M. Nixon, would write in his diary of Prime Minister Gandhi's "duplication action toward us at the time she saw me in Washington and the Bay of Bengal. The U.S. Permanent Representation to the U.N. George Bush, acting under orders from President Nixon, told the Security Council that India was responsible for the war. The Soviet vetoed the American resolution of condemnation, Prime Minister Gandhi signed a Treaty of Friendship with the Soviet Union and set-off a nuclear explosion.

Once again, the U.S. was thinking about the Soviet Union and not about India. Pakistan was arranging for Secretary of State Henry Kissinger to fly to Peking to prepare for a visit of President Nixon that would bring China into play as part of a "global balance of power." Hence, we would "till" toward Islamabad. The Author hesitates to offer a harsh assessment of the American role. In their memoirs, Nixon and Kissinger assert: their handling of events scared the Soviets into calling of their South Asian proxy, India, from attacking West Pakistan and showed the Chinese that the U.S. was willing to offer steadfast help to a friend during an unpopular crisis. Kissinger went so far as to claim that administration policy saved a "major American initiative of fundamental importance to the global balance of power and that the very structure of international order was endangered by the naked recource to force by a Soviet partner."

It is hard to agree with these assertion. Far from a diplomatic victory, the whole affair proved an unnecessary and embarassing diplomatic setback for the United States. Through their misreading of the crisis, and their pro-Pakistan bias, Richard Nixon and Henry Kissinger succeeded in needlessly transforming a regional dispute into one which threatened to become a great power showdown. The main consequences were severe and long-lasting damage to U.S. relations with India and enhanced Soviet influence with New Delhi.

That is about how matters rested for the remainder of the first half-century of Indo-U.S. relations. At the end, however, a most surprising event occurred. The Soviet Union broke up! This was a blow to India, which had invested for more than she ought to have done in that relationship. But the U.S. were left the world's only superpower, the price of victory was considerable. We would have been well advised to learn from the subcontinent as we pursued that protected conflict. By the 1970s, the U.S. had opted for a "global balance of power" strategy, the sort of thing seminars are made of, but not the real world.

The strategy simply assured continued existence and viability of the USSR. Whereas that should have been the first question to be raised. Would the USSR remain intact? Was it not another of those vast empires that had been breaking up all through the twentieth century? Wasn't the Indian sub-continent another such empire? Was it breaking up? Along religious and linguistic and ethnic lines? And mind, ought not India have given some thought to this possibilities? Prime Minister Gandhi and her son Rajiv Gandhi both cruelly, mindlessly assassinated, but not by instrumentories of the Cold War. Rather, by agents of indigenous nationalisms.

All that is now past. The author remarks that all things considered, "it is surprising the estrangement has not been worse". Things surely are better than they have been, not least owing to a marvellous migration that has brought over a one million Indians to the United States, with no sign of stopping, such is the welcome accorded these remarkably gifted individuals. The U.S. has cut off all military aid to Pakistan; it is hard to imagine any resumption.

Certainly, there would be no strategic grounds for

anything of the sort. Whatever injuries that Americans have done India, they never intended then, save possibly in that intervention in 1971.

In a sense, then, it is now India's turn. The author writes "Relations are unlikely to become more cooperative if India decides almost viscerally that opposing the U.S. is the natural state of affairs for Indian foreign policy." May a friend suggest that that *is* a temptation which needs watching. As far the U.S., there is a related disposition to assume that estrangement it is the natural state of his relation. It is nothing of the sort, and American should watch *that* temptation!

REFERENCES

1. At first seemed as feasible idea. Toasts of the President and Prime Minister Indira Gandhi of India, March 28, 1966, *Public Papers of the Presidents, Lyndon Johnson* 1966, Volume I.

   Fortunately, for all concerned on further consideration India decided not to go ahead with the foundation for higher education. But it had.

1

Roosevelt: The United States Meets India

The history of India -U..S. relations begins on the eve of America's entry into the World War II. Before then, the U.S. had scant contact with India even though, in 1772, only three years after he became President, George Washington appointed Benjamin as Consul in Calcutta, then the capital of British India.

Over the next century and a half, with India, part of the British Empire, political relations was virtually non-existent. Economic relations were also insignificant, except for a brief flourishing of trade during the Napoleonic wars.

In the later 1930s, for example, U.S. investment in India amounted to less than $ 50 million, with half in missionary schools, hospitals, or other non-business activities. U.S. missionaries were in fact, the principal link to India, yet numbered only a few thousand, for fewer than the Americans active in China.

In the period between the two World wars, India's struggle for independence won the support of American progressives, but did not gain widespread public backing. After Mohandas K. Gandhi—familiarly called the Mahatma, Hindi for "great spirit"—assumed the leadership of the Indian National Congress, the major nationalist organisation, his non-violent protest campaigns against British rule generated considerable press coverage.

The saintly figure wrapped in a bedsheet like garb became a sympathetic—if rather puzzling figures for Americans. On the negative side, Katherine Mayo's 1927 book, *Mother India*, dealt a heavy blow to India's image. This withering depiction of Indian society as depraved, squalid and without redeeming virtues sold a phenonenal 256,697 copies in 27 editions.

When Franklin D. Roosevelt entered the White House in 1933, New Delhi liberals, influenced by the anti-imperialist tradition of the Democratic Party, sympathised with India desire for independence. Neither Roosevelt nor Secretary of State Cordell Hull, however actively engaged U.S. influence in support of the Indian nationalist cause in the 1930s, on the eve of World War II India renamed a country about which U.S. had little contact.

American images of India flickered between erotic Hollywood portrayals of the British Raj and the adventure tales of Rudyard Kipling, Bejwelled Maharajas and British Colonial Sahibs, impoverished beggars and fakirs, maosine demonstrations of Indian nationalists and the complex problems of untouchability, caste and Hindu-Muslim communalism all made for a bewildering melange.

For India's, the U.S. was equally unfamiliar terrain, a distant land that seemed vastly different from their own dusty, impoverished sub-continent—as late as 1940, the census counted only 2,400—mostly Sikh farmers who had immigrated to California from the Punjab in northwest India at the turn of the century.

Educated Indians tended to look at the U.S. through the often critical British bus, as a country dominated by materialism and crime. Racial discrimination against non-Whites, especially segregation in the U.S. South, added to the unfattering picture.

Indians, like other Asians, deeply resented U.S. laws barring then from immigrant status and citizenship. Well-publicised incidents further tarnished the American image. Rabindranath Tagore, for example, cut short a lecture in 1929 when the Nobel Prize winner felt insulted by a U.S. immigrant official.

Pandit Jawaharlal Nehru, who in the late 1920's became one of Gandhi's principal Lieutenants and foreign policy spokesman for the Indian National Congress. Initially, found the U.S. not only racist, but imperialist. In 1927, the Indian leader joined in criticizing U.S. foreign policy toward Latin America at the Brussels International Congress against Colonial Oppression and imperialism. A year later Nehru wrote, "It is the U.S. which offer us the best field for the study of economic imperialism."

After the Democrats came to power in 1933, Indian nationalists, including Nehru, gradually developed a less negative attitude. Franklin D. Roosevelt gained popularity in India for his new deal domestic reforms and his anti-colonialists attitude. The President's decision to grant independence to the Phillipines in 1946 impressed Indians; Roosevelt's action sharply contrasted with British refusal to offer a timetable for Indian self-rule.

By the late 1930s, Nehru and other nationalists began to look to the United States as a potentially powerful support in their struggle for freedom for colonialism. Nehru, who had gained favourable attention in America as an articulate and sensitive Asian leader through his well-received autobiography, presented India's case for independence, for the informed U.S. audience in articles in *Foreign Affairs* in 1938 and the *Atlantic Monthly* in 1940.

By the time, the British were slowly and grudgingly reforming the Indian political structure to greater self-government. Following periodic civil disobedience movements organised by the Indian National Congress and lengthy negotiations with Mahatma Gandhi and other Indian political leaders, the Government of India Act of 1935 introduced democratically elected governments at the Provincial Level, Winston Churchill then the Conservative Party back bencher, bitterly opposed the reforms.

After farming well in 1937 in the first provincial elections under the reforms, the Congress Party was able to form governments in eight of eleven provinces. A brief period of cooperation followed between the Congress, assuming genuine responsibility at the provincial level, and the British imperial authorities, who continued to control the government of India in New Delhi. The Chief Executive remained the British Viceroy who, in turn, reported to the Secretary of State for India, a member of the British Cabinet and head of India Office in London.

When World War II broke out between Britain and Germany in September 1939, the Viceroy Lord Linlithgow declared war for India with little semblance of consultation with nationalist political leaders. Reaching against the Viceroy's unilateral action, the Congress Party refused to give its blessings to the War efforts despite the fact that many of its leaders including Nehru, emotionally supported the Allied cause against the Nazis. Congress Party members of provincial governments resigned their posts to protest against the Viceroys disregard of Indian sensivities.

A dour, unimaginative old style man of Empire, Linlithgow thorough disliked—even despised—key Indian National Congress Leaders like Mahatma Gandhi and Pandit Nehru. Leo Amery, Secretary of State for India shared Linlithgow staunchly conservative views and his dislike for Indian naturalist politicians.

After the Nazis swept through Western Europe in mid-1940 and Winston Churchill succeeded Neville Chamberlain as Prime Minister—Britain sought to allay the nationalists by offering a pledge of `eventual' dominion status after the war.

This gesture failed to mallify Congress leaders who wanted more tangible steps toward self-government in return for full backing for the war effort. The Indian Congress Party's unwillingness to support the struggle against Nazi Germany infuriated the British who were fighting for their national survival against Hitler.

Prime Minister Churchill's view on India remained rigid. From the start of the war, he warned against "the slippery slope of concessions and welcomed Hindu-Muslim differences as a "Bulwark of British rule in India." Even the firmly colonialist, Secretary of State for India, Leo Amery was at times critical of Churchill's old fashioned imperialism. "He has never really sympathised with the development of self-government in the Empire, "Amery commented"... as regards India (Churchill) had never got beyond the early Kipling stage."

The United States Develops an Interest in India

In Washington, the question of India's status became a matter of interest at the senior levels of government in early 1941. Although anti-war sentiment remained strong in the U.S., the sympathy of the President and his administration for the allied cause was clear. The initiation of selective service, the provision of 50 destroyers to Britain, and the start of Land-Lease assistance were all signs that the U.S. was gearing to become the "arsenal of democracy" in the fight against fascism.

As American leaders looked mere closely at India, they saw possibilities of the sub-continent's making a major contribution to the war effort, but soon became disenchanted with the British attitude. According to Secretary of State Condell Hull, he and President Roosevelt "were convinced that the Indians would cooperate, at least after the war." At the same time, however, Hull said he and Roosevelt suspected that it was a delicate question as to how far the U.S. could punish for Indian Independence in view of London's sensitivities on this issue.

With Britain fighting for its life against Nazi Germany, U.S. policy was to "take no step and utter no words that would impede her struggle". What Hull called the "delicate question" became the policy dilemma for U.S. leadership in dealing with India during the war: how hard could the U.S. push the British on Indian independence without impairing the alliance.

In order to facilitate U.S. support for the war effort in India—by then ruled eligible to receive Lend-Lease assistance as Indian representative to Washington to deal directly with the U.S. authorities. Until then, the government of India followed the cumbersome procedure of views through the India and foreign offices in London and then the British Embassy in Washington.

The State Department quickly accepted the British proposal, in turn, suggesting a reciprocal arrangement under which the U.S. would establish an office in Delhi. Washington found it highly unsatisfactory having to deal with the Government of India through the Consulate General in Calcutta nearly thousand miles away from New Delhi. As U.S. interest in India mounted, the U.S. wanted easier access to British authorities and Indian nationalist leaders.

At first, Lord Linlithgow halted worried that an official U.S. presence in Delhi would be inconsistent with India's status as part of the Empire. After a number of exchanges in the subject, Washington, London, and New Delhi finally agreed on an arrangement conveying something less than full diplomatic status to the envoys.

In Washington, the Viceroy's representative was to be called the Agent General of India and attached to the British Embassy.

In New Delhi, the U.S. would establish an office, the head of which would be called the Commissioner. The Viceroy designated a Senior Indian Civil Service Servant, Sir Girja

Shankar Bajpai, as Agent General in Washington, the State Department named Career diplomat Thomas Wilson, the Consul General in Calcutta, to become U.S. Commissioner in New Delhi.

In keeping with their unusual semi-diplomatic status, Bajpai and Wilson presented President Roosevelt and Viceroy Linlithgow personal letters of introduction rather than the unusual diplomatic letters of credence.

The first expression of discontent with British policy toward India came in May 1941 proposal by Assistant Secretary of State for Economic Affairs Adolf A. Berie, a New Deal Liberal—for pressure on London "to explore the possibility of making India equal of other members of the British Commonwealth."

Berie argued that with India's vast pool of manpower, the country could achieve a dominant position in supplying certain strategic war materials "if it became an active rather" than a passive partner in the war effort.

Despite the fact that Under Secretary of State Sumerwells convinced Hull "it was undesirable to upset Indian apple cart" by a formal demarche, Hull informally raised the subject of India with British ambassador Lord Halifax.

Having served as Viceroy from 1926 until 1931—when he was known as Lord Irwin—Halifax was obviously for more knowledgeable about India than U.S. officials. Although regarded as a liberal Viceroy in 1941 Halifax shared the prevailing conservative party view that it was preferable to stand up on Indian political arrangement and make no political gestures toward the Indian National Congress. Halifax's predictable response to Hull: it was not "feasible or even necessary now to make further liberalising concessions" to the Indian nationalists.

U.S. interest in India, nevertheless, continued to grow. Just before the August 1941 mid-Atlantic summit between

Roosevelt and Churchil, John Winant, the American ambassador in London, suggested urging the British to set a date, for granting India dominion status. Winant's recommendation won the warm endorsement of Assistant Secretary Berie but foundered like Benies own earlier suggestion with Sumer Wells, who opposed telling London "What the status of India should be."

Under Secretary Wells commented, "were the President disposed to take the matter up, I should imagine, he would wish to discuss it in a very personal and personal way with Mr. Churchill."

The President was quite ready—according to his son Eliot Roosevelt to raise the topic of India with Prime Minister Churchill when the two leaders met in the mid-Atlantic Ocean in August 1941. Roosevelt took the opportunity during an after dinner talk the next evening of the Conference to criticise British colonialism. British imperial policies, the Pesident charged, represented 18th, not twentieth century views, taking resources out of the colonies and giving nothing.back to the people when Roosevelt stressed the need to develop industry to improve sanitation, and to raise educational levels and standards of living in colonies, Churchill's anger rose. Beginning to look apopletic, the Prime Minister growled, "You mentioned India."

"Yes," the President responded, "I can believe that we can fight war against fascist slavery and at the same time not work to free people from over the world from a backward colonial policy." According to Elliot Roosevelt the two leaders continued to argue over colonialism at length and without agreement.

In the closing statement of the Conference of August 14, Roosevelt and Churchill issued the Atlantic Charter, the declaration of principles that served as the basic statement of Allied war aims. Their differences over the colonialism was apparent in later arguments about the third article of the Charter that the United States and Great Britain" respect the right of all peoples to choose the form of government under which they will live; and that they wish to see sovereign rights and self-government restored to those who have been forcibly deprived of them.

The Americans held the articles concept of self-determination had universal application, including the right of colonies to become independent. The President, Secretary Hull and Under Secretary Wells all make this point in public statements the following year. The British took a narrower view. Speaking in Parliament of September 9, 1941 Churchill stated that—as far as Britain was concerned—the article applied only to territories seized by the Nazis, and not to the Empire. Just before entering the House of Commons heard a plea from Ambassador Winant not to make the statement. Rebuffing the U.S. envoy, Churchill proceeded with his restrictive interpretation of the Charter.

The Prime Minister's statement cause bitter disappointment in India and dissatisfaction in Washington. Although the State Departmen'ts Near Eastern Division that the President press Churchill to extend the Atlantic Charter to India, under-secretary Summer Wells again proved the stumbling block. Wells agreed the Atlantic Charter should apply to India, but argued strenuously that the U.S. government should not press Churchill, during that difficult time, to take a step on India, he consistently opposed U.S. entry into the War in December 1941, vastly raised India's strategic importance in Washington as well as American willingness to express its views on the Indian political situation to the British. U.S. War planners saw the sub-continent as a key bastian for supporting China and a potentially enormous source of manpower and war goods for the Allied cause. The Assistant Chief of the Army's War Plans Division Duright D. Eisenhover then a Brigadier General, wrote "We have got to keep Russia in the War and hold India!!! Then we can get ready to crack Germany through England."

When Prime Minister Churchill visited Washington

during the Christmas 1941, Roosevelt apparently brought up India "on the usual American lines." There is no U.S. record of the discussions but Churchill wrote,"I reached so strongly and at such length that he never raised it (India) verbally again." Roosevelt's closest adviser Henry Hopkins said no American suggestions during the war were "so wrathfully received as those relating to the solution of the Indian problem."

It was indeed one subject on which the normally broad-minded, good humoured give-and-take attitude which prevailed between the two statesmen was stopped cold. It may be said that Churchill would see the Empire in ruins and himself buried under them before he would concede the right of any American, however great and illustrious a friend, to make any section as to what he should do about India".

Perhaps sensitised to Churchill's outlook, Roosevelt did not directly react to Britain's initial refusal to allow India to sign the United Nations Declaration, although agreeing with Henry Hopkins, he did not "understand why they don't include it." At Hopkins suggestion he asked Secretary of State Hull to provide them a little. "Two days later" Lord Halifax advised the State Department that the Viceroy and the War Cabinet had changed their minds. On New Years' Day 1942, Indian Agent General Bajpai was among the twenty-six signers of the United Nations Declaration.

As 1942 began, officials in Washington continued to worry about the projects for rallying Indian support for the war effort, with the allies reaching in Asia, the fall of September on 15th February triggered new concerns. A Senate Foreign Relations Committee hearing ten days later made clear the Congress shared administration anxieties.

Assistant Secretary of State Brackenridge, noting a "serious uncurrent of anti-British feelings," reported to Secretary Hull that the Senators demanded "India be given a status of autonomy. The only to get the people of India to fight was to get them to fight for India." The Senators declared, "Gandhi's leadership became part of America's Military equipment."

On February 25, Roosevelt took the initiative, instructing Averell Harriman, his Special Representative in London, to sound Churchill out about a "new relationship between Britain and India." After taking with the Prime Minister, Harriman cabled that the British leader remained strongly opposed to "Stirring the pot". The United States, Churchill asserted, was misreading the Indian situation: The war effort was tied to the support of the Muslims, not the Congress Party and the Hindus.

The Prime Minister claimed (wrongly) that 75 per cent of the Indian Army were Muslims and largely opposed to the Indian National Congress Party. Making a gesture toward the Congress would only offend the Muslims and not aid the war effort, the British leader argued. Appeals from China's President Chiang Kai Shek added to the pressure on a reluctant Churchill. During a visit to India in mid-February, Chiang strongly urged Britain to grant India independence—much to the dismay of the Viceroy Lord Linlithgow. The presence of the British Labour Party as a coalition partner in the war cabinet added further weight to the calls for action in India. Long at odds with the Conservatives over the pace of colonial reform, Labour Party of India Specialist and Lord Privy Seal, Sir Stafford Cripps, challenged Secretary of State for India Amery to rethink the policy of sitting tight.

Under mounting pressure, the war cabinet approved the idea—pressed vigorously by Cripps "issuing a firm offer of post"—war independence and of taking steps to give Indian political leaders a substantially larger government role during the war.

Out of the concern, for the Muslim minority, a quarter of India's the then four hundred million population, and the agitation by its major political grouping, the Muslim League, for a separate homeland— Pakistan—the cabinet declaration left open the possibility of creating more than one independent state.

The War Cabinet decided to send a senior figure to India to discuss the declaration rather than simply issuing the proposal. Not one to lack self-confidence offered to take on the task, reasonably hopeful he could gain the agreement of the many Indian friends, including Gandhi and Nehru.

In New Delhi, the Viceroy disliked the whole idea. Upset the Cabinet in effect pushed him aside by designating Cripps to present the proposals, Linlithgow offered to resign. He agreed to stay on only after a personal plea from Churchill. The Prime Minister explained, "It would be impossible owing to..... the general American outlook to stand on a purely negative attitude and Cripps Mission is indispensible to prove our honest'y of purpose."

Just before Sir Stafford Cripps left for India, Churchill informed Roosevelt about the War Cabinet proposals. Hearding sounding enthusiastic, the British Leader reiterated that Britain must not "on any account" break with the Muslims, the main element in the Army. Churchill commented, Naturally we do not want to throw India into chaos on the eve of an invasion." With Burma having fallen to the Japanese, an attack on India loomed as a real threat.

Roosevelt's response should have shaken the Prime Minister's composure. Disagreeing with the cautions, Lawyer-like approach of the Cabinet proposals, the President suggested the British would immediately establish a "temporary dominion government" on the lines of the U.S. Articles of Confederation.

> Perhaps, the analogy of some such method to the travails and problems of the U.S. between 1783 and 1798 might have a new start in India itself, and it might cause the people there to become more loyal to the British Empire and to stress the danger of Japanese domination, together with the advantage of peaceful evolution as against Chaotic revolution.

Surely aware that these words would not make his friend Winston very happy, Roosevelt ended his message diplomatically, "for the love of heaven, don't bring me into this, though I want to be of help. It is, strictly speaking, none of my business except in so far as it is a part and parcel of successful fight that you and I are waging."

The Johnson Mission: Roosevelt tries "to be of Help"

Circumstances soon provided the President a chance "to be of help". Discussions about how the U.S. could aid Indian production of war goods, initiated by Indian Agent—General Bajpai resulted in a decision to send a War production mission to India.

On March 6, 1942, the State Department announced that Colonel Johnson, a former Assistant Secretary of War and prominent West Virginia Democrat, would head the Mission, supported by former Assistant Secretary of State Henry Grady and three other industry specialists.

Before Johnson departed three weeks later, his role democratically changed. Instead of leading the mission, the Colonel became President Roosevelt's Personal Representative to India. Although the documentary record is lacking, it is reasonable to assume the President Johnson's assignment so that the U.S. would play a more active role in helping the British and Indians reach a political settlement in order. To engage Indian energies more fully behind the war effort.

A former Commander of the American Legion and Wheeler Johnson was an unlikely candidate for a sensitive diplomatic mission and later an unexpected convert to Indian nationalism. A strong supporter of preparedness as Assistant Secretary of War, Johnson was well qualified for the war production mission. His knowledge of India, however, was nil; Johnson admitted the only books he read on the subcontinent were *Kipling Kin* and Henry's with *Clive in India*.

By the time arrived in New Delhi on April 3, the Cripps Mission seemed near failure. Several weeks of intensive talks failed the Congress Party's agreement. Mahatma Gandhi was the main obstacle—disliking the loophole permitting the creation of Pakistan.

With the Allied position crumbling in Asia, moreover, Gandhi spoke of a British political pledge as a cheque drawn on a failing bank. Although Gandhi had a majority with the Congress Party leadership, a substantial minority including South Indian Leader. C. Rajagopalachari urged acceptance of the Cripps Plan and full support for the war against the Axis, Congress President Maulana Azad, a respected Muslim and Jawaharlal Nehru were sitting in the fence.

About to leave India in failure, a depressed Cripps delayed his report after Shiva Rao, a prominent pro-Congress Journalist, although a compromise on the management of India's defense, might salvage the negotiations. Although not optimistic Cripps asked authorization to try to work out a revised arrangement on defense, subject to agreement of the Viceroy and the Commander-in-Chief of the Indian Army, General Wavell.

Churchill replied he would seek agreement of the War Cabinet, expressing satisfaction that Cripps effort has been "most beneficial in the U.S. and large circles here." By offering the proposals Churchill believed the British received a better press in the United States allaying criticism of Burma's policy toward India.

One American who did not share the Prime Minister's appraisal was President Franklin Roosevelt. Talking with Indian Agent General Bajpai of April 2, Roosevelt criticised the Cripps proposals as not going far enough, expressing the view that the British should have offered India virtually complete autonomy.

Roosevelt's Personal Representative in India Louis Johnson was, in any event, not about to give up without a fight. As soon as the former Assistant Secretary of War arrived in New Delhi, he plunged into the meddle of negotiations. Delivering a message from Roosevelt to Congress President Maulana Azad urging acceptance of the British proposals, Louis Johnson found the Congressites and Cripps eager for his assistance. Delighted have help, Sir Stafford told a colleague that Roosevelt had sent Johnson pest-haste to lend a hand in achieving an Indian settlement. And lend a hand Johnson did, shuttling between Cripps and Pandit Nehru in a desperate effort to shape a compromise.

Although the Viceroy at first found Johnson engaging—he liked the fact that Johnson bluntly warned the Congress leadership that India would lose U.S. support if it rejected the British offer—Linlithgow worried that Roosevelt's Personal Representative concerning himself too closely in detailed negotiations between HMG and Indian politicians.

Just two days after reaching New Delhi, Johnson cabled Roosevelt and Hull to recommend that the President intercede with Churchill. In Johnson's view, both the Viceroy and General Wavell opposed an alleged Indian defense role, a step the U.S. envoy believed the President had to deal directly with Churchill.

The answer from Washington was a polite turndown. After considering the Colonels request, the President decided against a further personal appeal to the Prime Minister. Under Secretary cabled, "You know how earnestly has tried to be of help... it is feared that at this moment he interposed his own views, the result would complicate further an already overcomplicated situation."

Not easily detered, Johnson continued his whirlwind efforts in New Delhi with Sir Stafford's concurrence, he redrafted the proposals to retain full British control but to provide a better sounding Indian role. When both sides seemed agreeable to the revisions, Congress acceptance suddenly seemed possible, indeed likely. Johnson sent off an enthusiastic cable to Washington on April 9 stating that

Nehru was going to accept his modified defense proposal and that Wavell and Linlithgow also agreed.

Ending with patriotic flourish, Johnson cabled euphorically, Both Nehru and Cripps have expressed their appreciation for the revival of negotiations. The magic name here is Roosevelt, the land, the people would follow and leave, America."

An elated Cripps reported to Churchill—in less flamboyant language—that as a result of Johnson's help he now hoped to gain Indian agreement. Sir Stafford urged the Prime Minister to send thanks to the President for Johnson's assistance.

Neither Johnson nor Cripps realized that Linlithgow fuming over being elbowed aside, and increasingly incensed by Johnson's involvement was lomberding London with back channel telegrams. The Viceroy was furious that Cripps had allowed Johnson to show the revised defense formulation to Nehru before the Viceroy saw the proposal. Linlithgow also raised a more fundamental problem looking in the shadows of the Cripps discussions. What would the role of Viceroy be under the revised governmental arrangements.

Cripps had implied he would become a constitutional head of State, with the cabinet dominated by Indians possessing genuine authority. Was this really what London wanted, the Viceroy asked? Linlithgow worried that it would be harsh for the British to reject the Cripps-Johnson formula if the Congress Party leadership accepted.

"We cannot run the risk of the Governor-General (Viceroy), the (Commander-in-Chief and HMGS' being unwilling to honour a formula agreed between HMG's emissary and Roosevelt's personal representative," an anxious Linlithgow cabled the Prime Minister.

At this point, with the prospects for success of the Cripps Mission brightening, the fates intervened. Presidential aide Harny Hopkins was in London with U.S. Army Chief of Staff General Georges C. Marshall for discussions on wartime strategy. The Prime Minister unexpected called Hopkins to No. 10 Downing Street on April 9 to talk about India. Brandishing and cable from the Viceroy, Churchill told Hopkins an awkward situation had developed in New Delhi.

The Prime Minister claimed the Indians were going to accept the original British proposal but Cripps and Louis Johnson developed new idea without consulting the Viceroy. This development badly upset Linlithgow, who was also disturbed by the fact that Johnson was acting and talking as though the President sent him to India to mediate an Indian political settlement. It was possible, Churchill continued, the war cabinet would reject Johnsons proposals, something that would be embarrassing for the President.

Believing it important to down play Johnson's role rather than risk a public relations problem for Roosevelt, Hopkins promptly responded that he very sure. Johnson was not acting as the representative of the President in mediating the Indian business." Hopkins said Roosevelt's instructions on India discouraged becoming engaged in trying to resolve matters unless both sides so requested, and unless India and Pakistan assured him they would accept his ideas.

The President did not want to be placed in the public position where the contending parties turned down his proposals. Hopkins assumed, "Cripps was using Johnson for his own ends, Cripps being very anxious to bring Roosevelt's name into the picture.

In Hopkins presence, Churchill immediately wrote out a message to New Delhi that Johnson was not Roosevelt's Personal Representative except for munitions questions and that the President was opposed to anything like intervention or mediation.

Later that day, Churchill persuaded the War Cabinet to repriman Cripps for exceeding instructions and to raise questions about the appropriateness of Johnson's role in the discussions.

A reined in Cripps met for the final session with Congress Leaders Maulana Azad and Pandit Nehru. Instead of coming the negotiations with success, the April 10 meeting marked them final elapse of Sir Stufford Mission. When the Indians pressed for elaboration on the Viceroy role under the plan, a depressed Cripps could only temporize. He was unable to give even verbal assurance that the Ministers in the new government would possess real authority.

Nehru made clear the Congress Party's reluctance to work with the Viceroy and the traditional government of India machinery for the nationalists, the very symbol of British imperialism. Cripps left dejected, Nehru, in turn, sent a gloomy letter to Johnson, describing the meeting as a "entirely unsatisfactory" and indicating that the "very premises" of the discussions were unjustified.

Apparently unaware of Hopkins session with Churchill, Johnson reported the collapse of the talks to Washington, praising Cripps sincere but lacking authority for even minor concessions. Roosevelt's personal representative charged that London, in effect, wanted the Congress to refuse, penetrating the British as defeatists, ready to lose India during the War to reclaim it at his peace treaty. Johnson praised Nehru as "magnificent in his cooperation with me. The President would like him and on most things they agree.... He is our hope these."

Faced with the collapse of negotiations reversed field. Although he had rebuffed Johnson's earlier appeal for help, he now instructed Harry Hopkins—still in England to convey a blunt personal message urging Churchill to make every effort to prevent a breakdown in the talks.

Refusing to agree with Churchill's assessment that public opinion in the U.S. believes that the negotiation have broken down in general broad issues', Roosevelt stated:

> The general impression here is quite the contrary. The feeling is almost universally held that the deadlock has been due to the British government's willingness to concede to the Indians the right of self-government, notwithstanding the willingness of the Indians to entrust technical, military and naval defense control to the competent British authorities.

The President warned that if, after the failure of the talks, Japan successfully invaded India, "the prejudicial on the American public opinion can hardly be over-estimated. Asking that Churchill have Cripps postpone his departure. Roosevelt reiterated his suggestion that the British offer the Indian something like the Articles of Confederation. If the Indian rejected the proposal, Roosevelt said responsibility for failure "must clearly be placed on the head of the Indian people and not upon the British government."

Such a strong message from Roosevelt required a careful response from the Prime Minister. Drafted with Hopkins' advice, Churchill reply avoided the main thrust of the Presidents' argument—the British offer was not good enough. Churchill, instead stated (incorrectly) that he could do anything further since Cripps had already left India. Churchill also asserted that he would have to place the issue before the War Cabinet. He could not take responsibility for the defense of India if everything has again to be thrown into the melting pot at the critical juncture.

Leaving on the private nature of Roosevelts' cable to the "former naval person," the Prime Minister said he would not bring the message to the Cabinet's attention unless the President asked Appealing emotionally to Roosevelt, Churchill said, anything like a serious difference between you and me would break my heart and surely injure both our countries at the height of this terrible struggle.

A day later, Roosevelt received his first and only communication from Jawaharlal Nehru sent through Louis

Johnson, the message expressed sometimes not far from the President's own views. Although Indians preferred full "freedom and independence," Nehru said they were ready to accept a truly national government that could "organise resistance on a popular basis." Nehru stressed, "How anxious and eager we were, and shall are, to do our utmost for the defense of India. Over sympathies, Nehru wrote to Roosevelt, are with the forces fighting against fascism and for democracy and freedom." Roosevelt sent Nehru a friendly and prompt reply. Saying he was deeply gratified by the message, the President assured Nehru the United States would to the utmost extent of its ability" help India "resist Japanese aggression." Roosevelt, however, made no mention of Indian independence.

Although development clearly upset the President, he felt able to press Churchill only so far on India without damaging the war time alliance. When the Secretary of the Interior Harold Ickps urged support for Indian independence, the President replied "you are right about India, but it would be playing with fire if the British Empire told me to mind my own business."

Perhaps, had Roosevelt intervened sooner with Churchill, heading Johnson's, April plea or had to fates not placed, Harry Hopkins in England on April 9, Johnson's compromise formula on defense arrangements might have won acceptance. Still the gap between what the British were willing to offer and what the Indian Congress wanted was so wide and there was so much mistrust between the two sides—that an agreement over defense matters might soon have founded over more fundamental differences.

As Nehru told Louis Johnson in a private note, "It is exceedingly difficult to find a formula" to satisfy both Indian nationalists and British for between the two there is intradictable and permanent conflict." Nehru wrote further, "The two cannot exist together or cooperate with each other, for each dislikes and distrusts the other."

Quit India: British Arrest Congress Leadership

The failure of the Cripps Mission left everyone despendent, except Winston Churchill, pleased that the effort improved the British image in the United States without his having to relinquish any power to the Indians. In India, the nationalists regarded the British offer as inadequate and insincere, a view that has been echoed in later assessments by Nehru, Azad and others.

Sir Stafford Cripps believed the Congress Working Committee was prepared to accept Johnson's formulation on defense but after a two hour telephone conversation with Gandhi voted 8-4 against the proposal. The Labour Party Leader refused to blame Churchill or Linlithgow for undercutting him, either from Loyalty to the War effort or from ignorance of what happened behind his back.

Johnson remained in active contact with Nehru during the month after Cripps departure desperately trying to find some way to restart the negotiations. When rejected a proposal by Johnson for a statement of Pacific war aims that would appeal to Indian nationalists, he again urged the President to intervene with Churchill.

"American alone can save India for the United Nations cause" Johnson cabled Roosevelt on May 4. Presumably with his earlier inability to move Churchill in mind, the President accepted the State Department's approval that Johnson's proposal was unlikely to succeed and would only make matters worse in India. He cabled back a polite but firm rejection.

Johnson, who developed medical problems from the dust in India, underwent surgery in New Delhi before retiring to the United States in mid-May to recuperate. Once back in Washington he stressed his opinion that the British rather than the Indian Congress Party, were to blame for the political impasse, State Department officials agreeing the Churchill may have been pleased with the breakdown of the talks questioned that he actively undercut Cripps as Johnson alleged.

Once London got wind of Johnson's criticism, Churchill countered his charges, cabling Harry Hopkins," Frankly we do not think his comments have very much weight.... We do not at all relish the prospect of Johnsons return to India." When Hopkins replied that Johnson was sick and had no plans to go back to India, the British were relieved. Two months later, Johnson resigned from the State Department to become head of General Dyestuffs Corporation. After the war in the Truman administration, he returned to public life to become Secretary of Defense, loosing his job after the start of the Korean war.

The British were, on the whole, more than satisfied with the impact of the Cripps Mission on American opinion, especially the shift in the U.S. press from being critical of the British to criticizing the Indian Congress for rejecting the proposals, Graham Spry, a Canadian Member of Cripps party toured the U.S. for two months to put across the British viewpoint. In his assessment Spry asserted that Americans liked the Cripps' proposals and thought that Congress should have accepted them.

One person who seemed not to share this view, however, was the President. Why Spry called at the White House on May 1, 1942 Roosevelt pointedly asked if the British cabinet switched instructions during the later stages of the Cripps negotiations. Regarding, Louis Johnson's role, Roosevelt stated he sent the Colonel to India to be `helpful.' Smiling broadly, the President said, "Perhaps some of your people over there thought he was interfering."

Roosevelt also criticised the Cripps proposals when British Embassy Minister Sir Ronald Campbell came to lunch at the President's home at Hyde Park during the summer.

Roosevelt told the British diplomat that London would have been wiser not to have proposed a post-war constitutional procedure but reiterating the view he put to Churchill in March—should have followed the American example of an interim system settling on constitutional reforms only after a period of error. The idea of offering parts of India the right to secede, the President said, "sounded terrible" to American ears after the Civil war.

In the wake of the failure of the Cripps Mission, there was a widespread sense of gloom among Indians. Reflecting his frustration, Mahatma Gandhi unsettled Washington by a number of critical comments about the U.S. in his journal *Harijan*. "A never ending stream of soldiers from America... amounts to be end to American influence, if not American rule added to British." Churchill wrote on April 26.

A month later, the U.S. mission heard Gandhi was planning to launch a mass Civil disobedience movement, apparently "unmoved" by warnings that such a movement could cause absolute chaos, and make India an easy prey for the Japanese." A worried Nehru just back from a holiday in the Himalayas sent a message to Louis Johnson in Washington, warning that "events seemed to be marching toward internal crisis."

On June 4, Nehru cabled Colonel Johnson that Gandhi did not want to embarras the present war effort... American opinion should not misunderstand him, he has emphasised Indian independence as this is the only way for India and progressive nations to utilise India's great resources in cause of world freedom.

Fresh calls by Gandhi for the British to withdraw their troops from India and criticism of the moral basis for American participation in the war because of U.S. race policies hardly reassured Washington, whatever Nehru might say about Gandhi's intentions.

Apparently aware of the negative impact of his remarks, Gandhi to modify his position in talking with American Journalists and in his statements. In the *Harijan* of June 14, he wrote that an independent India would permit the Allies to stay. Gandhi also asked the U.S. to use its influence to help India with the British and followed up a personal letter to President Roosevelt, which he sent through journalist Louis Fischer.

Speaking as a "friend and well-wisher of the Allies, Gandhi reiterated Indias' willingness to cooperate with the Allies—if given freedom. Gandhi probably spoke the positive impact of the letter by undiplomatically seemed "hollow so long as .... America has the Negro problem in her own home".

The President's short reply to Gandhi dated August 1, 1942 skirted the Mahatma's, call for help. Roosevelt, instead, expressed the hope that our common interest in democracy and righteousness will enable your countrymen and mine to make common cause against a common enemy." By the time the President's message reached India, Gandhi was in jail. The letter rested for two years undelivered in the U.S. mission until the British released the Congress leader in late 1944.

As events in India headed towards crisis, the continuous flow of unfavourable war news placed an even greater premium on allied units and reduced the chances that Roosevelt would risk Churchill by pressing him to make concessions to the Indian National Congress. In the Middle East, General Roosevelt forces were advancing to within 100 miles of Alexendria, threatening to capture the Suez Canal, Soviet armies were ruling under renewed Nazi attacks. Although Japanese had rejected to invade India, the threat remained.

On July 14, the Congress Working Committee despite strong opposition to Nehru, in favour of civil disobedience campaign—known as the Quit India Movement. The next step would be formal adoption of the proposal by the All India Congress Committee.

With the United States closely following developments, Nehru told U.S. Mission Political Officer Lampton Berry that the Congress would be willing to cooperate in the war effort if Britain declared India independent and established a provisional government. Nehru's ideas sounded surprisingly like President's own pet solution for India: from a provisional government and work out the details later.

Following up Nehru's comments and remarks to the press by Congress President Maulana Azad, Mission on July 21 made a last ditch proposal to avert the civil disobedience campaign. The Mission suggested that the U.S. stand guarantor to a British pledge of Indian independence immediately after the war, and help the Indian political parties in setting up a provisional war time government.

The medicine too strong for the State Department, aware of the President's disinclination to challenge further on India. The proposal never made it out the Near Eastern Division.

Roosevelt gave another sign of his unwillingness to intervene over India he rejected a plea from Chiang Kai Shek. The President cabled Churchill after turning down the Chinese Leader, "we would not, of course" wish to pursue any course undermines the authority of the Government of India at this critical time."

Meeting in Bombay on August 8, the All India Congress Committee formally adopted the Quit India resolution, calling on Britain to withdraw or face a mass civil disobedience campaign. The day before, Acting Prime Minister Attlee informed President Roosevelt that the Government of India would arrest all Congress Leaders as soon as the Congress adopted the resolution. Despite some domestic pressure for U.S. action, Washington remained silent about the arrests of the Congress Party Leadership, in effect acquiescing in the British crackdown.

The American Leadership could hardly fathom Gandhi's tracting of mounting the Quit India campaign—certain to disrupt the war effort—at the moment the struggle against the Axis being in the balance. In U.S. eyes, it was one thing to launch a civil disobedience movement as part of a peacetime struggling for freedom, quite another in the midst of world-wide war against fascism.

Harry Hopkins told British Embassy Minister Campbell several days later that Roosevelt remained anxious about India, although he did not see what could be done. Even Pandit Nehru might say all the right things, Roosevelt advisor commented, "It would be Gandhi who would decide and we all knew what Gandhi was."

In India, the British authorities, to their display faced widespread violence and sabotage after the arrests. A shaken Viceroy spoke alarmingly of the most serious challenge to the Rey since the 1857 mutiny.

By the end of August, however, the government regained control, with official statistics indicating more than 1,000 dead and more than 3000 seriously injured in the Quit India disturbances. The British arrested over 100,000 nationalists, many for the duration of the War.

The summer of 1942 markedly the high watermark of the Axis powers. On the frontiers of India, after the Japanese advanced stabled in the jungles of Assam, the threat of invasion receded. In the Middle East, Montgomery defeated Rommel at El. Alamein driving him out of Egypt. Russians stopped the Nazi tide at Stalingrad. Preparation went forward for the invasion of North Africa.

By the time, the U.S. military build up of India as a major staging area to supply the China theater and to reconquer Burma was beginning to move into geer. The U.S. established the China-Burma-India (CBI) command under the inspired albeit ascertic, leadership of Lt. General Joseph Stilwell. With his Headquarters in New Delhi, planned the campaign for China, trained troops for the fight against the Japanese, and dispatched supplies for Chiang Kai Sheks forces by air over the Himalayan mountain, the famous "over the hump" route.

By wars' end, the U.S. had assigned 250,000 American soldiers in India, almost entirely in supply and engineer functions and mainly concentrated in eastern India, in Bengal and Assam, where they built numerous air fields. Sensitive to potential Indian criticism that this large military presence meant U.S. support for British policy, the President approved the State Departments' statement, on August 12, that U.S. forces were not to become involved in Indian internal affairs and were in India only to fight the war against the Axis.

Washington found it difficult to deal with the large scale American military presence—by for the most extensive contact the U.S. had ever with India. Although the war effort remained the primary concern, the U.S. government did not want the presence of so many troops to suggest support for the way the British were dealing with India.

Roosevelt never really found a satisfactory way around this problem—how to show Americans backing for Indian aspirations for in defence without offending the British, his principal wartime ally and partner.

Personal impressions of Americans about India and Indians of Americans were mixed. Many like General Stilwell, depressed what they found unfavourably compared the Indians and the Chinese. "In China they have their heads up.... appear to have object in life. India is hopeless." Stilwell wrote Indians, in turn, found the American GI's more approachable, friendlier and informed them the stand offish British. They were, however, put off by U.S. racial policies that rigidly separated GIs into segregated units according to colour. A few publicised racial incidents against Indian's by white GI's offended Indian sensibilities.

Phillips Mission "Amazingly Radical for a Man like Bill"

While Lord Linlithgow, in New Delhi had a frosty view of Americans after his experience with Louis Johnson, Churchill, Foreign Secretary Anthony Eden, and other thought that the U.S. could be brought around if properly handled. The Viceroy pretted when White House aide Lauchin Currie, passing through New Delhi, met with Shiv Rao, a leading pro-Congress journalist.

For once even a diehart like Churchill grew unsympathic about the Viceroy's complaints. The Prime Minister commented that even though the British could probably bloc visits by Americans, could not the Viceroy "Captivate and convert them." The Prime Minister went on. "I always make a point of seeing these prominent Americans and make sure they get a good show, and the results have been most satisfactory."

Anthony Eden considered Linlithgow's, reaction, to Currie mistaken. The Foreign Secretary indeed, believed the U.S. send a high calibre envoy to India to replace Louis Johnson. "I am very doubtful whether we can expect to get the results we want unless the tale (about India) is told to the President and to America by an American," Eden wrote Leo Amery, head of India Office. The War Cabinet agreed with the idea of "more authoritative U.S. representation" in India on the understanding that the new envoy—unlike Louis Johnson—not become involved in the Indian political situation.

During the fall, the British pressed the idea in Washington, and also on the reluctant Viceroy. After the Johnson episode, the senior career diplomat, preferably someone with President Roosevelt. London's favoured choices were too of the Americas— top diplomats, Joseph Gnew, former ambassador to Japan and William Phillips, former ambassador to Rome, then serving as the head of the London Office, the office of Strategic Services (OSS), the U.S. wartime intelligence service. Within the State Department, officials urging the same two names on the President, who seemed in no hurry to replace Johnson, perhaps—as Gary Hess wrote—because he was unsure how to handle India.

In the meanwhile, pressure in Washington for doing something about India was building up. Although the U.S. press approved the suppression of the "Quit India" movement, public opinion shortly swung in favour of fresh effort by the British to negotiate with Indian nationalists. After Churchill virtually slammed the door in a attack on the Indian National Congress in Parliament on September 10, Roosevelt came under increasing pressure.

In October, the pot boiled over. In a nation-wide radio address, former 1940 Republican Presidential Candidate Wenddell Wilkie—reporting on his around the world tour focussed attention on India. During his talks in Asia, Wilkie said:

> "Many asked: What about India... by our silence we have already drawn heavily on the reservoir of goodwill in the East... . They cannot ascertain from our government's wishes wanting attitude toward the problem of India what we are likely to yeel at the end of war about the other hundreds of million of Eastern people."

The Wilkie speech forced Roosevelt's hand. Talking to the press the next day, the President reaffirmed that the Atlantic Charter's right of self-determination applied to all peoples—those subject to colonial rule as well as Axis conquest. Secretary of State Hull told newsmen that looking for ways to deal with the Indian problem.

The President acted to fill the vacancy in New Delhi, selecting William Phillips to replace Johnson as his new Personal Representative. In early December, Roosevelt announced the Phillips appointment playing down the idea the envoy was not anything than a normal diplomatic mission.

If Louis Johnson typified the back slapping, rough and

American politician, William Phillips personified the American East coast aristocracy. Having spent his youth in a baronial mension on Bostons Commonwealth Avenue, Phillips graduated from Harvard in 1902. He entered the diplomatic service a year later as Private Secretary to Joseph Choate, the Ambassador to London.

Advancing rapidly the diplomatic ladder, Phillips caught the eye of P.resident Theodore Roosevelt and later served Woodrow Wilson's Assistant Secretary of State. Phillips and Franklin Roosevelt, Willsons' Assistant Secretary of the Navy, became friends.

In the 1920s Phillips reached the top of the Career Service, becoming Under Secretary, the No. 2 post in the State Department, and later serving as an envoy to the Netherlands, Belgium and Canada. Roosevelt reappointed Phillips as Under Secretary in 1933, and four years later sent the Boston to the sensitive post of ambassador to Mussolin's Italy.

After Phillips retired in 1941, Colonel William Donovan asked the diplomat to head the OSS London Office. Phillips had a reputation as cautious, conservative and pro-British. It was hard to imagine "someone less likely than William Phillips to sympathetic with the Indian Nationalist leaders, much less with masses.

Before leaving London, Phillips talked with a wide variety of Indians and British including V.K. Krishna Menon, the Congress Party's representative and a close friend of Jawaharlal Nehru. Foreign Secretary Anthony Eden urged Phillips to get the whole picture and report it to the President. Winston Churchill followed his own advice about giving Americans a good show. Hosting on lunch for Phillips he spoke with "great earnestness" about the assignment, saying "much might come out of it" but offering few specifics.

In a personal touch, the Prime Minister set the new envoy his lettered copy of *Twenty One Days in India*, a book Churchill himself read on the eve of his departure for India as a young cavalryman nearly half a century ago.

Phillips instructions from Secretary that posted a different challenge: he was to try to move the British toward a political settlement with Indian nationalists without appearing to exert pressure or to suggest U.S. intervention.

Although Phillips thought the reference to a political settlement with Indian nationalists without appearing to pressure or to suggest U.S. intervention.

Although Phillips though reference to a political settlement was "naive", he reorganized that this task was the heart of his assignment. The envoy arrived in India in January 1943. When his plane touched down at Karachi airfield as Indian western edge, the scope of American military aspirations at the air base surprised Phillips.

After reaching New Delhi, Phillips spent his initial days in Viceregal luxury as Linlithgow's guest at the Viceroy's vast palace. The Viceroy hosted a formal dinner in Phillips' honour the night of his arrival.

With Indian footmen standing behind each of 38 guests at the long dining table, a five-man bagpipe orchestra provided music for the occasion. Taken aback, Phillips wrote in his diary, Linlithgow had obviously adopted the outward forms of royalty to a pronounced degree.

At first the Viceroy reacted positively to Phillips. "It is hard," he wrote Amery, "to imagine a greater contrast to Johnson.... (Phillips) seem to me better really than anything we could reasonably have hoped for." Gradually, the attitude changed as Phillips developed his personal view on India and the British role there. The first jolt came two weeks after the Americans' arrival.

In a talk with Viceroy, Phillips expressed his opinion that

progress toward a provisional government and a political settlement would be good thing. Phillips added that British officials in London encouraged him to help this process along.

The discussion trigged a frantic exchange of telegrams between the Viceroy and India Office Chief Amery, who assured the worried Linlithgow that somehow Phillips had ministerpreted what he heard in London namely that the British would welcome his views, but not his intervention.

Had the Viceroy been reading Phillips letters to President Roosevelt, Linlithgow would have even more grounds for discontent. Describing his initial impression, on January 22, 1943, Phillips wrote that both Hindus and Muslims lacked confidence in British provinces to free India.

Although Phillips found many in Britain ready to grant independence if the Indians agreed among themselves, he was unsure if Churchill and the Viceroy "old colonialists" shared this view.

In a February letter, Phillips wrote "Reluctantly" he wrote the President, "I am coming to the conclusion that the Viceroy, presumably responsive to Churchill is not in sympathy with any change in Britain's relationship with India." The Ambassador worried that the presence of so many American troops in India, as well his own assignment there, was creating the impression among Indians that the U.S. supported British imperialist policy.

It was important, Phillips stressed to correct this impression. When Phillips requested policy guidance from Washington, the State Department replied that the President wanted the Nehru to return to Washington for consultations in May.

On February 10, Mahatma Gandhi with, alongwith the rest of the Congress Leadership was in prison, commenced one of his famous fasts in order to attract world situation to the political situation in India. Despite the fact that Churchill belittled the impact that the fast would have in America, official Washington become agitated.

On February 16, Hull cabled Halifax to express concern lest Gandhi die in custody. Two days later, he instructed Phillips to make an informal demarche with the Viceroy, Linlithgow took a rigid line, he was convinced "that present policy was right" and "faced with equanimity of Gandhi's death."

When doubts mounted about the survival of the 73-year old Gandhi, Secretary Hull cabled Halifax again to the State Department. During that February 20 meeting, President Roosevelt telephoned to emphasize his extreme embarassment about "sitting with hands folded doing nothing on an issue that likely to have grave international reactions."

Stressing the undesirable consequences should the Indian leader die, Roosevelt wondered if it were not better to release Gandhi from prison. Although Halifax urged Hull not publicise the demarche, the State Department let the press know that the Secretary had conveyed U.S. concerns about Gandhi's condition.

Writing the President a day after Gandhi ended the fast—defying predictions that he die—Phillips said he was deeply moved by Gandhi's willingness to sacrifice himself for Indian independence and found unfacting the Viceroy's cold reaction. He added that most Indians, believing Great Britain had no intention of granting independence, were turning to the U.S. for help in breaking the deadlock.

Surprised by Phillips, criticism of the British and sympathy for the Indian nationalist cause, Roosevelt told Harry Hopkins that Phillips suggestion was "amazingly radical for a men like Bill." Although the President did not respond directly, he asked Hopkins to show the message from Phillips to the visiting Anthony Eden. One can only surmise that Eden, after reading the letter, may have regretted having probed the assignment of Phillips so vigorously.

In order to gain more detailed impression of India before returning for consultations, Phillips widely toured in March and April. The fact that the Congress Party leadership was in Jail limited the scope of his contacts with the nationalists. The American envoy made a pain, nevertheless, of seeing Congress supporters whenever possible. Before visiting Bombay, Phillips requested permission to see Gandhi, who was still in Jail. When the Viceroy refused, the envoy accepted the turndown in apparent good grace.

Among the political figures Phillips met Mohammad Ali Jinnah, the leader of the Muslim League, the principal political organisation for India's 100 million Muslims. Although Jinnah impressed the American diplomat as being highly articulate and intelligent during that nearly four-hour session, Phillips disliked his proposal for Pakistan—the separate Muslim Homeland that Jinnah was demanding.

The more he studied Jinnah's Pakistan the less he appealed to him as the answer to India's communal problem Phillips wrote, "To break India into two separate nations would weaken both". History had proven him right.

As the dates for Phillips departure drew nearer, he renewed the request to see Mahatma Gandhi. Phillips believed a meeting with the jailed Indian Leader would help "make Indian feel that America is with them and in a position to go beyond more public assurances of friendship." Phillips concluded his usefulness would be over if the record did not show he tried seriously to meet Gandhi.

Tipped off to Phillips, intention by the American Minister in Afghanistan, Cornelius Van Engert, the Viceroy informed London he would not agree to a Phillips'-Gandhi meeting. Increasingly exhausted, Linlithgow asserted, "I am quite sure that the only possible time to adopt with Americans over the Indian affair is that it is our affair and not theirs."

"Although Linlithgow personally found Phillip friendly and distinguished, the Viceroy worried about the Viceroy talks with Indian political leaders. London reassured the Viceroy. Anthony Eden promised to take a tough line during an upcoming visit to Washington. Churchill was ready to cable Hary Hopkins."

In exchange with the State Department, Phillip was skeptical of the Viceroy's agreeing to his request, but pressed for official authorization. He wanted to make clear that America and the British were not marching together on the question of self-government for India.

Summer Wells remained stubbornly negative, arguing that the British would interpret an official request for a meeting as a change in U.S. policy toward India. In the end, Secretary Hull gave himself a loaf, agreeing that Phillip make the request to see Gandhi on a "personal" basis.

Although annoyed by Washington's lukewarm backing Phillip pressed ahead. An unusual opportunity presented itself with Linlithgow invited the American for a tigerhunt in the Himalayan foothills near the Viceroy mountain lodge at Dehradun. Swaying back and forth together on top of an elephant for three hours during the tiger hunt, the envoy pressed Linlithgow to agree to his seeing Gandhi. The Viceroy refused to budge although he did assent to Phillips' telling the press about the request. "My visit to Dehradun" the envoy wrote, had been a hunt for "Gandhi rather than a tiger. I had failed in my principal objective and had to be content with second best."

Disappointed but not surprised, Phillips returned to New Delhi. At a cocktail party for the press before Phillips departure, Herburt Mathews of the *New York Times*, promised the envoy asked about the Gandhi meeting. Phillips lost most of his guests as soon as he responded that he had asked the Viceroy to see Gandhi and had been turned down."

"There was an immediate rush for the doors to break the news," Phillips wrote, "My Mission was over." As he hoped, the news of his attempt to meet Gandhi received positive press play in India, improving the U.S. image as well as Phillips' own.

Nonetheless, the envoy left India frustrated Phillips summed up pessimistic impressions in a April 19 letter to the President. The British were sitting pretty. They had locked up the Congress leaders and would agree to no political change during the war. Militarily, the British were not likely to offer more than "token assistance" for the war effort.

The U.S. would have to bear the burden. Looking to the future, Phillips worried that, in Asian eyes, America seemed to be supporting British imperialism. He voiced concern about a "Vast bloc of Oriental peoples" with a growing dislike and distinct of the accidental".

The only remedy, Phillips argued, was "to try with every means in our power to make Indians feel that America is with them and in a position to go beyond mere public assurances of friendship."

On May 14, Phillips arrived in Washington, briefly met the President, and then drafted a summary report for President Roosevelt. This report forcefully argued that India was unlikely to cooperate fully in the war effort unless the British made a major gesture toward independence. The U.S. should have a voice, Phillips asserted not accept the British view that "this is not of your business."

Roosevelt agreed with Phillips' analysis but knowing Churchills' views on India, was reluctant to intervene directly. If a year earlier during the Cripps Mission—when the U.S.

possessed for greater beverage—Roosevelt failed to budge the Prime Minister, there was no realistic prospect he could so in May 1943 with the beginning to turn in favour of the Allies and India no longer in imminent danger of invasion. Phillips is sufficiently pursuasive that the President agreed to recommend that Churchill send Eden to India to take soundings with all leaders, including Gandhi. Roosevelt later passed on the idea to British press barron Lord Beaverbrook, who argued to raise it with Churchill apparently without result.

Since Churchill happened to be visiting Washington at the time, Roosevelt asked Phillips to present his views frankly to the Prime Minister. Their meeting at the British Embassy was not pleasant. After Phillips outlined his ideas, the Prime Minister placed back and forth across the room angrily confronted the American: "My answer to you is this: Take India if that is what you want. Take it by all means! But I warn you that if I open the door a crack there will be the greater blood-bath in all history. Mark my words" he said, shaking a finger at Phillips," I prophesised the present war, and I prophesy a bloodbath." Phillips wrote in his diary, "It was helpless to argue. It is only too clear he has a complex on India from which he will not and cannot be shaken."

After his stormy session with Churchill lunched at the White House with the President. Although the Ambassador was taken aback by Churchill's angry reaction, Roosevelt seemed "rather amused but glad that I had spoken so frankly." Without the President having to risk a direct clash with Churchill over India, the message had been put across.

That evening Phillips saw Roosevelt again over drinks "as old friends". Phillips raised the question of his returning to India, saying he saw little point unless a change in the British attitude enabled him to be of help in negotiating a settlement. Roosevelt agreed, he know there was little the U.S. could do as long as Churchill continued to dig in his heels.

Phillips never went back to New Delhi, although he technically remained the President's Personal Representative for India until his retirement in March 1945, just weeks before Roosevelt's death.

In the fall of 1943, Phillips returned to London, assuring new responsibilities as General Eisenhower's Political Adviser, a function he filled until his retirement. Phillips maintained an active interest in Indian developments and sympathy for nationalist aspirations. In keeping with the Roosevelt's policy, he undertook no initiative with the British authorities.

The war produced two unusual U.S. envoys to India, Louis Johnson and William Phillips. Despite their radically different backgrounds and styles—the Johnson, the political wheeler-dealer who hardly knew where India was, and Phillips the consumate diplomat, four times a U.S. envoy and twice Under Secretary of State—they reached the same conclusions. Both believed that they did not want to give up India.

Both thought the U.S. should actively press for Indian independence. Both ultimately failed to move Roosevelt into a battle that he was likely to lose with the closest war time ally of the U.S.

1943-1945: Roosevelt Remains Inactive in India

In Phillips' absence, leadership of the American diplomatic mission in New Delhi fell to George Merrell a mere junior diplomat. Even though the staff continued to report closely on the Indian situation remaining critical of the British attitude, U.S. diplomats in India—like Phillips in London were passive, rather than active, observers.

In late 1943, Linlithgow retired, replaced by Lord Wavell, the previous Commander-in-Chief. Although more liberal, Wavell was kept on a tight leash by Churchill, who remained adamently opposed to political concessions. Thus, a new Viceroy brought no change in Britain's policy of starting pat on India.

By the end of 1943, President Roosevelt was becoming uneasy about reports in the press and from the mission in New Delhi that the U.S. unwillingness or inability to influence British policy—and the large scale presence of American troops— was causing anti-American sentiments among Indian nationalists. To counter this, the President took the initiative on February 4, 1944, to declare again that the sole reason for the American military presence in India was to defeat the Japanese.

Roosevelt's action helped to some extent, in allying Indian disappointment about U.S. policy. A few months later, a leak of William Phillips final report to the President gave an even stronger boost to U.S. standing with Indians.

After columnist Drew Pearson on July 25, published parts of the envoy's report to Roosevelt, the story created a sensation in India and in Britain although it caused little reaction in the U.S. Phillips' scathing comments about the British and his support for nationalist aspirations delighted Indians. The British were furious about Phillips depiction of them as unbending imperialists scarcely concerned about winning the war against Japan.

When the British pressed for an official disavowal by the U.S. government, Hull successfully argued with Roosevelt against this on the grounds that the State Department agreed with Phillips' views.

The U.S. refusal to repudiate Phillips angered the British, boosting U.S. stocks further in India. Roosevelt told Phillips' wife that he assumed Summer Wells was the source of his leak. After learning the State Department in 1943—in contrast to his strongly pro-British stance when he was Under Secretary.

Pearson and Senator "Happy" Chawler of Kentucky,

stirred additional controversy by leaking some government of India telegrams, including one that said Phillips' would be *persona non grata* if he tried to return to India.

Word of this message—apparently leaked by an Indian member of Bajpai's staff—proved enormously embarrassing to all concerned.

When Phillips tried to retire in August 1944, supposedly for family reasons, Roosevelt decided the envoy should remain as his Personal Representative for India in view of the fuss. By undescoring the continuing policy differences with the British, the President's refusal to accept Phillips, resignation provided a further fillip to U.S. understanding in India.

Just before Christmas 1944, the Indian nationalist came in the U.S. received a substantial least from the extended visit of Jawaharlal's sister, Vijaya Lakshmi Pandit, she flight to NY U.S. air force Commander General Stratmaye with the blessing of the State Department.

Although Mrs. Pandit's ostensible purpose to see two daughters at College in New England and to attend a Pacific Affairs Conference, prominent friends of the Indian Scientist cause, such as author Pearl Brick and *Time Office* publisher Harry Luce, introducing Mrs. Pandit to many top Americans.

Nehru's sister also undertook a well publicised and successful cross-country speaking tour on behalf of Indian independence. Partly in response to the pressure Mrs. Pandit generated the State Department reaffirmed U.S. settlement in a political settlement in India. Acting Secretary of State Joseph Grew told the press on January 29, 1945 that the U.S. would be happy to contribute in any appropriate manner to a satisfactory settlement.

He has close ties of friendship both with the British and with the people of India. When the President was attending the Yalba Conference, Mrs. Eleanor Roosevelt invited Mrs.

Pandit to lunch at the White House—a further sign of U.S. desire to keep a good terms with Indian nationalists.

Just a month before his death, Roosevelt spoke again of his concern about colonialism in Asia, this time in a talk with State Department adviser Charles Tassig. The President commented that much of the Orient is ruled by a handful of whites and they resent it, "The President told Tassig, our goal must be to help them achieve independence—1,100,000,000 potential enemies one dangerous. Churchill does not understand this."

"Churchill Does not Understand This"

These words—"Churchill does'nt understand this"—summed up the problem Roosevelt faced throughout war in dealing with India. Supporting nationalist hopes for independence and worried about post-war Asian attitudes toward the United States, the President strongly disagreed with standpoint of imperialism of his ally Churchill.

At the time of the Cripps Mission when India itself was threatened with invasion—Roosevelt pressed Churchill hard to grant India *de facto* independence. Their written exchanges over India are among the sharpest the two wartime leaders who so admired and respected each other.

Gandhi's tactics—appalling to America—of launching the Quit India Civil Disobedience campaign at the height of the War in August 1942 and his earlier criticism of the U.S. played into the hands of British hardliners. Winning the war came first in Washington. Those opposing the war effort in effect what Gandhi was doing although he claimed he was not —got short shrift.

Had the Indian National Congress not launched the Quit India Movement, Roosevelt might have been willing to press more vigorously for further negotiations. With the entire Congress leadership in Jail, there was instead little Roosevelt could do given Churchills' rigid imperialist attitude.

Aware U.S. standing among the nationalists was slipping. Roosevelt worried about the implications for future U.S.-Indian relations. The President succeeded to some extent in distancing the U.S. from the British through symbolic gestures, such as statements on the role of the U.S. military in 1942 and 1944, sending Phillips in 1943, and then refusing to disown the leaked Phillips report in 1944.

If the U.S. attitude toward India was ambivalent support for independence yet disappointment over the attitude of the nationalist toward the war effort—the Indian reaction to U.S. policy was simply ambiguous. The Indians appreciated the indictions of the support for the nationalist cause. Johnson and Phillips views, were known during the War. Roosevelt's sharp exchanges with Churchill were revealed in later years.

At the same time, Indians felt let down by the U.S. specially after Roosevelt refused to intervene in August 1942, our Quit India Movement and thereafter remained unwilling to press the British to make for the political concessions.

Between Indian nationalists and Americans the priorities ultimately differed for Indian Congress Party leaders, even for those like Nehru, who were emotionally supportive of the Allied cause, the pot remained that of ending British rule and gaining India's independence. For Roosevelt, winning the war was the top order of business.

Everything else came second, including the independence for India, if as was the case this would risk a serious rupture with his British Allies. Because Indians and Americans expected—and thought they deserved—for each others 'support, the course of events during the war shortened mutual disappointment. This first interaction between the U.S. and India foreshadowed the frustrations that would follow during the next five decades.

2

Truman: Dealing with Neutralism

Harry S. Truman—even the name sounded unfamiliar—assumed the Presidency with Nixon, and indeed the world, stunned by the death of Franklin D. Roosevelt, who led the U.S. for twelve difficult years through the Depression and World War II. A compromise candidate for Vice President, Truman was in office barely a month when he became the President. The former Senator from Missouri had little experience in foreign affairs and no special knowledge of Asia or India.

One of his first tasks, just ten days' after Roosevelt's death, was to convene the San Francisco Conference to establish the United Nations the post-war organisation on which Roosevelt placed high hopes as a mechanism for keeping the peace. Thanks to Roosevelt's pressure in December 1941, India was a founder Member although still under British rule in April 1945. The Indian delegation selected by the Viceroy Lord Wavell, included Indian supporters of the British Raj, but no Congress nationalists. Except for Gandhi, released in 1944, the party leadership was still languishing in prison.

To protest the composition of the Indian delegation, Nehru's sister, Vijaya Laxmi Pandit, who was visiting the U.S. led the Nationalist delegation to San Francisco, claiming to be the true representative of India. Although Mrs. Pandit's attempt to challenge the official Indian delegation appointed by the Viceroy got nowhere, the effort proved a public relations success.

Representative of France, the Phillipines and most important the Soviet Union, called on Mrs. Pandit. Soviet Foreign Minister Malafor won friends in India by declaring her delegation the true voice of India. Although the U.S. gave no sign of support for the nationalist at San Francisco, President Truman invited to meet with him at the White House before she left for India. The gesture was appreciated.

The State Department also accepted the advice of William Phillips to urge the British to adopt a more liberal approach toward the subcontinent. Secretary of State Edward Stettinius and Under Secretary Joseph Grew raised the India question with visiting Foreign Secretary Anthony Eden in April and May 1943. Although the American received a non-commital response. U.S. pressure may have played a role in the British Offer of an interim government in June 1945.

Just before the Allied victory for Europe on May 8, 1945, the British released Nehru and other Congress Party leaders from jail.

During the three years of Congressites were imprisoned, Mohammad Ali Jinnah and other Muslim leaders, who remained free, won much increased support for a goal of separate Muslim homeland—Pakistan.

Two months later in July 1945, after the British Labour Party defeated the Conservatives Clement Attlee replaced Winston Churchill as Prime Minister. Unlike Churchill, Attlee and the Labour Party favoured the early handover of power in India.

With Labour in power, Indian independence was no longer in doubt. Although the U.S. continued to follow events closely, pressure from Washington on London to end Colonial rule was not needed. U.S. officials believed it was upto Indian political leaders and the British to workout the modalities, and did not see the need for trying to influence the process. In fact, as the Truman administration grappled with a host of post-war domestic and foreign policy problems, South Asia was scarcely visible on the lader system.

As the U.S. military presence wound down after the Japanese surrender in August 1945, some GJs find themselves entangled in heightened Indian domestic tensions. One U.S. servicemen died and more than thirty were injured in riots in Calcutta in November 1945 to protest trials of Indian National Army (INA) members—the captured Indian troops that fought for the Japanese.

In February 1946 following the convictions of an INA Officer some 37 Americans were among 400 casualties in Calcutta riots. In Bombay, a mob waving the Congress Party flag burned the U.S. Information Service Office.

These troubles were the exception on the whole, the 250,000 U.S. troops in the CBI Theatre departed India without problems. Except for strong racial incidents, they left behind a good impression. The GI's seemed friendlier and less staudoffish than the British. The U.S. soldiers, however, carried away remarkably few positive memories from the first extensive contact between the U.S. and India.

For more GIs, India was an ordeal, in which jungles of Assam and the slums of Calcutta erased any Hollywood, stereotypes of glamour and Romance in the mysterian East. The Indian Theater during World War II, according to political scientist Harold Isaac, produced hardly any nostalgia at all, let alone any significant literature or movies.

From New Delhi, American diplomat began to report of self-determination for all peoples in October 1945, Pandit Nehru welcomed the statement, but added his hope that it represented "something more than an expression of vague goodwill." Although everywhere in Asia and Africa people looked upto America, Nehru commented critically, "there has been some disillusionment in India in regard to American championing the independence for freedom."

Commissioner George Merrile, who succeeded Phillips as head of the New Delhi Office, kept Washington,informed regarding on-going Indian criticism of the U.S. failure to press British, French and Dutch allies for decolonization of their remaining holding in Asia. When the Phillips formally framed their independence on the 4th July 1946, Pandit Nehru sent a cabled message of congratulations. Some countries that are called independent are far from free and are under the economic or military domination of some great power, Nehru cabled, "we hope that is not with Fillipinos." Within the Congress Party leadership an aging Gandhi played a less active role. Nehru had the more conservative Sardar Vallabh Bhai—like Gandhi from Gujarat in Western India—emerged as the two senior leaders. Although in domestic matters, two shared authority, in foreign policy, Nehru, because of his outstanding position as a Congress spokesman and his unusually broad knowledge was unchallenged.

During 1946, Pandit Nehru was at first vague in talking about the foreign policy an Independent India would pursue, but the seeds for neutralism were already germinating. "We want to be friendly with the three principal powers—America, Russia and England—it is impossible for me to say what military and other alliances a free India may approve. Generally speaking it would not like to entangle itself in other peoples' feuds and imperialist rivalries", he told journalists in March. In August 1946, talking with the *New York Times*, he took much the same approach, mainly stressing Indian support for decolonization in Africa and Asia.

A month later, in September, after the formation of the interim government in which Nehru served as Deputy leader and foreign minister, he was more precise declaring, "India will follow an independent policy, keeping away from the power politics of group aligned one against another." The concept of neutralism was, thus, articulated a year before independence.

In the period of intense negotiations between the British, the Congress and the Muslim League over the future of British India, the U.S. watched with interest and generally supported British efforts hoping, like London, that some compromise—such as that envisaged by the British Cabinet Mission Plan of 1946—could be found to permit an Independent India to remain united.

The battle lines were, however, sharply drawn following the 1946 Indian general elections. In contrast to the balotting in 1937, the League swept the seats reserved for Muslims, lending for greater credibility to its demand for a separate Muslim homeland—Pakistan.

After the British formed the interim government in September 1946, which the Congress, not the League, initially joined. Acting Secretary of State Dean Achesan sought and received President Truman's approval to raise the U.S. and Indian Diplomatic Missions to full Embassy status, a more designed to bolster the standing of the interim government.

Technically, still under British rule, India made its *defacto* international relations in the fall of 1946. Ironically, Mrs. Vijaya Laxmi Pandit—an outsider in 1945 at San Francisco—became the leader of the official Indian delegation to the UN's first General Assembly Session at Lake Success, New York. Her instructions from Nehru, her brother and the foreign minister called for India's sheering clear of the democratic and communist power groups.

Although stressing "we have to be on friendly terms with both Russia and America" Nehru added—fore shadowing in his later slant on non-alignment—"Personally, I think in this world-wide tug of war there is on the whole more reason on the side of Russia, not always of course."

Also revealing of Nehru's sensitivities, and pride was the advice he gave Asaf Ali, a senior Muslim Member of the Congress Party, who became India's first ambassador to the U.S. in late 1946. "The U.S. are a great power", Nehru wrote, "and we want to be friendly with them for many reasons.

"Nevertheless, I should like to make it clear that we do not propose to be sub-servient to anybody... we have plenty of good cards in our hands and there is no need whatever for us to appear as suppliants before any country."

When the Indian envoy paid to initial protocol call on the Secretary of State George Marshall on February 26, 1947, Asaf Ali seemed to have forgotten Nehru's advice. His remarks—as recorded by Marshall were at some variance from the Nehru line. Asaf Ali urged India's political and economic development so that "it would be a baston for the world against the great northern neighbour which now castes its shadow over two continents, Asia and Europe." Asaf Ali also referred to India's need for economic help. "A number of Tenesse Valley authorities" were projected for India and it was specially in regard to these that the ambassador would call upon me for assistance," Marshall recalled.

A more accurate preview of the troubled relationship occurred on January 1947, when John Foster Dulles—a Republican Party adviser to the U.S. delegation to the UN criticised alleged communist influence in the Indian interim government in a speech to the National Publishers Association in New York city.

Nehru reached with "surprise and regret," telling the press Dulles comments "show lack of knowledge of facts and want to appreciation of the policy we are pursuing." The State Department promptly instructed the New Delhi Embassy to tell Nehru the U.S. government did not share Dulles' views and indeed, was "favourably impressed with India's avowed intention to pursue an independent but cooperative policy."

In a letter to State Department official Henry Villard, Dulles explained he did mean to suggest India was a Soviet puppet but based his comments on his impression of the Indian delegation to the United Nations and particularly of delegate Krishna Menon, who he thought a confirmed Marxian and a protege not only of Nehru but of Soviet Foreign Minister Viacheslov Molohov.

As the impasse between the Congress and the League continued, Washngton became increasingly concerned about the future of India. "Any help in the constitutional process there may well cause widespread chaos similar to China which would last for many years and could have world-wide repercussions," a worried State Department cabled the U.S. embassies in London, and New Delhi on the eve of a last ditch British effort to break the dea lock by the flying Nehru, Jinnah and other top Indian leaders for talks in London.

On December 3, 1946, Dean Acheson, then Acting Secretary, spoke out strongly during a press conference in favour of mutual concessions to permit a United India. Acheson urged both the Indian National Congress and the Muslim League to accept the British Cabinet Mission Plan for a federation. Acheson pressed confidence that the plan would permit an Indian Federal Union in which all elements of the population have ample scope to achieve their legitimate political and economic aspirations. The Department instructed the Embassy in London to convey words to Nehru and Jinnah and the Embassy in Delhi to review the text with Sardar Patel.

For the next several weeks, U.S. diplomats in London, New Delhi and Karachi forcefully urged League Leader Jinnah and his Chief Lieutenant, Liaquat Ali Khan and Congress Leaders Nehru and Patel to accept the Cabinet Plan without qualifications.

The efforts led nowhere. Saying it was upto the Congress to make the initiative, the League refused to move. The

Congress leaders, in turn, spurned the bulge from the U.S., expressing doubts about the sincerity of the League—and of the British.

In February 1947, disheartened by failure to achieve a compromise formula on independence the British decided upon shock treatment. Prime Minister Attlee announced Britain's intention to depart from India later than June 1948 with or without agreement on the future political structure. He named Lord Louis Mountbatten to replace Wavell as the Viceroy to implement the new policy.

As a courtesy—and a sign of the U.S. global leadership role—the British ambassador in Washington, Lord Inverchapel, informed Secretary George Marshall of the decision a day in advance and also left a top secret analysis of the background to the British decision.

Four months later in June 1947, Attlee called in Lewis Douglas, the U.S. envoy in London, to give him advance word of the decision to make the date of independence ahead to August 1947, and if a last try by Mountbatten failed to attain agreement on a United India, to accept partition into a Hindustan dominion and a Pakistan dominion." Attlee, Douglas reported was in "sober mood, at times tinged with sorrow."

In the spring of 1947, the State Department sent career diplomat Raymond Hare, stated to assume charge of South Asian affairs, to spend three months leaving about the subcontinent. Within the Department, the Near Eastern Division became an office, covering the Near East, South Asia and Africa, with Loy Henderson, a former specialist in Soviet Affairs, named as the first Director.

Meeting leading political personalities, the Viceroy, Gandhi, Nehru, Patel, Jinnah and others and travelling widely through the sub-continent, Hare had an unusual opportunity to witness the last days of the British India and to ponder how the U.S. should deal with independent India.

Hare's meeting with Mahatma Gandhi began with a lengthy discussion by the Indian Leader on the "beneficial mental effect" of spinning cotton "in times of emotional stress such as the present" when Hare commented he found little enthusiasm in his travels for independence, Gandhi replied the America was right. "The reason was simple", the Mahatma stated, "It was partition." When Hare asked how sympathies between the U.S. and India could be deepened, Gandhi answered, "By the employment of unselfishness, hitherto unknown in international relations."

During talks with Nehru, Hare inquired about India's post-independence foreign policy. The Congress leader, expected to become India's Prime Minister, said the country would stay "out of entanglement in the current power struggle in the belief that such was the best for India, and best for the world peace." Nehru added "there was a general fear of American economic penetration," but he thought "India would have to depend on the U.S. for certain types of support." Overall, he emphasised India's desire for friendly relations with the U.S.

Hare puzzled about what the U.S. role should be in dealing with an independent India. U.S. thought foreshadowed many of the questions that would occupy U.S. foreign policy planners dealing with India in later years:

> In the past our policy had been revolutionary war hang-over of anti-materialism and helping colonial peoples to gain their independence, in other words we had needled the British to take a more liberal attitude vis-a-vis the Indians.... But things have changed, India was apparently getting its break but, more important we had graduated, from the role of Kibizing and were playing the hand ourselves. How should we play the Indian trick? Could we do anything to bring them in actively on our side? If not,

did it make any particular difference? Could the Russians make any real headway in India? Might it be too much for them to handle as it might be for us.

When India finally gained freedom on August 15, 1947, sadness over the turmoil and bloodshed that followed partition mingled with the joy of freedom from the British rule, Washington paid only limited attention to the dramatic events in the subcontinent.

At the very moment, India and Pakistan were emerging as independent nations, the U.S. was shaping the concept of containment of communism that become the driving force behind U.S. national policy for the next 44 years.

During the summer of 1947, the U.S. foreign policy status lay on the mounting difficulties in relations with the Soviet Union. In April, President Truman announced the policy of aid for Greece and Turkey after Britain decided it could no longer shoulder the burden. In June, Secretary of State George Marshall launched the economic recovery programme for Europe that bears his name.

India's already expressed desire to have a foreign policy independent of the two power blocs that were then forming did not create too many worries in the State Department. The main American concern in Asia related to the sinking fortunes of China's Nationalist Leader, Chiang Kai Shek and the growing strength of his Chinese communist rivals.

In India, as expected Pandit Nehru, in addition to his duties as Prime Minister, continued as Foreign Minister. In many speeches and writings on international issues over the years, and especially in 1946 and 1947, Nehru had already articulated the broad outlines of the foreign policy India would follow:

First and uppermost at independence, was India's support for rapid decolonization—the end of European overseas empires. Free after its long struggle with the British, India wanted the rest of Asia and Africa to gain freedom from Western colonialism.

Foot dragging by the West European colonial powers, especially by the Dutch in Indonesia and French in Indo-China and U.S. reluctance to press its European friends too hard—disappointed Nehru. The Indians, on the other hand, were pleased by consistent Soviet support on decolonization although they recognized this was hardly disinterested.

Second was Nehru's desire that Asia's destiny rest in Asian hands and that Europe play a reduced role. Nehru envisaged a close partnership with China and its leader Chiang Kai Shek a supporter of Indian independence during the difficult years. The Indian Prime Minister soon became free Asia's best known and most articulate spokesman sponsoring a pan-Asian Conference in New Delhi in 1947.

Third was deep Indian sentiment about racial prejudice and discrimination, particularly against non-whites in South Africa, where a million Indians lived and also racial segregation in U.S. South. Nehru made South Africa India's top issue at the very first U.N. General Assembly in 1946.

Finally, there was Nehru's desire that India play an active role in world affairs without joining either of the two power blocs. Nehru favoured a policy of "Non-alignment—the term he used at the time" to ensure that India would not see its independence abridged by joining one of the two blocs, presumably the U.S. led Western group.

By standing apart, Nehru believed India would preserve its freedom of action, increase its international stature and reduce the possibility that foreign affairs would emerge as a domestic issues. In any case, as the strongest power in South Asia, India did not need external support to bolster its foreign policy position.

The first U.S. ambassador to India was Dr. Henry Grady, a businessman and former Assistant Secretary of State. No stranger to the sub-continent from his service as head of the 1942 war production mission, Grady arrived in New Delhi in June 1947, two months before independence with the interim government still in office. In a July meeting, Nehru gave Grady his thought on policy questions:

- India desired to avoid involvement with either of the power blocs, but at the same time, wished warm relations with the U.S.
- The Soviet held attraction for India as an example how a backward country develops rapidly. Politically, however, India disliked the undemocrate and totalitarian nature of the Soviet regime.
- India had concerns American economic power would, in some way impinge on her sovereignty. At the same time, India needed and desired, U.S. capital goods to help the country's development.
- India's economy would probably broadly the British Socialist model. As in Britain, basic heavy industries would be nationalised.

Four months after independence, in December 1947, State Department officials dealing with South Asia Paul Alling and Henry Grady, the ambassadors to Pakistan and India, met in Washington to review the situation. The record of their discussions indicated less concern about U.S. relations with India and Pakistan than about their relations with each other—strained by the continued exodus of Hindu and Muslim refugees and the outbreak of fighting over Kashmir.

The consensus of the meeting was that the U.S. should promote some sort of loose economic cooperation between the two states. Beyond expressions of goodwill and friendship, U.S. policy toward South Asia remained nebulous. Independent India was not a matter of high priority in Washington.

The Kashmir Dispute: U.S. Reaction Disappoints India

Neither the Cold War, dollar diplomacy nor anti-colonialism caused the first major bilateral differences between the U.S. and independent India. The problem arose over the unfinished business of partition—the dispute over the partition— the dispute over the princely state of Jammu and Kashmir.

Under the British ground rules, the rulers of the several hundred princely states were encouraged to join either India or Pakistan, taking into account factors such as geography and the religious make up of their populations. By August 1947, all but three of more than 350 states had acceded to India or Pakistan. Two of the three still standing apart were, unfortunately, the largest states, Kashmir and Hyderabad.

Strategically located in the Himalayas in the north-west portion of the subcontinent, Kashmir had a Hindu ruler and Muslim majority population. The natural beauty and cool climate of the central valley or vale of Kashmir had attracted the Mughal Emperors and then the Britain as a haven from the scorching heat of Indian summer.

When the temperature mounted in May to over 100 degrees on the plains, the British flocked to house boats on the lakes near the 5000 foot high capital of Srinagar, where the soaring Himalayas' provided a magnificent backdrop.

The Hindu ruler of Kashmir, an unpopular despot, hesitated. Before the British relinquished power, he took a preliminary step toward Pakistan but failed to complete the act of accession.

Communal disorders broke out in many parts of the State in mid-summer. In October 1947 two months after independence, as the Maharaja continued to dither about accession, Pathan tribes from Pakistan Northwest Frontier province, known for their fierce fighting qualities and their

Islamic formation, swept into the State, advancing swiftly the capital of Srinagar. In panic, the Maharaja appealed for Indian help. Under pressure from Delhi, he executed the documents of accession to India.

Governor General Lord Mountbatten convinced Nehru that Kashmir's accession should be conditional until the people of the state could vote on the final status. Mountbatten's acceptance of accession for the Government of India stated explicitly that when Law and order were restored, and the invaders gave the question of the state's accession should be settled by inference to the people. A few days later, in a November 2 radio broadcast, Prime Minister Nehru similarly stated that a plebicite would settle the state's fate.

A dramatic airlift of Indian troops secured the Kashmir airport, preventing the fall of Kashmir's capital. The Indian soldiers then gradually drove back the Pathan tribesmen, the invaders having failed to seize Srinagar when it lay defenders wasting their advantage on looting and pillaging. After attempts to end the fighting failed Nehru—following Mountbatten's counsel—took the issue to United Nations Security Council, behaving that India's legal and moral case against Pakistan was strong.

Quite apart from political considerations Jawaharlal Nehru had a strong emotional attachment to Kashmir his family's homeland. The Indian leader was a Kashmiri Pandit, a Brahmin subcaste that ranked now the top of the Hindu social order. Nehru was also a personal friend of Sheikh Mohammad Abdullah, the Charismatic leader of the Nationalists in Kashmir, to whom the Maharaja turned over effective power after joining India. Politically the Sheikh had close ties with the Indian Congress Party supported the idea of a secular state and opposed the concept of Pakistan.

Initially, the U.S. was reluctant to become involved in Kashmir problem when British Commonwealth Secretary

Noel Baker presented detailed ideas in January 1948 for conducting a plebiscite under international control, the State Department's response was lukewarm.

Near East Office Director Loy Hinderson—soon to become ambassador to India—urged Acting Secretary of State Robert Lovett to stay out of the dispute. He argued the U.S. was already overcommitted globally, should avoid making a choice between giving support to the interests of India or Pakistan, and should not through U.S. involvement provide the Soviets an opening to mix into the affairs of South Asia. State Department officials were also skeptical the U.N. would prove effective in resolving the dispute.

The U.S. nonetheless, cooperated with the British when the Kashmir question came before the U.N. Security Council. The initial presentation by India and Pakistan made clear the enormous gap between the two parties. As Indian political Scientist Sisir Gupta wrote, "Both appeared as aggrieved parties both as the complainants. To India, Pakistan had committed aggression and violated her territory, to Pakistan, India always was hostile and was intent on undoing the creation of Pakistan its e.g.

With the U.S. and British delegations the time moves, the Security Council on April 12, 1948 adopted a resolution setting it the UN Commission for India and Pakistan (UNCIP). The Indians reacted sourly, angry that the U.N. failed to condem Pakistan as the aggressor and seemed to be treating the two countries as equal parties to the dispute. Based apparently on what Belgian ambassador Prince de Ligne told him, Nehru saw the U.S. stance on Kashmir as influenced less by the merits of the dispute than by U.S. global interests in light of the tensions with the Soviets.

Expressing great distress to the Viceroy Lord Mountbatten, Nehru called the American and British attitude on Kashmir, "completely wrong," warning their stance would have far reaching results in our relations "write his sister he charged, "The U.S.A. and the UK have played a dirty role." Nehru hold British Commonwealth office Under Secretary "Gordon Walk the "motives of the U.S. were to get military and economic concessions in Pakistan."

During most of the summer of 1948, UNCIP shuttled back and forth between Pakistan and India trying in vain to reach an agreement on arrangements for a cease fire and a plebiscite. A major hurdle was a basic agreement over who would control Kashmir during the plebiscite. Pakistan wanted a U.N. administrator. The India wanted Sheikh Abdullah to remain in charge of the State, aided by U.N. observers. When India eventually accepted the UNCIP proposal in August, Pakistan rejected the plan.

In October 1948, as UNCIP continued its work, Secretary of State George Marshall at the urging of British Foreign Secretary Earnest Bevin—discussed Kashmir with Prime Minister Nehru during the U.N. General Assembly session in Paris. According to Marshall, Nehru was touched during their discussions finding it difficult to remain calm while talking about Kashmir. Before the issue of Pakistan aggression, Nehru asserted with much emotion that the fate of Kashmir was important for Indian policy of secular democracy which be contrasted with Pakistan's idea of a state based on religion.

Eventually calming down, Nehru in the end said he was very conscious of the problem, was sincerely desirous of having it settled and he hoped that some solution could be worked out.

January 1, 1949 saw an important step forward as both countries accepted cease-fire. Although there was no agreement on the arrangements for holding plebiscite, the Security Council appointed Admiral Chester Ninitz, commander of the U.S. Navy in the Pacific during World War II, as plebiscite administrator.

The principal differences related to the pace of withdrawal of Pakistani and Indian forces from Kashmir administration during the voting. Unlike the previous year, the Pakistanis gradually shifted their position to accept almost all UNCIP proposals. It was India that began to dig in its heels in opposition.

U.S. pressure in support of UNCIP increasingly irked New Delhi. On August 15, 1949 reaching to charges India was not acting in good faith on Kashmir, Nehru called in Ambassador Lay Henderson—who had by then replaced by Henry Grady—to complain he was "tired of receiving moral advice from the U.S.... so far as Kashmir was concerned he would given an inch. He would hold his ground even if Kashmir, India, and the whole world went to pieces." Nor was Nehru any happier when President Truman urged him, in August 25, message to accept arbitration as a way to break the impasse on the plebiscite. The Indians rejected Truman's suggestion, along with a similar proposal from British Prime Minister Clement Attlee.

Kashmir figured prominently in the official talks during Prime Minister Nehru's visit to the United States in October and November 1949. After President Harry Truman raised the issue during a White House meeting and Nehru agreed on the importance of finding a solution—Secretary of State Acheson tried and failed in a subsequent talk with Nehru to pin the Indian leader down on specifics.

As exhausted Acheson invade, "I got a curious continuation of a public speech and flushes of anger and deep dislike for his appointments." Nehru's main points—according to Acheson— were that the U.N. should not deal with the merits of the dispute until the Pakistan forces withdrew from Kashmir, that a plebiscite on the basis of a religious state would be disastrous for the stability of his subcontinent and that the Pakistan had no legitimate claim to Kashmir.

Despite Nehru's negative reaction, the U.S. continued to press for Indian acceptance of McNaughten's ideas. In January 9, 1950 meeting with Mrs. Vijaya Laxmi Pandit, who had become Ambassador to Washington and External Affairs Ministry Secretary General Bajpai, Dean Acheson strenuously urged India not again to refuse UN Kashmir proposals.

Angry about the U.S. demarche, Nehru sharply replied via Bajpai that Achesons' message:

> Is not only unfriendly in tone and substance but appears to us to be seeking to bring pressure on our government under threat of consequences... it appears to be totally forgotten that we are not the aggressors, but that we are the victims of aggression. I would like to add that it is a matter of great personal request to me that Mr. Secretary Acheson should have sent us message of kind.

After the failure General McNaughten's effort, the Security Council sent prominent Australian jurist Sir Aven Dixon to South Asia to try his hand. Arriving during the oven like heat of May, Dixon toiled through the summer of 1950, working quietly with Nehru, Pakistan's Prime Minister Liaquat Ali Khan and others. When he concluded that a statewise plebiscite was impracticable, the Australian suggested an approach similar to an idea put forward earlier by Girja Bajpai limiting the vote to the valley while partitioning the rest of the state on religious lines. In the end, this proposal failed after Nehru rejected the idea of U.N. control of the valley during the plebiscite.

The Australian who, perhaps came closer to reaching a Kashmir settlement than any one else, left disappointed at the end of the summer. In his report to the Security Council, Dixon wrote, "I have formed the opinion that if there is any chance of settling the dispute over Kashmir's by agreement between India and Pakistan now lies in portion and in some means of allocating the valley rather than an overall plebiscite." He recommended that the UN not pursue the mediation effort on Kashmir, letting the two countries seek a political settlement on their own.

The U.S. notwithstanding Dixon's recommendations did not favour letting the issue drop. In November 17, 1950 meeting between the Secretary Acheson and Pakistan's Foreign Minister Zaffrullah Khan, Acheson said, "I need advice, and guidance. We have very discouraged by India's attitude and had been trying through our Ambassador to make India see what could be done with what success. I do not know." In the discussion that followed, Acheson was in basic agreement with Zaffrullah's position that unless Indian troups were removed and a UN administrator appointed for the vale, it would not be possible to have a fair plebiscite.

In 1951 saw a renewed effort to tackle Kashmir with Dr. Frank Graham appointed as UN mediator. A former President of the University of North Carolina and U.S. Senator, Graham had gained an excellent reputation for his work in resolving the Dutch-Indonesia dispute. His approach was to package ideas into a series of detailed points and then seek agreement on these by both sides. By October was down to three outstanding questions: the number of Indian troops to remain in Kashmir after demilitarization, the length of the demilitarization period, and the date of formal appointment of the plebiscite administrator.

Although the assassination of Pakistan's Prime Minister in October 1951 and India's first general election in January 1952 delayed Graham's work, he toiled away, Graham impressed the Indians. Nehru describing him as "a sincere and earnest man anxious to do what he can to further a settlement."

Chester Bowles, who replaced Loy Henderson as ambassador in November 1951, quickly injected his own ideas on Kashmir. The contrast between the two American envoys was striking. Henderson was a veteran career diplomat, whose service in the Soviet Union helped shape a strong an-anti-crimes bent.

Conservative in outlook he had few hopes that Indo-American relations would be smooth, although Henderson established a good working relationship with Secretary General Bajpai, his dealing with Nehru were often tense and blunt. Henderson's cables even down to earth and terse.

Bowles came to the job after losing a bid of re-election as Governor of Connecticut in the 1950 elections. A pioneer, in modern advertising in the 1920s and 1930s, Bowles had gained a natural reputation as the successful head of the Office of the Price administration during World War II. He became active in politics after the war as a member of the Democratic Party's liberal wing. Following the communist takeover of China, Bowles felt people would look closed at India to see if democracy could provide an alternative to communism as a path to economic development in Asia.

Bowles urged the U.S. to restrict its role to serving as a friend to both countries, willing to help in solving the dispute without taking sides. The State Department responded unsympathetically to Bowles views, instructing the envoy to continue giving full and firm support to Graham's efforts.

Bowles reported, "Nehru acting wholly in unreasonable manner and will probably continue to do so." The Prime Minister, Bowles continued, hoped in the problem would away since he knew India had a weak position internationally.

At the U.N., the Russian generally remained silent during Kashmir debates until 1952. They abstained from voting although their propaganda portrayed dispute as an Anglo-American imperialist plot. By not openly taking sides, they presumably hoped to avoid danger in their relations with either India or Pakistan.

Soviet delegate Jacob Ralik, thus caused surprise when in January 1952 he sharply criticised Dr. Frank Graham's report to the Security Council. Taken aback by Soviet support called in the American charge 'd' affairs. Stressing that India had not asked the Soviets to intervene, Bajpai emphasised that India did not want Kashmir to become embrailed in the cold war.

Chronic friction between Washington and New Delhi over Kashmir inevitably had a negative impact on bilateral relations as Nehru predicted. In October 1952, Nehru wrote G.L. Mehta, the Bombay businessman he appointed to succeed Mrs. Pandit as ambassador to Washington, that India has told the State Department in the clearest language that we consider their attitude in this matter, completely wrong and unfriendly to India and that this in the way of the development of cordial relations between India and America, that all of us , more than anything else.

For Indians, the Kashmir question was a central and vital foreign policy issue inevitably limited with the traumatic partition of British India and the creation of Pakistan. As Joseph Corbel one time Chairman of UNCIP, wrote:

> The struggle for Kashmir in every sense another battle in the continuing struggle and by now irrational war of ideas. In the minds of Nehru and the Congress, Kashmir is in miniature, another Pakistan and if the Muslim nation can be successfully governed by India, then their philosophy of secularization vindicated.

The U.S. looked at Kashmir quite differently. Washington regarded the problem as a serious dispute between two countries with which U.S. had friendly relations, but as an issue involving vital U.S. interests. Kashmir also appeared to be type of regional dispute that the U.N. should be able to resolve, especially as India's original suggestion for a plebiscite provided a basis for settlement.

The concern in Washington was that in the absence of a settlement fighting would again break out between India and Pakistan.

Although at first Washington took no strong position on the merits, the U.S. backed the U.N. call for a plebiscite and gradually became exhosperated by Nehru's backsliding on this question and by incremental steps New Delhi took to formally incorporate Kashmir into the Indian Union. George McGhee, Assistant Secretary of State for near Eastern and South Asian affairs through much of this period, commented that the main U.S. concern was about the possible outbreak of war over Kashmir. We wanted to avert full scale war between India and Pakistan—this was always a threat. Our efforts failed because of Nehru," Mc Ghee assaulted.

Bilateral Relations: Mutual Misunderstanding: Quite apart from Kashmir, the U.S. and India found themselves at odds at many foreign policy questions unrelated to the Cold War. International control of atomic energy, Palestines, and the creation of Israel, Indonesia and Indo-China were issue on which the two countries differed. Although Nehru's insistent independence from the West annoyed U.S. policy makers—ambassador Grady told him "India should get on the democratic side immediately—Washington enthusiastically accepted India's policy not to become entangled.

The overall orientation of Indian policy was not directed against the U.S. In the late 1940s, India's relations with Moscow were fosty. Soviet dictator Joseph Stalin regarded Jawaharlal Nehru with suspicious as a "bourgeois democrat and lacky of British imperialism. Even though Nehru sent his sister as India's first envoy to Moscow, the Soviet Leader never once received Mrs. Pandit during her two years in the Soviet Union.

On March 8, 1948 when Nehru elaborated India's foreign policy before the Constituent Assembly, he made a point to have the Ministry of External Affairs inform ambassador

Grady that it would be unthinkable for India to be on the Russian side in the event of a World War.

Visiting Washington a month later, External Affair Secretary General Girja Bajpai made the same point in meeting with Loy Henderson, then Director of the State Departments office of Near East and South Asian Affairs and acting Secretary of State Robert Lovett. Bajpai stressed that the people in the U.S. who thought India was in the Soviet Camp, were wrong. In the event of war, India will side with the forces of freedom.

The desire for better relations with Washington paralleled the remarkable turn around in relation between India and Britain after independence. Contrary to the expectations and Indian Congress Party programme, independent India decided to remain in the British Commonwealth—a step which London and New Delhi regarded at that time as of great importance. After having improved ties with London, Nehru hoped in 1949, to firm up relations with the U.S. The Prime Minister wrote his friend Krishna Menon then High Commissioner in Britain, he was as prepared to align with the U.S. somewhat as long as it was not necessary to become subsequent. Personally, Nehru had ambivalent feelings about America, a country he had never visited. The Indian leader had a considerable bias that seemed to continue the anti-American social prejudices of the British elite and the anti-American policy views of the left wing of the British Labour Party. In foreign policy dealing, he found U.S. too cocksure about the rights and wrongs of the cold war, too insensitive to the aspirations of the colonial people and too patronizing in dealing with India.

Despite disappointments over Kashmir and difference on anti-colonial issues, Nehru remained, nonetheless, hopeful about relations with Washington, behaving the U.S. would be interested in friendly relations with India because it is well recognized today all over the world that the future of Asia will be powerfully determined by the future of India.

A note Nehru wrote on negotiation for a commercial treaty with U.S. spelled his antiviolent views:

> America is the most powerful and richest country in the world and can certain help India a great deal. There is no reason why we should not get that help and remove causes of friction between us. But it is true that America represents a reactionary policy in world affairs, I think a policy which will not succeed. The safest policy, therefore appears to be friendly to America to give their fair terms, to write their help on such terms, and at the same time not to tie ourselves upto much with their world or their economic policy.

In October and November 1949; the Indian leader paid his first visit to U.S. During the three weeks trip, Nehru travelled from the Atlantic to the Pacific coasts seeing much of America and meeting many prominent figures from a broad cross-section of U.S. life.

The Prime Minister cut an impressive figure in numerous public appearances as an eloquent advocate of India, explaining its neutralist policies and seeking friendship with the U.S. without becoming a political camp follower or a supplicant for an economic help. The public generally accorded him a warm welcome as a leading representative of free Asia. The liberal press landed Nehru as the hope of Asia specially after the fall of China to the Communists.

The official side of the trip went much less well. Nehru's antiviolence toward U.S. policy was matched by the skepticism of U.S. leaders toward the Indian approach. The Americans found Nehru's views on foreign affairs perplexing and imprecise. They received coolly his suggestions that the West should be more reasonable in dealing with the Russians and recognise Communist China. After a three hour informal private meeting, Secretary of State Dean Acheson wrote:

> I was convinced that Nehru and I were not destined to have a pleasant personal relationship. He was so important to India's survival and was so important to all of us, that if he did not exist-as Voltaire said of God—he would have to be invented. Nevertheless he was one of the most difficult men I had ever to deal with.

If the American leadership found the Indian Prime Minister stiff and vague, Nehru in turn both Truman and Acheson candidescending. The Prime Minister wrote Dr. S. Radhakrishnan the South Indian scholar philosopher who replaced Mrs. Pandit as Indian envoy to Moscow, "They had gone all out to welcome me and I am very grateful to them for it and expressed myself so. But they expected something more than gratitude and goodwill and that more I could not supply them."

The Prime Minister taken aback by the flanking of material wealth and what often seemed a lack of culture and good taste in the U.S. In New York, for example, the hosts at a lunch with businessmen made a joint boasting that the company's represented at the table were worth more than the $ 20 billion.

Nehru also found the conversation at the White House dinner less than intellectually scrutilating a main topic of discussion and Vice President Althen Barkley concerned the merits of Kentucky borurbon whiskey.

A few months after returning to India, Nehru was annoyed by the warm welcome given Pakistan's Prime Minister Liaquat Ali Khan in the U.S. writing to his sister in Washington, he corped:

> The Americans are either very naive and singularly lacking in intelligence. They go through the same routine whether it is Nehru or the Shah or Liaquat Ali. It does appear that there is a concerted attempt to build up Pakistan and build

> down, if I may say, India, it surprises me how immature in their political thinking the Americans are! In their dealings with Asia, they show a lack of understanding which is surprising.

The positive public relations impact of the trip also proved short lived. In the spring of 1950 the American Embassy in New Delhi, reported about increased anti-U.S. feelings in India. Although ostensibly directed at supposed U.S. faults (racial prejudice, pro-colonialist policies etc.) ambassador Loy Henderson thought the real causes were: the lack of economic aid, the U.S. position on Kashmir and fears that the U.S. was using its economic muscle to press India to shed its socialist policies.

With the communists on the Indian political left flaming the flames, Henderson the upsurge was unlikely to dissipate unless the U.S. backed up its rhetoric about friendly relations with concrete action, especially in the area of economic aid.

The State Department replied testily—reflecting growing distance for India—that friendly relations had to be based on more than loans or gifts. The message argued that the best way to win Indian friendship was to convince New Delhi that "our objectives are disinterested and constructive as we are confident the Inds wid (sic) wish their own to be disregarded. Present Ind (sic) attitudes subj (sic) these beliefs to serious doubt.

When placed alongside similarly pompted comments, Nehru was making about the U.S. in his letter to his sister and others, he exchange between the State Department and Henderson underscored the troubled nature of relations between India and America in the early months of 1950.

The Korean War: Indian Neutralism put to the Test

The cold war became a hot war after North Korean forces invaded South Korea on June 25, 1950. The initial Indian reaction to the outbreak of hostilities pleasantly surprised

Washington. Sir Benegal Rau, India's UN delegate, voted for the security council's condemnation of the invasion several days later, India voted for a second resolution calling for support to South Korea to repel the attack. Nehru delayed taking this action until the full Cabinet approve the Indian position. India appeared, thus standing with the West against the communists on a fundamental issue of war and peace.

There could be no. doubt that the North Korean government had committed aggression on a large scale on South Korea, Nehru wrote his Chief Minister to surrender to it was wrong and would have meant the collapse of the United Nations as well as led to other dangerous consequences.

Nehru was, however, extremely uneasy. Apart from fear that events would lead to a World War, he strenuously disapproved of President Truman's linking the Korean conflict with the problems of Formosa and Indo-China. He saw U.S. policy as threatening to enlarge the war in the defense of western interests.

Favouring Chinese cooperation of Formosa and the withdrawal of the French from Indo-China, Nehru saw both issues in terms of Asianationalism, as part of the struggle to free the region from Western domination rather than a contest between pro and anti-communist forces.

In early July, Nehru launched a coordinated peace effort with Indian envoys in Moscow (Radhakrishnan), London (Krishna Menon), New York (Sir Bengal Rau), Washington (Mrs. Pandit) and Secretary General Bajpai in New Delhi all the act. The heart of the proposal was that, for talks on Korea the Soviets would return to the Security Council and the Chinese communists would occupy the UN seat of the Chinese nationalists. Although Stalin temporised in his reply, Dean Acheson with Truman's blessing turned Nehru down flatly, his feelings. The Indian press, taking its cue from the government, blamed Washington for thwarting the peace initiative.

Being right about the Chinese interventions won Nehru no friends in the U.S. press or in the American Leadership. *The New York Times* once full of praise for Nehru, was critical. "Nehru purports to speak for Asia," the *Times* wrote, but it is the voice of obnegation, his criticism turnout to have been obstructive, his reply appeasement."

Mrs. Pandit reported that Truman supposedly told a Congressman that "Nehru has sold us down to Hudson. His attitude has been responsible for our loosing the war in Korea."

At a staff meeting of the U.S. delegation to the UN, John Foster Dulles—serving as a Republican adviser—said that since the Indians were eager to solve someone else's problem, perhaps, the U.S. should sit on the sidelines and let the Indians try to solve Korea. That might make them less willing in other peoples affairs, the future Secretary of State commented.

In early 1951, Secretary Acheson was less than enthused about a trust by the Indians—supported by the British—for a Korea cease-fire resolution that collided with a U.S.-backed drive for a UN resolution condemning the Chinese communist military intervention.

After difficult deliberations, Washington agreed to go along with the Indian proposal, which the General Assembly approved in January 1951.

When the Chinese communists rejected the resolution, the General Assembly proceeded to condemn the Chinese as aggressors by a resounding 50:78 majority. India and Burma were the only two countries to join the Communists in opposing this resolution. Nehru, then, temporarily gave up his peacemaking efforts, writing in exasperation to his friend Krishna Menon in London that we failed in the end before the big stick of the U.S.

Krishna Menon's aid tung and striking—almost diabolic

—looks soon make him a media celebrity at the UN. Since his barbed verbal thrusts were more often than not armed at the U.S., Menon presence added a new, and ultimately heavy burden to Indo-American relations.

After Dwight D. Eisenhower swamped the democrats in the November 1952 elections, the Indians and British feared that the incoming Republican administration might widen the war in Korea. They were eager to have a cease-fire in place before the new President took office in January 1953. Seizing the opportunity, Krishna Menon told franetically to shape a resolution that would bridge American and Chinese and North Korean differences over the fate of the thousands of the prisoners of war who did not want to return home.

Although Nehru agreed on the basic issue of no forced repatriation, Acheson found Krishna Menon exasperatingly difficult to negotiate with. Reporting to President Truman, the Secretary commented that Menon resolution as they say in the strike settlement lingo, gives us the words at the other side the decision. Menon, Acheson told a staff meeting, seemed to be "a master of putting words together, so that they convey no ideas at all. Menon's plan, the Secretary asserted was like a room with only one door, "powling to the north."

Running parallel to Indo-American friction over the Korean war was the continuing dispute about the recognition of the Communist China. Even before Indian independence, Nehru regarded good relations with China as a fundamental plank in India's foreign policy. He saw the two ancient countries and civilizations emerging from European domination to become pillars of the New Asia.

When the nationalist with whom he had friendly relations, fell from power, Nehru believed the communist victory due less to the attractiveness of Marxist ideology than the shortcoming of Chiang Kai Shek regime.

Another bone of contention between Washington and New Delhi was the peace treaty with Japan. Negotiated with John Foster Dulles, the treaty was for signature in the summer of 1951. To the dismay of Washington and Dulles, Nehru decided that India would not sign.

Nehru believed the treaty should have included the Soviet Union and Communist China and was also unhappy about the securing arrangements between Japan and the U.S.

The U.S. leadership, but especially the treaty negotiator Dulles, was put out by India's insistence on standing apart. Apparently suggested by the final Indian turndown, Dulles told ambassador Mrs. Pandit, "I cannot accept this. Does your Prime Minister realise that I have prayed at every stage of the treaty?" Nehru's sister was at a loss for words. Nehru recognised that India's decision would "naturally cause resentment and some disappointment" in Washington.

When the U.S. reply "was conched in language which is usual in correspondence between governments," Nehru was annoyed but decided against using "strong language in our answer."

In Kashmir, where Indian soldiers shed their blood against Pakistan, the U.S. attitude badly upset the Government of India. In Korea, where the U.S. soldiers were shedding their blood against North Korean and Chinese communist forces, the Indian attitude badly upset the U.S. government. India and the U.S. each wanted aggression punished and basic principles of international morality upheld.

Fearful of expanded conflict in the Far East, the Indians urged moderation and compromise in the case of Korea. Fearful of an India-Pakistan war, the U.S. similarly urged moderation and compromise in the case of Kashmir. Neither Washington nor New Delhi was friends in each others' capital by playing the peace-maker.

Economic Assistance to India: A Slow Start

Although in the 1950s and 1960s economic assistance became a major element of U.S. policy toward India, aid was not an important issue immediately after independence. The U.S. had yet to initiate assistance programmes for the developing world. It was only in 1948 that Washington launched Marshall Plan aid for nations of Western Europe.

With the U.S. at the peak of its economic power Nehru and other Indian leaders, nonetheless, looked to America for help. Even before the first anniversary of independence, Minister of External Affairs Secretary General Bajpai, during in April 1948 visit to Washington, sought aid for hydro-electric projects. Bajpai feels led nowhere.

There was also limited activity on the part of the U.S. private sector. Despite the fact that Washington encouraged investment in India, few U.S. businesses took this advice, except for large concerns—like the oil companies—already experienced in the international field. India's announced socialist economic policy, corporate finance about South Asia, and the reputation India soon acquired not only as having a terribly poor country but as a difficult place to do business-all acted as dampens on investment.

In India, the attitude toward foreign business was analogous. Although New Delhi wanted U.S. investment, there was, at the same time, fear the U.S. would use its economic might to interfere with India's sovereignty or to unfairly exploit the country's resources. Nehru himself thought the concerns were overdrawn.

The question of economic domination of India by U.S.A. is not that frightens me, he wrote. The political left in India was able, nonetheless, to exploitnaturalists fears about foreign business encroachment deeply rooted in the British economic exploitation of India during the colonial period.

In his January 1949 inaugural address, President Truman announced the programme of technical assistance to help poorer countries, known as Point Four. Although the idea inserted in the speech by White House staff without advance planning generated much interest, little actually happened for more than a year.

When Nehru visited Washington in October, 1949, obtaining U.S. aid was high on his agenda but, perhaps, out of pride—in talking with the U.S. leaders, "he mentioned this, though rather casually."

Just before Nehru arrived, ambassador Henderson made the first serious proposal on aid to India, recommending a five year $8500 million programme. With economic assistance, India might become a stalwart and worthy champion of the West in Asia; without aid, Henderson argued, India might degenerate into a vast political and economic swamp. Henderson was ahead of his time in making the proposal.

The Truman administration remained ambivalent about India, uncertain U.S. interests warranted an investment on so large a scale and uncertain the U.S. Congress would support such a programme. Nehru did not help the case for economic aid when he failed to press the issue seriously during his visit. A month later, in November 1949, the State Department informed Henderson his aid proposal was rejected.

India's most pressing economic need in late 1949 was for food assistance to starve off a possible famine. With this in mind Nehru asked the President for a million tons of wheat to provide a stronger food reserve. In spite of the fact that Truman responded positively, delays and misunderstandings including an attempt to barter the wheat for strategic materials frustrated an accord.

The upshot was ill will. The Indians that U.S. intriguely trying to use food aid as a policy level. The Americans complained the Indians never adequately followed up after Nehru talked with Truman. As the State Department cabled stiffly to Ambassador Henderson, "The USG may be pardoned, if it is puzzled to learn it is criticised for India's failure to obtain aid when no firm or formal request was ever made."

Despite the unfriendly reaction—confirmation of India's unpopularity with many in Congress—Truman decided to proceed with food aid legislation. Enlisting the support of former Republican President Herbet Hoover—who won fame for his role in feeding Europe after World War I. Truman sent a strong message to the Congress on February 12, urging two millions tons of wheat for India on both humanitarian and national interest grounds.

At first, things went smoothly but anti-Indian feelings led to procedural delays, especially in the Senate where Senator Cornwell refused to schedule hearing. After a plea from Truman, the Senator finally relented in mid-April.

Conservatives in the House of Representative Rules Committee then raised new obstacles that threatened to block the bill. Annoyed by Congressional foot-dragging and criticism of India, Nehru hit back. "We would be unworthy of high responsibility with which we have been charged if we bartered away, in the slightest degree our countrys' self-respect or freedom of action even for something we badly need," the Indian leader stated on May 1 over All India Radio.

Nehru's comments prompted an angry response among legislators in Washington, who postponed further action on the bill until the Indian government clarified whether in fact, still desired the aid. An additional complication was whether the wheat would be provided as gift—the Truman administration and Senate proposal—or as a loan—House of Representatives approach.

Realising the damage he has caused, Nehru spoke

positively about food aid in Parliament on May 10, indicating that, if given a choice India preferred a loan rather than a gift. Nehru's statement soothed Congressional nerves. The billion approving $190 million of wheat as a long-term loan finally passed in early June. On June 1951 President Truman signed the measure into Law, initiating the first of many U.S. food aid shipments to India.

The arrival of U.S. wheat ensured India could avoid famine. The extended haggling in the Congress and the outburst of anti-Indian sentiments, however, undercut any public relations benefits.

Nehru commended that, despite the best efforts of the U.S. administration, there has been a feeling of resentment in India regarding the obstructionist techniques of some people in the American Congress. In contrast, the Soviet Union received much applause for a smaller food shipment that arrived before U.S. wheat.

Although Chester Bowles first tour as ambassador to India lasted little more than a year, he made an ending impression. A master at public relations, Bowles `sold' America to Indians in a way that his predecessor Lay Henderson, a superb professional diplomat but no salesman or image-maker could not do.

Bowles spoke frequently with the Indian press, fielding with patience and understanding tough questions about U.S. racial discrimination, criticism of U.S. foreign policy and other subjects.

He travelled widely throughout India, visiting villages and improvised urban areas as well as holy nobling with wealthy elite. He focussed U.S. aid on India's community development programme to help India's poor.

Bowles enthusiasm and goodwill had a positive impact, helping to offset the policy imitants and friction between New

Delhi and Washington. He succeeded in showing Indians that America cared about them and their nation's effort to modernize within the democratic framework. He also had an impact on informed U.S. opinion.

When India held its first democratic election on the basis of universal sufferage in 1952, Bowles stressed the significance of India's adherence to the democratic system. He made some headway, especially among liberals, in gaining acceptance for his conviction that India deserved a greater attention from American foreign policy-makers. Bowles' achievement, in one start year was substantial.

U.S. Military Supply to South Asia: The Beginnings

After 1954, the U.S. military supply relationship with Pakistan would become a major irritant in Indo-U.S. relations from the Indian perspective the biggest single war to friendlier ties. Although Pakistan first requested arms aid barely two months after independence in the fall of 1947, when it received a flat state Department turndown, it was ironically, that first procured arms from the U.S. Before the Kashmir war, modest sales of military equipment to a former World War II ally posed no difficulty for the State Department.

The outbreak of fighting in Kashmir, however, led President Truman to impose an embargo on arms exports to either India or Pakistan in order to armed fuelling a conflict which the U.N. was trying to stop. After the cease-fire agreement in January 1949, the ban was lifted.

Pakistan's Prime Minister Liaquat Ali Khan renewed the request for U.S. arms without success during 1948 with Secretary Marshall, Liaquat line—similar to the approach Jinnah used when Raymond Hare called on Muslim League leader in 1947 was to seek military aid to bolster Pakistan and other Muslim states against the communists.

Liaquat continued the quest during his spring 1950 visit

to the U.S. In contrast to Nehru, the Pakistani leader Liaquat Ali made an excellent impression voicing his country's support for U.S. foreign policy at the same time he urged the U.S. to provide Pakistan military assistance.

During the Truman administration, arms for Pakistan, thus received consideration, but nothing concrete happened despite support from senior officials like McGhee and Byroade. Although there was some interest in the Defence Department in possible U.S. airbases in Pakistan, South Korea did have a high priority in the Pentagon's strategic planning funding for military aid was short.

Needs and priorities were greater elsewhere. Washington also knew arms for Pakistan would encounter a severe reaction from India. A comment by Secretary Dean Acheson best summed things up.

"The Pakistanis," Acheson recalled "were always asking U.S. for arms and I was always holding them off." After John Foster Dulles became Republican Secretary of State in January 1953, the situation would change.

Indo-U.S. Relations: Through the Prison of the Cold War

"India had become the pivotal state in non-communist Asia by virtue of its relative power, stability and influence." The policy paper hoped India would agree "voluntarily to associate itself with the U.S. and like-minded countries opposing communism," and supported ambassador Henderson's recommendations that an aid programme be initiated.

The continuing incompatibility of U.S. and Indian views was, however, underscored in April 1951 discussions that Assistant Secretary McGhee and ambassador Henderson had with Prime Minister Nehru in New Delhi. These talks confirmed a wide gap between U.S. and Indian thinking on the major foreign policy issues of the day-handling the war in Korea, the Soviet Union and communist China. As Henderson put it, there remained "a fundamental difference between U.S. about the aggressive intent of international communism."

Nehru told the Constituent Assembly on March 8, 1949:

> Our policy will continue to be not only to keep aloof from power alignments, but to try to make friendly cooperation possible. If, by any chance, we align ourself definitely with one power group, we may, perhaps from one point of view do some good, but I have not the shadow of a doubt from a greater point of view, not only from India, but of world peace, it will do harm.... Therefore, it becomes all the more necessary that India should not be lined up, with any group of powers which, for various reasons are full of fear of war and preparing for war.

Nehru behaved, firmly that the war in Korea proved that India's policy was right—just the opposite of the U.S. view. Nehru stated:

> I believe the policy we have pursued has been demostrably proved to be good for India and good for world peace. I think it has averted or helped in averting the spread of the Korean War.... the mere fact that both our friends and critics inevitably look to India to take up some step to breake the present impasse, in the world is significant of the virtue of India's foreign policy.

The Prime Minister remained consistently critical about U.S. policy toward Kashmir, continuing to believe his was motivated by an interest in aligning Pakistan with an Islamic bloc, under western against the Soviets—"Pakistan was easy to keep within their sphere of influence in regard to wide policies, while India was an uncertain and possibly unreliable quality." Still the Prime Minister doubted the U.S. would push too far, believing "it is thoroughly understood... in the USA that India counts for more than Pakistan."

By the end of the Truman years, Indo-American relations had fallen into the pattern of chronic friction that had so perplexed observes over the years. Although there were positive aspects, especially with Bowles as ambassador, a sense of estrangement was only too evident.

With hindsight, the reasons are not hard to find. After the Korean war made the Cold War a global struggle, U.S. and Indian World views were bound to clash shortly and did on fundamental security issues. The U.S. saw a worldwide threat from the Soviet Union and its fellow communist, states and felt peace could be secured only through a strong military posture and collective security.

India, in contrast, thought the communist threat over stated and saw East and West as gripped in mutual fear. Nehru's concern was that this security psychosis would end not in pressing the peace, but in provoking war. He saw peace had preserved through dialogue not force, pursuing this end as actively as the U.S. pursued a stronger security fortune.

Added to his fundamental difference of outlook was the friction over Kashmir—an issue of fargreater importance to India than the U.S. stung and annoyed by India's frequent criticism of U.S. policies. India's unwillingness to follow through with the plebiscite New Delhi itself had proposed seemed to Americans a far cry from the lofty moralism and principled views Nehru so often articulated.

Underlying the estrangement was a sense of mutual disappointment led by unrealised expectations. Democratic and secular India expected the support of the U.S. on issues like Kashmir. The U.S. as of the democratic world expected that free and democratic India would back the general thrust of U.S. policy in dealing with the Soviet threat.

Washington did not welcome India's effort to follow a path, western democratic and communist totalitarian camps, especially after the U.S. began to shed its blood in the war in Korea. And, thus, it was that Indo-U.S. relations got off a rocky start in the early year of independence.

3

Eisenhower I: Tougher on Communism

Dwight David Eisenhower became President on January 20, 1953. The incoming Republicans favoured a more conservative approach to the national problems—they wanted government at home and a tougher policy toward Communist adversaries abroad. Above all, Eisenhower pledged an early end to the Korean war, increasingly unpopular as the conflict dragged on into its third year.

The emphasis that incoming secretary of state John Foster Dulles placed on collective security arrangements worried the Indian leader, concerned, let us, sponsored military pacts embrace India's principal antagonist and neighbour Pakistan.

The new Republican administration also appeared more rapid than the democrats about economic assistance to the developing countries, a subject of growing interest to India as food production to lag.

India and Korean War—POW Repatriation

Soviet leader Joseph Stalin died in March 1955, after Eisenhower took office. A five-nation Neutral Nations Repatriation Commission (NNRC) chaired by India, with Canada, Sweden, Poland and Czechoslovakia as members would offer POW an opportunity to express their wishes about returning home. Since the NNRC would take decision by majority vote, neutral India was likely to have a key role. There was also talk of India's sending a military force to take charge of the POWs until their fate was decided.

The possible Indian role did not enthuse U.S. officials. Alexi's Johnson, then a senior State Department Far East expert and later Under Secretary of State for Political Affairs told the British, we were, of course, not discussing India but we would not be happy one such a choice as India all too often seemed to consider it necessary to more neutral towards the Chinese Communists than the UN.

South Korea's President, Syrigham Rhee, was more hostile. "Rhee feels very strongly," UN Commander General Mark Clark called Washington, "that India is not neutral and is opposed to have its (Indian) armed forces.... on his sovereign soil."

Although Dulles had yet to declare neutralism `immoral' he was known for his hard-line views on dealing with communists and his dislike for India's non-alignment. Given their conflicting policy approach, the meeting between Nehru and Dulles could not have been very relaxed. Korea was, perhaps, was the subject where their views most converged, despite their different appraisals of communist intentions.

Dulles asked India to send troops take custody of POWs not in shining repatriation. Nehru expressed willingness, but urged a greater effort to achieve an armistice, voicing concern that otherwise the conflict would broaden.

Dulles responded pointedly, "if the armistice negotiations collapsed the U.S. would probably make a stronger rather than a lesser military exertion and that this might well extend the area of conflict." Dulles commented in his report of the conversation, "I assumed this would be relayed (to the Chinese communists)."

Nehru, who regarded Rhee as an reactionary anachronism,

thought the US should have taken a tougher line with the South Korean leader instead of trying "to appease him by all kinds of assurances for the future."

Even though the Chinese communists were angry, Nehru refused to give ground out of concern the POWs would riot unless they were released. Thimayya told Ambassador Arthur Dean, UN Korean peace negotiator that Chou En-Lai had cabled Nehru, "They are our prisoners, not yours and you cannot release them. It would be better to let them break out on January 23 and then you must shoot them whatever happens." The Prime Minister reportedly responded to Chou that India would have no part in bloodshed and had the duty to see that the prisoners were treated in humanitarian fashions.

During the January 21, 1954, National Security Council Meeting, CIA director Allen Dulles described the POW affair as "one of the greatest psychological victories so far achieved by the free world against communism."

The Indian's, however, won few plantifs from Syrigham Rhee, who remained bitterly critical. Nehru, in disparaged Rhees commitment to peace, alleging that South Korea was acting in an utterly irresponsible manner.

The issue split the UN camp, with the countries of the British Commonwealth—except Pakistan—supporting India's presence. In the showdown vote, a majority of the UN Political Committee favoured India, but failed to nuster the third vote needed to overside US and Latin American opposition.

For India, the Korean war was equally important, putting Nehru's concept of neutralism to the test staying aloof from the two major powers, India was able to establish itself as the country in the middle between East and West, able to send as an honest broker and Channel of Communism between the Western and the Communist powers. Even though India received praise and often much criticism from both Cold war camps, Indian diplomacy proved successful.

India, in the process, gained prestige and influence for beyond its military or economic power. Whether one liked it or not in the mid-1950's and usually the US did not—India had become a factor in international affairs that could not be ignored, speaking for its people and articulating the desires of millions of others in Asia and Africa emerging from Western Colonial rule.

US Military Assistance to Pakistan

For Indo-American relations, the most important question during May 1953 visit of John Foster Dulles to South Asia was not Korea but Pakistan's membership in a pro-Western Middle East defense grouping and American assistance.

When Nehru mentioned India's concerns about these possibilities, Secretary Dulles replied with lawyer-like precision that the Middle East Defense organisation seemed unlikely to take shape as originally projected. He made no mention of the alternative northern tier system that he would discuss in public ten days later.

Regarding arms to Pakistan, the Secretary stated that the U.S. "had no present plans that would bring it into a military relationship with Pakistan which could be reasonably looked upon as unneutral as regards India." Literally accurate, Dulle's statement was misleading, for the Secretary was certainly considering providing arms to Pakistan even if nothing yet had been formerly decided.

The issue of reasonableness about U.S. arms for Pakistan—on which Dulles and other American officials would place importance—was, in a sense irrelevant since India regarded any U.S. military aid to Pakistan as "unneutral." In his report of the conversation, Dulles wrote "Nehru expressed satisfaction with the declaration" one wonders.

Dulles' next stop after New Delhi was Karachi, then the capital of Pakistan. The contrast in the welcome was marked. In New Delhi, the Indians were correct but formal, in greeting Dulles. Nehru saw no reason to butter if visitors from Washington.

In Karachi, the Pakistanis overwhelmed the Americans with the warmth of their reception. Eager to gain military support, the Pakistanis had every reason to const Dulles and his party. Like many senior American leaders, the Secretary was flattered by Pakistani hospitality—with an individual as doer as Dulles, no mean achievement.

The Pakistani leadership, especially Army Commander General Ayub Khan, forcefully urged U.S. military aid. Ayub "reiterated potential, both in manpower and bases that is available in Pakistan and that his country under the present government is extremely anxious to cooperate with the U.S."

The U.S. Ayub argued, should not be afraid to help those countries ready to receive help against the Communists. Ayub contended that a strengthened Pakistan would make Nehru less intrigent and more likely to agree to Kashmir settlement. Dulles was impressed, several days later, the secretary cabled fromTurkey that the genuine feeling of friendship encountered in Pakistan exceeded to a marked degree that encountered in any country on the trip.... Pakistan is one country that has more courage to do its fast resisting communism.

In Dulles opinion, "Pakistan would be a cooperative member of any defense scheme that may emerge in the middle East and that we need not await formal defense arrangement as condition to some military assistance.

Dulles reiterated his positive appraisal during June 1 NSC meeting just after returning to Washington. The Secretary declared that he was immensely impressed by the martial and religious qualities of the Pakistanis.

These qualities made him and Mr. Stevenson feel that Pakistan was a potential strong point for us.... In contrast the Secretary's assessment of Jawaharlal Nehru was hardly flattering. Dulles described the Indian leader as an utterly impractical statesman.

Assistant Secretary of State Henry Byroade, who drafted the speech while accompanying Dulles on the trip, said that the address provided vehicle for getting the Secretary's agreement on the northern ties defense concept to replace the still born Middle East Defense Organisation.

The idea that later became the Baghdad Pact was, thus, put on the table for public discussion with official blessing. Although Byroade, a strong supporter of the northern tier, hoped the concept would become a reality, he was unsure and in no hurry to force a decision.

If the U.S. was in no hurry, the Pakistanis were eager to conclude the arms agreement. After the assassination of Prime Minister Liaquat Ali Khan in 1951, control of the country fell into the hands of the conservative military and civil service leadership which desperately wanted to bolster Pakistan security against India through association with the U.S.

They seized the opportunity presented by Dulles public discussion of the northern tier concept to urge a decision by Washington on arms aid. When Karachi heard positive sounding words but no signs of action, General Ayub Khan came to the U.S. in the fall of 1953 in order press Pakistan case.

When Ayub met with Dulles, the Secretary assured the visiting Pakistani he supported arms aid regardless of the Indian reaction.

Dulles explained to an impatient Ayub it would take time before the issue could formally be put to President Eisenhower. Byroade asked Ayub to avoid premature publicity during the time administration was reviewing the proposal.

Despite the fact that Ayub agreed, he leaked that what was going on to the *New York Times* correspondent shortly after returning to Karachi.

The story appearing on November 3, provoked a loud public outcry in India. Prime Minister Nehru at first reached only in private, warning Pakistani Prime Minister Mohammed Ali Bagra:

> If such an alliance takes place, Pakistan definitely enter into the reign of cold war.... It must also be a matter of grave consequence to us, you will appreciate, if vast arms are built up in Pakistan with the aid of American money... All of our problems will have to be seen in a new light.

Nehru roundly criticised the U.S. as being unable to "think of anything else but of getting bases all over the world to fight for them." Nehru assented:

> A military pact between Pakistan and the U.S. changes the whole balance in this part of the world and affect India more especially. The U.S. must realized that the reaction in India that this arming of Pakistan is largely against India or might be used against India, whether the U.S. wants that or not... They imagine that such an alliance between Pakistan and the U.S. would bring such overwhelming presence on India as to compel her to change her policy on non-alignment. That is rather a naive view because the effect on India will be just the opposite, that is, one of greater resentment against the U.S.

Worried about being politically outflanked by rightists and communists, Nehru soon dropped his restraint and entered the fray publicly doubtless as Ayub hoped.

Nehru warned the U.S. arms to Pakistan would bring the Cold War to the region and would have very far reaching consequences on the whole structure of things in South Asia and especially in India and Pakistan.

When Indian Ambassador Mehta raised the arms issue with Dulles, Secretary replied that, given India's military superiority over Pakistan, any possible aid would pose no reasonable' threat to India. Dulles added that the U.S. could not indefinitely postpone strengthening an important region of the world just because India and Pakistan were at odds. Hardly a heartening response from the Indian standpoint.

By raising a public fuss Nehru may have availed domestic political problems in India, but his outcry upset many opinion matters in the U.S., where India had relatively few prominent political supporters apart from former ambassador Chester Bowles and Senator Herbert Humphrey liberal—democrats unlikely to carry weight with the Eisenhower administration.

As the American press considered the issue, the balance of opinion swing in favour of aid to Pakistan, even the *New York Times* criticised the Indian attitude. Ayub's leaks, thus achieved its purpose provoked Nehru into making so much threatening noise that he backed the U.S. administration into a corner. The question became less whether to go ahead with arms for Pakistan than whether to back down because of India's protests.

The basic idea remained one of providing greater stability to the northern region through association with the U.S., making it easier for these countries to deal with the presumed communist threat. Because Washington saw the danger more as political and psychological than military, the Defense Department placed almost no role in the decision-making process.

The Pentagon undertook little serious planning for an arms aid programme for Pakistan. Byroade himself was thinking of a largely symbolic programme perhaps 20 million for less than the amount of assistance the U.S. later provided.

The Secretary stressed the effect that not going ahead would have in light of Nehru's strong and public objections. If the U.S. backed down Dulles believed this step would "do a great deal to establish Nehru as leader of all of South-East Asia nations in that region would henceforth be reluctant to proceed in matters with the West without obtaining Nehru's support." Eisenhower gave his approval but again expressed concern about the Indian reaction. He directed every possible public and private means at our disposal he used to ease the effects of our action on India.

The President made two principal points: he offered military aid to India and pledged to act against any misuse by Pakistan of U.S. military assistance against India.

After reading Eisenhower's letter carefully, Nehru smiled, looking silently at his cigarette for a few moments before responding. When Nehru spoke he adopted a pleasant, almost cordial tone, commenting it was not "U.S. motions" that disturbed him, but the possible consequences of this action," both internationally and internally on India and Pakistan.

The intense and emotional Indian reaction had a far more profound effect on Indo-American relations than anticipated. The U.S. government know the action would cause problems, but, like allen, policy-makers hoped the impact would not be too diverse or long-lasting.

The revised U.S. South Asia Policy document NSC 5409 under consideration in tandem with the decision to provide arms to Pakistan reflected this view. NSC 5409, in typically qualified U.S. officials stated, "A result may be an intensification of differences in U.S.-Indian relations and possibly more friendly relations with the Soviet Union, although there would probably not be any major change in India's foreign policies."

The U.S. Intelligence Committee also under-estimated the impact. June 1954 national Intelligence Estimate (NIE) regarding the implications of the arms decision concluded that although the Northern tier security arrangements would:

> In some degree, increase Indo-U.S. tensions, it would unlikely that an open rift would develop between the U.S. and India as a result of this factor alone.. Should Pakistan be materially strengthened as a result of U.S. aid, India would also seek to build up its own forces. In any event, it is extremely unlikely that India would move more significantly closer to the Soviet bloc.

For Washington the main consideration was relatively simple: through arms to Pakistan, the U.S. thought it was taking an important step in advancing the policy of containment of communism by strengthening the chain of collective security arrangements around the borders of the Soviet Union. In the administration's eyes, as reflected in NSC 5409, the action strengthened the defense of region against the communist threat and was not intended to make Pakistan the dominant state in South Asia.

The U.S. joined in Pakistan a new ally in the Cold War, a muslim country with a proud military tradition and, on paper at least, a substantial number of fighting troops that would be available for the defense of the oil rich Persian gulf.

Although Washington recognized Pakistan's primary motivation was to strengthen itself against India, the U.S. leadership believed Pakistan was also concerned about the threat of communism. The Pakistan is pointedly played their alleged worries about the danger from the Soviet Bloc in talking with American officials.

Neither Byroade nor John Foster Dulles were concerned that U.S. arms would upset the South Asia power balance. Because India was for stronger than its neighbour, the small amount of arms then contemplated—NSC 5409 projected only $ 10 million annually could hardly enable Pakistan to present a credible military threat to India.

Reflecting on the decision over three decades later, Henry Byroade acknowledged having under-estimated the depth of Indian and Pakistani animosity, we know they disliked each other, misjudged the intensity of the feelings.

Nehru rejected angrily to the U.S. decision. Despite what Washington said, the action psychologically strengthened Pakistan in its dealing with India—this was after all, the basic reason why Pakistan wanted the ties with the U.S. until 1954, the politically and psychologically weak Muslim State Chief Ministers, "Behind Pakistan will stand a great and powerful country, the U.S.A. In fact, the giving of military aid to Pakistan is an infriendly act to India."

Ingrained the psyche of South Asians was a sense that Muslims were for more martial than Hindus.

As Winston Churchill emphasised President Roosevelt in 1942, the Muslims were the fighters, not the Hindus. In 1954, many Pakistani heroes to the martial tradition of Muslim dominion of the subcontinent still believed, and many Indians feared, that one Muslim soldier was worth ten Hindus.

The amount of aid concerned Nehru less than the qualitative change from the arms decision. "Pakistan," he stated, "will become definitely build up with the Western powers and a region of Cold War now and shading war, perhaps." Nehru thought the U.S., in deciding to give arms to Pakistan, was, in past motivated by its opposition to Indian neutralism. Until 1954, the Indian leader hoped to develop an area of peace, a region that stood apart from the two power blocs, based loosely on the Arab-Asian group of independent states, then, emerging from colonialism.

Burma, Indonesia, and Egypt were, in Nehru's view, leaning in this direction. By accepting U.S. military aid, Pakistan, whose foreign policy until then was mainly concerned with Kashmir issue—"breaks up this Arab-Asian group and enlarges the possible area of war".

The public reaction in India to news of the arms decision was outcry against the U.S. whatever Washington might say by way of explanation the action, the U.S. standing in India plummeted.

The ruling Indian Congress Party at its meetings at Kalyani sharply criticised the U.S. foreign policy decision. Nehru became even more disappointing of U.S. foreign policy stating in Parliament on March 1, that U.S. military aid amounted to intervention in South Asia that would have a direct effect on the Kashmir issue.

Nehru demanded the immediate removal of American members of the UN Kashmir truce observer group, assisting the U.S. was no longer neutral because of its new relationship with Pakistan. In the end, the Prime Minister relented somewhat, permitting the U.S. observers group to complete their tours but only on the understanding that no Americans would be sent as replacements.

Whatever the cause, the consequences of the U.S. decision to arm Pakistan were far reaching for relations with India for U.S. South Asia policy. After initially trying to avoid taking sides in India-Pakistan disputes—despite friction with India over Kashmir—Washington opted to develop a close security relationship with India's principal enemy. Pandit Nehru wrote K.M. Pannikar, then ambassador to Egypt:

> The United States imagine that by this policy they have completely outflanked India's so called neutralism and, thus, will bring India to her knees. Whatever the future may hold, this is not going to happen. The first result of all this will be an extreme dislike of the U.S. in India.

Kashmir Dispute: Prospects for Settlement

The Kashmir dispute was deadlocked when Eisenhower took office in January 1953. Dr. Frank Grehans try at mediation on behalf of the Security Council ended in failure in March.

Despite the unpromising outlook, President Eisenhower endorses Secretary Dulles' suggestion to send Foundation head Paul Hanffman, former Chief of the Marshall Plan, as a private Presidential envoy to South Asia. Eisenhower told Dulles, "Our world cannot simply afford an outbreak of hostilities between these two countries, and I would risk a great deal to prevent any such eventuality.

Nehru who saw little future in continuing the UN Kashmir effort, agreed to meet bilaterally with Mohammad Ali Bogra, Pakistan new Prime Minister.

The Eisenhower administration initially was less fixed on the idea of a plebiscite than its predecessor. During Dulles visit to India, the Secretary told Nehru partition of Kashmir might prove a better solution. Dulles noted the plebiscites in the inter-war period stirred much emotion while failing to resolve territorial disputes.

Not surprisingly, Nehru agreed that a plebiscite was not desirable solution, commenting that he envisaged a Kashmir settlement on the basis of the cease-fire line established in 1949 with minor adjustments—a posture he would support to his death in 1964. After Dulles encountered still Pakistani opposition to giving up the plebiscite he backed away from shifting U.S. policy in the question.

The Prime Minister faced a problem of a different sort-rising concern in New Delhi about the attitude of Kashmiri Premier Sheikh Muhammad Abdullah. Upset by communal agitation instigated by Hindu extremists, the Sheikh began to sound less eager for the Union of Kashmir with India. His talking about the possibility of an independent State greatly upset the India.

As the dominant political leader in the State, the Sheikh's opinion carried weight and could underline Indian Control over Kashmir. To prevent this happening, the Sheikh was ousted from power in August 1953 by his deputy, Bakshi Ghulam Mohammad and arrested a few days later.

The U.S. to its dismay, found itself embroiled in Kashmir's internal political crisis. Opponents of Abdullah alleged he was conspiring with American offering bases in return for U.S. support for Kashmiri independence. A meeting in May 1953 with former Democratic Presidential candidate Allen Stevenson was cited as "proof" that Washington was encouraging the Kashmiri leader to seek independence. The Indian Press reported implability that Eisenhower was using Stevenson, the man he had defeated in a bitter presidential election, as an envoy to Abdullah. Ambassador Allen took the criticisms sufficiently seriously that he received State Department to give Nehru a flat denial. Despite this official disavowal charges that the U.S. was upto no food in Kashmir continued to circulate. The Embassy cabled Washington, practically every high Indian official and writer had become firmly convinced a story manufactured out of whole cloth."

Even though Sheikh Abdullah's ousters caused an uproar in Pakistan. Mohammad Ali Bogra procalled with bilateral talks, leading a large delegation to New Delhi where, in keeping with the love-hate relationship between the two countries, he was warmly received by the populace.

Surprisingly, the negotiations registered progress. In the August 20 communique, Nehru and his Pakistani counterpart agreed to name a new plebiscite administrator by the end of April 1954—something to which the Indians previously refused to agree.

The improved atmosphere were short lived. Indeed of taking advantage of Nehru's more forthcoming attitude to cement plebiscite arrangements, Karachi reverted to a tougher line. Pakistan was the only member of the Commonwealth to vote against Indian participation in the Korean political conference, a move hardly to sit well with Nehru.

The Pakistani press, contrary to an accord to tone down criticism, rescued strident attacks on India. When Nehru annoyed by Indian exclusion from the Korea Peace Conference and suspicious of U.S. activities in Kashmir—balked at having an American replace Nimitz, the Pakistan insisted on having a U.S. citizen as the new plebiscite administrator.

Senior Indians, including Ministry of External Affairs Secretary General N.R. Pillai, who succeeded Bajpai and Dr. S. Radhakrishnan, who became India's Vice President after serving as envoy to Moscow, urged Ambassador Allen to seek a postponement of the arms decision, arguing this step would boost the chance for progress on Kashmir and avoid the two issues. Allen refused to recommend a delay to Washington, apparently inconceived Nehru was sincere about seeking a Kashmir settlement.

Once the arms decision was firm Nehru carried out the threat to toughen India's stance on Kashmir. The bilateral discussions collapsed within the year, the Indians were refusing to talk about a plebiscite as a way to settle the dispute. Since then, New Delhi's position has remained that the people of Kashmir had spoken for India by electing the Constituent Assembly and, therefore, there was no need for a plebiscite to determine what Kashmiris wanted.

India Edges Closer to Moscow

Nehru was now prepared to edge India closer to the Soviet Union to offset U.S. support for Pakistan. Post-Stalin Moscow was too willing to reciprocated. In a sign of shifting Cramlin policy toward India, G.M. Malenkov, Chairman of the Council of Ministers, in an August 1953 speech, praised India for its role in promoting peace in Korea and call for better relations.

If the U.S. disliked neutralism as contrary to Western policy goals, the new Soviet leadership viewed the Indian approach in a much more positive light. Since much of the thrust of neutralism was directed against Western colonialism, Moscow could cheerfully support the policy without risk to its interests. As a time when West was seeking to contain the Soviets—vigorously trying to Moscow's contacts with the newly emergent nations—the chance to expand relations with the largest non-aligned country was an opportunity the Russian eagerly seized.

As one indication of warning relations, Nehru paid a successful official visit to the Soviet Union in June 1955. During his stay, the Indian Leader became the non-Communist leader to address the Soviet people on the Television. Even if Nehru remained easy about the totalitarian nature of the Soviet State, he was impressed as he had been on his first visit in 1928—by signs of economic progress. He also approved of the mere pragmatic foreign policy approach of the new Soviet Leadership, believing in their policy slugh reduced the chances of global conflict.

In November and December 1955, Communist Party General Secretary Nikita Khruschev and Premier Nikolei Bulgarin paid a reciprocal state visit to India, they toured the country for almost a month, receiving an enormously warm welcome wherever they went. What was particularly called the `B&K show'—because of the colourful artices of Khruschev reached its high point in December 9 in Srinagar, the capital of Kashmir. To the delight of his hosts, Khruschev dropped Soviet neutrality on Kashmir to proclaim support for India's position. The Russians seconded the Indian view that the ratification of Kashmir accession by the States Constituent Assembly was proof that the people of Kashmir had already expressed their will at the ballot box. The Communist Party General Secretary declared:

> The Kashmir of Kashmiri as one of the Constituent States of Indian Union has already been decided by the people of Kashmir. Facts show that the pulation of Kashmir do not wish that Kashmir became a toy of imperialist forces.

Khruschev's policy change boosted the Soviet Union's popularity in India. If Pakistan could count on the U.S. for support, India now had a powerful friend of its own. The Soviet shift also had the practical advantage of making it herde for the UN to seenage itself actively in efforts to settle the Kashmir dispute. India could, henceforth, rely on a Soviet veto to bloc Security Council moves which New Delhi opposed.

During their visit, the Russian leaders won further friends on November 28 by calling the existence of Goa, the nearly four country Portugese colony along the Arabian Sea Coast in Western India, "a Shame to civilization." After British granted independence, the French agreed to handover to India Pondicherry and other small French colonial holdings.

Lisbon, however, stubbornly refused to give up Goa, asserting the territory was not a colony but a province of Portugal. Soviet support on Goa contrasted with the ambivalent U.S. position that Washington's sensitiveness for its NATO ally Portugal.

The difference between the U.S. and Soviet positions was further under-scored when John Foster Dulles angered New Delhi by joining the Portugese Foreign Minister on December 2, in criticising Soviet statements concerning Portuguese provinces in the Far East.

Khurschev and Bulgarin offered India economic aid as well as support on Kashmir and Goa. The Soviet agreed to build a million ton public sector steel mill financed by $112 million low interest loan and to provide other economic assistance for industrial development during the second Five Year Plan, which was stated to commence in 1956.

At the same time, Moscow and New Delhi expanded cultural and educational exchanges and increased trade with India. In deference to Nehru complaints, Moscow ostensibly distanced itself from the Communist Party of India, the winner of more than 5 per cent of the popular vote in the 1952 general election.

Even though the trend in relations pleased Nehru, he remained somewhat reserved about the Russian embrace, refusing a proposal for a non-aggression pact embodying the principles of peaceful coexistence.

India similarly showed only limited interest at this point in procuring the Soviet military equipment, despite the offer of easy financial terms and growing concern about the increase in Pakistan military strength after military aid started flowing in.

Vietnam, Bandung, and Hindi-Chini Bhai Bhai

As if to compensate further for diplomatic defeat India supposed when Pakistan gained U.S. military assistance, Nehru worked hard through 1954 and 1955 to buttress Indian Foreign Policy, pressing for a settlement in troubled French Indo-China, playing the leading role in the first Afro-Asian summit and Bandung, and relations with Communist China.

In a speech at Colombo on April 28, 1954, he coined the phrases "non-alignment" to describe India's policy, prefering this to neutralism, since it applied on active rather than a passive approach.

In Indo-China, the Vietnam victory at Dien Bilen Phu signalled the end of French colonial domination. Dien Mende's France came to power in Paris pledging to bring peace to the region. In 1954, Nehru proposed a six point plan for a settlement, which the U.S. disliked. Even-though not a formal participant in the Geneva Conference on Indo-China, India was forcefully represented by the Krishna Menon.

The unofficial Indian envoy shuttled from different delegations with whom he had roughly 200 interviews during the three weeks of Conference. Because India was the only

Asian state present, apart from communist China, the other delegations listened to Menon's views. In the end, the Conference asked India, alongwith Canada and Poland, to serve on the three International Central Commission's (ICC) established to monitor the Geneva accords in the Indo-China states. Nehru felt particularly gratified India could play this role, so in keeping with his policy of nonalignment and his desire to promote peace in Asia.

Lukewarm about his Geneva accords, the U.S. promoted an anti-Communist collective Security Pact for Southeast Asia that became a reality in September 1954 as the Southeast Asia Treaty Organisation (SETO). Headquartered in Bangkok, SETO's membership underlined its narrow required support—the only Asian countries to join were the Phillippines, Thailand and Pakistan. Geographically, the oldest participant Pakistan took the initiative to seek membership, eager to strengthen its security to the U.S.

Although Dulles recognised the problems inherent in including the Pakistanis, Washington found outmanouvered by Karachi and in the end had to agree to their joining. Quite apart from annoyance over Pakistan's membership, Nehru regarded SETO as "harmful to Asia as well as the cause of peace." He commented, "the habit of the West to carry" white mans' burden in the East still continued, even through conditions in the world and in Asia have changed greatly."

Although tough on communism at home, Nehru pursued close relation with Communist China, as well as the Soviet Union. In the spring of 1954, China's Premier Chou En-Lai visited New Delhi, where he succeeded in easing Indian worries about Chinese policy towards Tibet. The upshot was a new Sino-Indian agreement, in which India relinquished the special privileges it inherited from the British in Tibet. The preamble contained the so called Five principles—in Hindi, *Panch Sheel*.

These concepts of non-interference and mutual respect, although not in themselves new or earth-shaking, soon gained wide recognition as the articulation after desire of Asians to shape their relationship on Asian rather than simply reiterating the languages of Western statecraft.

Nehru hoped the accord would ensure peace along the Himalayan front ushering in a long period of friendship between India and China. The era of Hindi-Chini Bhai-Bhai lasted, however, only five years—until the Himalayan border dispute became a matter of public knowledge in 1959.

In 1954, Nehru travelled to China where the communist leaders amazed for a wildly enthusiastic reception. In the bilateral talks that took place Nehru raised a question of concern to the Government of India—Chinese maps showing parts of the Ladakh region in Northern Kashmir and of the Northeast Frontier Agency (NEFA) that India claimed its territory as Chinese. Chou En Lai's response that those were maps, which the people of Republic had yet to revise—satisfied the Prime Minister. Unfortunately Nehru did not take up Chou's suggestion for a joint communique at the end of the stay.

This might have dealt publicly with the map question, sharing much grief when India and China later fall out over their differing border claims. On his way back to India, Nehru visited the four Indo-China states. North Vietnam leader Ho Chi made an excellent impression. South Vietnam produced a completely opposite effect, Nehru stated.

In 1955, Afro-Asian solidarity, a subject dear to Nehru's heart, received a major boost with the first gathering of the leaders of the independent nations of his two continents at Bandung in Indonesia. Initially lukewarm about the summit for fear the gathering would become entangled with the Palestine issue. Nehru gradually came around to see Bandung as a means to promote his foreign policy aims, by asserting the importance of Asian and African views in dealing with the regions problems and by stressing the importance of peace.

At home, after the 1952 general elections, Indian democracy seemed well launched politically. Economically the country was poised to adopt another of Nehru's goals—socialist planning—as a means of accelerating economic development and promoting social justice.

Even Nehru's old foe, Winston Churchill, sang the Indian leaders praise, "I hope you will think of the phrase "light of Asia". "It seems to me that you might be able to do what no other human being could in giving India the lead, at least in the realm of thought, throughout Asia, with the freedom and dignity of the individual as the ideal rather than the communist party drill hook."

Indo-U.S. Economic Relation: Thorium Nitrate Aid

Meanwhile in Washington, Eisenhower was unhappy about the downturn in Indo-US relations. Eisenhower was less antagonistic toward India and more concerned about relations with former colonial states than his Secretary of State. He worried if the West failed to support decolonisation and economic development, the countries of Asia and Africa would become anyway and found communism attractive.

Concerned over India's economic development was not a popular theme in the early days of Eisenhower administration. One of Secretary Dulles first decision regarding India was indeed, to shast the economic request.

The summer of 1953 saw India and U.S. embroiled in an acetic dispute over the Battle Act—a U.S. law sponsored by Congressman Larie. Battle, Democrat of Alabania—leaning American aid to any country that traded in strategic goods with Communist China.

The trouble arose after American officials became aware the Indian government's Rare Earths Corporation had shipped to China a strategic commodity called Thorium Nitrate used in the production of Uranium. When ambassador Allen raised the issue with Nehru, the Prime Minister reacted vehemently, stating flatly India would now permit the U.S. to tell with whom it could trade as a price for aid.

Although American officials explained U.S. Legislative requirement tied their hands, the Indians refused to budge. Secretary General of the Ministry of External Affairs Pillai pleaded with Allen to bear in mind that the GOI is young and, perhaps, super sensitive its sovereignty. Since other developing countries accepted Battle Act conditions, Americans were puzzled why India was making such a fuses. The fact Nehru himself authorized the shipment—admittedly unaware that he violated U.S. law—for the complicated matters.

The lesson ambassador Allen drew from the affair was that the U.S. had been too soft with the Indians in aid. Instead of insisting on clear cut request, Allen felt the U.S. allowed the Indians to simply act as know how much aid they needed without having to ask anyone for anything.... I believe continuation of the essentially dishonest fiction would be fraud on American people as well as continue to place U.S.-Indian as a false and, therefore, unsound basis. The upper echelons of the State Department applauded Allen's tough line but shrank from his recommendations.

And reviewing the record, it was also realised Allen was wrong in asserting the India's had never asked for aid. The ambassador was apparently unaware of Nehru's expect request made at the insistence of Ambassador Loy Henderson in May 1951. Admitting he did not have the facts, Allen, none-the-less, emphasized that the U.S. should not be thursting aid on India.

Having new quarrels with Allens' views, the administration posture was to maintain—but initially not to increase the bilateral assistance programme initiated toward the end of the Truman administration.

The main focus continued to be an agriculture and moral

development with the Community Development Programme initiated by Bowles the top priority activity. Despite the frictions in relations, the administration, a year later, as part of an overall increase in economic development assistance, supported a $104 million allocation for India. In 1954, a new agricultural Commodity bill—Public Law 480—also became a law. PL 480, it was soon known, permitted the U.S. government to dispose of mouring surplus farm products in return for blocked rupees.

For India, struggling to raise its Food to keep pace with the mounting population, the protect of U.S. food in term for readily available blocked rupee instead of scarce foreign exchange was tempting. New Delhi soon sought another larger food assistance package. Washington was initially slow to respond.

Although Eisenhower, and even Dulles supported the push for increased assistance for India, the effort into stiff opposition. Part of the difficulty was the lack of support for foreign aid generally among Republicans but part was the dislike for India's policies. Meeting with Congress leaders, Dulles responded to criticism from arch-Conservative Republican senator William Knowlamb of California about rewarding neutralism.

"We are not rewarding policies we dislike", the Secretary declared, "we are simply trying to prevent India from moving towards communism."

Within the State Department, hard-line anti-communists like Assistant Secretary of State for Far Eastern Affairs Walter Robertson also opposed helping India. An internal review in November 1955, chaired by Under Secretary of State Robert Murphy, murmured Congress criticism.

The India desk (Burn Smith) urged to increase to help those supporting "Sounder policies" and communist efforts to penetrate the region. Senior Economic specialists (Kalijari and Proschrow) supported the increase "despite the often times unfriendly or difficult statements of Mr. Nehru." Robertson strongly disagreed. Calling Nehru, a communist supporter, he charged aid to India only served to build up a government unfriendly to U.S.

Concerned about poor relations with India Eisenhower wanted Cooper to make a special effort to become friendly with Nehru, noted that the Indian leader seemed to be swayed as much "by personality as by logical argument." The President asked Secretary Dulles to try to avoid burdening the new envoy with chores that would cause problems in his developing rapport with the Prime Minister.

The Cooper Nehru relationship prospered despite the relatively short period in Kentuckian spent in New Delhi after year Cooper returned to U.S. politics to win back his Senate while in India.

In early March 1956, during a stop in New Delhi the Secretary Dulles, ambassador Cooper proposed a larger aid programme to provide substantial U.S. support for the just announced Indian Five Year Plan. Cooper's ideas, "A feasible programme of U.S. Economic Assistance for India," called for $ 500 million development aid and $ 300 million food aid over the five year period— an annual total of $ 160 million. Cooper justified the boost in assistance in terms of counting the increased Soviet effort to penetrate South Asia and of supporting India's efforts to develop her economy by democratic means.

Secretary Dulles set up a special study group which agreed with some but not all of all Cooper's recommendations. The result was an administration request for 80 million in development aid and approval for proceeding with the new PL 480 agreement.

Despite Cooper's friendly relation with Nehru, relations between New Delhi and Washington remained strained as Eisenhower's first term neared its end. For many Americans, Krishna Menon, now a fixture at the U.N., had become the symbol of India—a country that preached non-alignment and high moral principles in international affairs but hypocritically favoured the communists and cold bloodly pursued its interests in Kashmir in disregard of UN resolution.

A typically negative reaction was that of President Eisenhower on whom Krishna Menon called at the White House in March and June 1955 to discuss Indian efforts to help reduce tensions between the U.S. and China. Eisenhower described the peripatetic Indian emissary a menace.

For Indians, Menon's American counterpart was John Foster Dulles. Although hardly in Menon's league when it came to sarcasm and the Secretary of State was given to sermonizing on the global struggle between good (the free world) and evil (the Communist bloc).

Dulles barely concealed his distance for India's Foreign policy, indeed on June 9, 1956, the Secretary spoke his mind plainly, telling an "Iowa State University audience that" except under very exceptional circumstances, neutralism was an moral and short-sighted conception.

Dulles role as the architect of Pakistanis' alliance with the U.S. added to Indian dislike of the Secretary of State. In December 1955, Dulles further soiled the waters by appearing the support the Portugese position on Goa.

Nehru and Dulles disagreed again in their assessment of China. The Indian leader also attacked Dulles creations—SEATO and Baghdad Pact asserting Pakistan had entered the alliances against the Soviets but he get strength to use against India. Calling the Pakistan "a martial people and a fanatical people who could really attack India," Nehru blamed U.S. arms and for forcing India to increase defense spending.

In responding, Dulles claimed others had pressed Pakistan to join SEATO, admitting Pakistan had no business to be there. The Secretary reiterated the standard U.S. pledge that arms assistance to Pakistan would not be used against

India, and denied that U.S. arms to Pakistan were causing an arms race.

Although Nehru did not know it, one important point did get through to Dulles—the extent of India's anxiety about Pakistan.

Cabling President Eisenhower from Colombo a day after his talks with Nehru, Dulles stated:

> The one distinct impression that I gained is their almost pathological fear of Pakistan. I know, of course, that they did not like an alliance with and armament programme for Pakistan, but I never appreciated before the full depth of their feeling.... I do not think, we can alter on Pakistan relationship which is of great value but I do think we must try to handle it in ways which give maximum assistance to India, that our military aid will be only used for defensive purposes.

After his discussion with the Secretary, Nehru also reflected on bilateral relations with the U.S. his very different from those of Dulles. The `singularly misconceived and harmful' U.S. positions on Kashmir and Goa `have come in the way of better relations between India and the lest more than anything else,' Nehru wrote the Chief Minister.

Some believed relations depended on how much aid the U.S. gave, but this was "a complete misapprehension" Nehru stated.

> Whether the U.S. give us much or little or nothing at all, our relations with them will not be affected much, provided other factors are satisfactory. It is these other and political factors that are constantly coming in the way. Our general approach to the world situation differs from that of the U.S. which is based largely on military considerations. We think that there can be no solution of the major problems of the world if the approach is chiefly a military

one. Indeed we have seen a progressive deterioration because of this military approach.

Bilateral relations thus, sank to a low point during Eisenhower's first term in the White House under the burden of policy differences between Washington and New Delhi.

As in the Truman years, the friction focussed on conflicting Indian and U.S. perception of the communist threat and the differing policy responses. During Eisenhower's first term as President, however, the U.S. response to the Communist threat by establishing a military relationship with India's enemy Pakistan in 1954 directly affected South Asia, India's home territory.

The U.S. believed the U.S. gains in acquiring a new ally, Pakistan, would more than offset the losses sustained with India. Eisenhower would shortly call this judgement in question, but could not reverse history.

4

Eisenhower II: Improved Relations

Dramatic overseas events—the simultaneous Suez and Hungary crises—almost pushed the presidential election off the front page. In the case of Suez, Nehru reached rapidly, angrily condemning the Anglo-French-Israeli attack on Egypt on a flagrant violation of the UN charter.

"I cannot imagine a worst case of aggression, Nehru cabled Dulles, the whole future of the relations between Europe and Asia hangs in the balance."

Eisenhower's insistence that the British, French and Israelis withdraw impressed Nehru. He had not expected the U.S. to take such a firm stand against its allies in favour of Nasser, a neutralist with whom Washington had poor relation.

In contrast, the Indian leader was slow to react critically to Russian use of force in Hungary. In a November speech in Hyderabad Nehru pillored Britain and France for their attack on Suez, but said nothing about the Red Armys' crushing the anti-communist revolt in Budapest. In a November 9 speech in Calcutta, Nehru seemed to accept explanations of their actions in Budapest, describing the crisis as an internal Hungarian affair.

The same day at the United Nations, Krishna Menon voted against a resolution called for the withdrawal of Soviet forces from Hungary. India was the sole non-communist country to caste a negative vote.

J.P. Narayan warned Nehru, "if you do not speak out, you will be held guilty of abeting enslavement of a brave people by a new imperialism more dangerous than the old because it masquerades as revolutionary. "Bruised at home and abroad, condemning the Soviet repression in a November 14 statement with the Prime Ministers of Indonesia, Ceylon and Burma and in a November 19 statement in the Indian Parliament, Nehru about face, somewhat weakly explained by his having received fuller information about the Hungarian situation repaired some of the damage done to his reputation as a statesman who stood for high principle and morality in international relations. The Hungary episode nonetheless, left a bad appetaste.

A month later, in December 1956, Nehru paid his second visit to U.S. Apart from his interest in reviewing world affairs and discussing South Asian developments with President Eisenhower, as Prime Minister was well aware that India needed more economic assistance from the U.S. to bolster its development efforts. In contrast to Nehru's 1949 talks with Harry Truman, the 1956 visit was a success.

In their substantive talks, Eisenhower and Nehru broke little new ground, essentially restating the clashing policy views of their two governments in particular, on the dangers of communism.

Nehru, however, refused to agree with the President that the Soviet Union was seeking world domination or represented a new form of colonialism. Not denying the logic of this view, Nehru believed that overtime, communism would defeat itself.

The President observed, "It was rather cold comfort to realize that historically inevitable doom of dictatorship often occurred only after the passage of much time, the loss of life, the postponement of peace."

The two leaders continued to differ on communist China. Nehru argued for Peking's acceptance into the family of Nations. He thought it only a matter of time Formosa fell. Eisenhower believed the Chinese needed to follow basic norms of international conduct before they joined the U.N.

Regarding India's non-alignment, Nehru emphasised that this approach helped keep defense expenditures down since the policy minimised the chances of conflict on the Himalayan borders, the only logical security threat to India. In an argument that impressed Eisenhower, Nehru asserted that, given his country's economic weaknesses, having India as an ally would "serve to weaken rather than strengthen" the Western bloc.

The Prime Minister took a tough line on Pakistan. Touching on Indian worries about U.S. arms aid, Nehru said that many of his countrymen felt that Pakistan was going to attack India, an idea fanned by fanatics. "He called partition an egregous blunder, arguing that the Pakistanis got their independence only through the successful struggle of Indian Nationalists.

Nehru claimed the people of Kashmir wanted to belong to India but he did not have to justify his opposition to a plebiscite as Eisenhower forgot to ask this point. Nehru gained the impression Eisenhower agreed that no good would be served by stirring up public interest regarding Kashmir in the near future.

On economic assistance, Nehru reported that Eisenhower was enthusiastic in offering American support for India faltering economic development plans. Eisenhower's version of the talks was different, indicating that Nehru did not directly ask for American aid but talked at length and eloquently about India's development hopes.

The President must have been listening to Nehru, a few

weeks' later he was well versed about Indian economic plans during a spirited discussion in the NYC with the Secretary of Treasury George Humphrey, an opponent of aid to India. Showing for more knowledge than Humphrey, Eisenhower shortly defended U.S. assistance and sympathetically explained India's plans to develop public sector industries.

New Forces and New Nations were Stirring

In his second inaugural address in January 1957, Eisenhower signalled his concern that communism would prove attractive to the newly emerging nations unless they enjoyed adequate economic development. "New forces and new nations" were stirring across the earth ... one third of all mankind has entered an historic struggle of a new freedom: the freedom from grinding poverty, the President declared.

To counter the Soviets and their allies more effectively in the developing world, Eisenhower sought a substantial increase in foreign aid during his second term, arguing strongly that such a step was in the U.S. national interest.

As the "winds of change" signalled the demise of European colonialism, may newly independent nations followed India's lead in adopting a non-aligned policy, in trying to walk a middle road between the Western and Communist camps. With Europe and Far East stable—despite periodic crisis at flash points like Berlin and Taiwan straits—the Cold War focussed increasingly on the uncommunist nations.

To a considerable extent, the East-West contest seemed to turn on how best to persue economic development, to meet what was called at the time "the revolution of rising nations". A group of U.S. economists and social scientists at the Massachusetts Institute of Technology Center for International Studies (CENIS), led by Professor Walt Rostow and Max Milliken, developed a theory of underpining to support the view that a substantial input of foreign aid would permit countries such as India to take off for `self sustain' economic growth under democracy and free enterprise.

Rostow and Milliken in their influential *A Proposal Key to an Effective Foreign Policy,* that appeared in 1957, offered a comprehensive argument for expanded foreign aid. Rostow and Milliken, and their colleagues asserted that more economic assistance could spur development, lead to stable societies and thwart communist efforts to gain the upper hand in the developing world.

India, because of many factors—its size and population, the use of English, Nehru's prestige, the country's economic planning (then much in vogue), and its adherence to democracy because the model for many of the MIT theoretical studies. As Rostow wrote, "Rightly or wrongly, we believed the success or failure of India with respect to both its development and its politics would be widely influential."

In 1957, India had its second democratic elections since independence. Nehru's Congress Party again won a sweeping victory, although the opposite parties on the left, the socialists and communists increased their share of the vote.

The election shocked which many alms hells in Washington was the communist victory in Kerala, a Southern Indian state with India's highest level of literacy and its longest Christian population.

The Kerala election marked one of the rare times a communist government gained power in a free vote. The lesson Washington drew was that communists won in Kerala because the economy failed to improve rapidly enough to satisfy the populations expectations.

U.S. experts feared that if Pandit Nehru's Indian National Congress Party failed to achieve adequate economic growth, communist strength would continue to expand, presenting a real, if long-term danger. Preventing additional Kerala's became an important argument for augmenting U.S. assistance to India.

Although the Kennedy-Cooper resolution passed the Senate in 1958, it lacked support in the House of Representatives and died in the joint Senate House Conference. The resolution, nontheless, proved a major spur to the aid India effort.

In addition to boosting bilateral assistance, the U.S. became the major source of funding in implementing the Indus Waters Agreement, for which the World Bank succeeded in obtaining India-Pakistan agreement in 1959.

U.S. funds covered half the $ 1 billion worth of dams, irrigation works and other construction project envisaged under the accord. Bank's President Engene Black worked closely with Under Secretary Dillon, who in August 1959 got President Eisenhower to approve $ 517 million, with other donors providing the remaining $ 250 million.

Although Dillon correctly regarded the Indus Waters Agreement as a major step in improving relations between India and Pakistan, he was overly optimistic in telling an April 1960 NSC meeting that the accord showed that the Kashmir dispute could also be settled. Dillon overlooked an essential difference between the two disputes.

The World Bank was able to make both India and Pakistan winners in the Indus Waters settlement, since each country received more irrigation water as a result of the agreement.

In the case of Kashmir, as long as both India and Pakistan coveted Srinagar and the valley and saw the dispute in highly emotional and ideological terms any conceivable settlement would inevitably make one side or the other conclude itself the loses.

As to size of bilateral aid increased the U.S. officials paid more attention to the programs impact, especially in comparison to that of Soviet economic assistance. In May 1959 Embassy New Delhi informed reported Moscow was prepared to give New Delhi virtually everything the Indians sought on favourable repayments terms, including a pledge of upto $ 1 billion for India's Third Five Year Plan.

The Soviet emphasis on a big `show projects' and aid to Indian public sector industries was likely, in the Embassy's view, to earn to Russians much credit with Indian public opinion. To counter the Soviet Embassy New Delhi urged U.S. assistance to Indian public sector projects, including a million ton Steel Mill, to be built in Bokaro in eastern India.

The question of U.S. aid to an Indian government owned steel mill (the Soviets, British and West Germany) became a sensitive issue undertaking for a number of years. Symbolically, for many Indians and some Americans U.S. willingness to fund Bokaro became a litmus test of U.S. support for India's industrial development. Other Americans, including most Republicans, opposed using U.S. dollars to pay for Bokaro.

Question the wisdom of India's Socialist economic policies, they did not think completion for favour with the Soviets provided a sufficient reason for Uncle Sam to find a public sector steel mill. Although Bokaro received considerable high level attention in Washington during the Eisenhower administration, the Republicans reached no decision, passing the issue on to their Democratic successors.

Less in public eye was possible U.S. financing for an atomic power plant. After President Eisenhower proposed the Atoms for Peace programme in 1955, India's Atomic Energy Chairman Homi Bhabha, gifted scientist and energetic administrator, sought to interest Washington in building a nuclear power plant in India as a dramatic way of demonstrating U.S. support for peaceful uses of atomic energy in the Third World.

Ambassador Bunker argued in favour of the project, stressing that India needed the power and would get the plant from the Soviet should the U.S. refuse.

The U.S. Atomic Energy Commission, at first, doubted the economic feasibility of the project and also questioned whether India was technologically ready. The AEC agreed to consider the power plant seriously only after Prime Minister Nehru raised the subject during Eisenhower visit to India and the State Department strongly supported sending a survey mission.

The team was impressed by the Indian atomic energy programme found the costs of nuclear power production in India competitive with conventional power, and concluded the project made sense. Washington agencies had the proposal under consideration when the Eisenhower administration left office in January 1961.

After 1957, expanded foreign assistance became an important foreign policy goal supported by a broad bi-partisan coalition, the administration pushed through a major expansion of U.S. assistance to India and energised the World Bank and U.S. allies to increase their help.

The Eisenhower administration, ironically ended up with the type of commitment to India's development programme that Chester Bowles had proposed in vain in 1952.

NSC 5701: Neutralism Not Against American Interests

By 1957, President Eisenhower concluded that India's neutralist policy was not against American interests. Quite the contrary, Eisenhower told his advisors on a number of occasions that he supported India's staying non-aligned. Echoing a variation on what Nehru told him, Eisenhower stated—during a January 1957 NSC review of South Asia policy—there would not be enough money in the U.S. to support India should that country become an ally.

Further standing U.S. policy on his head, Eisenhower criticised "our tendency to rush out and seek allies" as not `very sensibly.' The President called the accord with Pakistan "perhaps the worst kind of a plan, and decision we could have made. It was a terrible error, but we now seemed hopelessly involved in it."

NSC 5701, a revised South Asia policy that Eisenhower approved on January 10, 1957 marked shift in emphasis from the 1954 policy contained in NSC 5409 even if the new policy did not fully reflect the President's outburst over the consequences of arming Pakistan.

NSC 5701 characterised South Asia as an important Cold War front where the Soviet Union was seeking to roll back support for the West through a vigorous diplomatic, economic, and propaganda assault. Perceiving the competition between India and China as a struggle between democratic and totalitarian development, models, NSC 5701 concluded that despite India's frequent opposition to U.S. policies:

> The risks to U.S. security front a weak and vulnerable India would be greater than the risks of a stable and influential India. A strong India would be a successful example of an alternative to communism in an Asian context and would permit a gradual development of the means to enforce its external security interest against communists Chinese expansion into South and South-East Asia.

On the issue of arms assistance to Pakistan, the revised policy accepted past U.S. promises of aid those having resulted in a `symbolic' $ 10 million annual programme projected the NSC 5409 balooning into a substantial $ 471 million by 1957 - but opposed further increases in aid levels. Perflecting the adjustment in policy that was then in train, NSC 5701 stressed better relations with India and placed greater emphasis on economic rather than military means in meeting the Soviet challenge.

During the Eisenhower's second term, the attitude towards India gradually mellowed. This process was helped along by Elworth Bunker, whom Eisenhower named to John Sherman Cooper an ambassador to India. A businessman and a democrat, Bunker earn praise as Harry Truman's ambassador to Argentina and Italy and later as the President of American Red Cross. Dulles suggested his nomination to India after Eisenhower said he would be glad to "send a Democrat to one or two diplomatic posts," a somewhat unexpected step during a period of considerable partisanship.

During the four years in India Bunker, a reserved New Englander, added to his reputation as a highly effective diplomat. One measure of his skill was Bunker's ability to earn the respect of Nehru and other Indian leaders without losing credibility in Washington.

The warming in Indo-American relations even survived a testy-period during and after January 1957 U.N. Security Council debate on Kashmir. When Krishna Menon delivered an impassioned two-day defense of the Indian position. Nehru was annoyed the U.S. agreed to have Kashmir come before the Council and continued to support the idea of a plebiscite—contrary to the idea he received from Eisenhower during the talks. The vitrio U.N. debate provided Menon a platform to gain popularity in India and to stir even deeper antipathy among Americans.

Fighting sarcasm and venon at Pakistan and acidly attacking the U.S. and Britain for challenging India's right to Kashmir, Menon spoke vituperatively for two days, interrupted only twice when—with theatrical flourish—he fainted. After the Soviets vetoed a resolution calling for the stationing of U.N. troops in Kashmir, the Council agreed to send its President, Swedens' Gunnar Jarring to the subcontinent. Jarring travelled to South Asia, talked with Indian and Pakistani leaders, and to none one's surprise reported back to the Council that the Kashmir dispute remained deadlocked.

Later in the 1957, the Pakistanis again brought Kashmir to the Security Council. On the occasion, Nehru instructed Krishna Menon to tore down his comments after the U.S. complained some of his remarks. The result of the debate was Security Council approval for another mission to South Asia by Dr. Frank Graham, who had unsuccessfully in the early in 1950s to mediate the dispute.

Graham's effort proved as fruitless as his earlier attempt at finding a settlement. In Karachi, he found the Pakistanis willing to accept any arrangement that permitted a plebiscite. In New Delhi, Graham ran into a sponewall. In so many words, the Indians told the UN representative, "The matter is settled, Kashmir is ours."

After the 1954 arms pact with Pakistan an enthusiastic U.S. found itself under periodic presence to keep the Kashmir alive internationally through discussion in the U.N. and by mention in SEATO and Baghdad Pact countries.

Although this process is no way improved the chances of solving the dispute—Dulles frankly admitted as much in talking with Pakistan's Foreign Minister Feroz Khan in November 1957—continued attention kept the issue on the international agenda and showed the Pakistanis that their American friends, at least rhetorically, supported them. At the same time, Karachi was not unhappy that discussion of the Kashmir issue internationally for served as a chronic irritant in Indo-American relations.

Despite the difficulties, Eisenhower persisted in pressing for better relations between India and Pakistan. The American observers looking at the subcontinent, one conclusion struck home: the enmity between India and Pakistan rendered South Asia vulnerable to external threats, especially from the Soviet Union or China.

A closing of ranks between the two antagonus seemed

the logical step; Eisenhower made his views clear when Indias' Vice President Servapalli Radhakrishnan met the President during a March 1958 visit to Washington.

Recalling his discussions with Nehru, Eisenhower said "to his mind it was incomprehensible that there had not been a settlement of the issues between India and Pakistan.... Nothing could be more wonderful for peace than a rapproachement." Eisenhower added that the U.S. was trying to be friends with both countries and not have sides between them. Dulles had rather different sentiments.

When he met Pakistani Finance Minister Amjad Ali and General Ayub Khan in April 1958 he said that "U.S. feeling for Pakistan were, in a sense, politically different from those for India.... The basic relationship with India was intellectual in contrast to its relationship with Pakistan which came from the heart.

To help the process of rapproachment along, the administration launched a sincere, if ill fated, to tackle outstanding India-Pakistan differences. Originally suggested by the American Embassies in Pakistan and India the proposal linked together in a simple basket the three major areas of India-Pakistan friction—Kashmir, the military competition between the two nations, and Kashmir dispute over the use of major rivers in the Indus Valley.

The strategy called for using U.S. leverage mainly through economic programme, to press for a simultaneous solution of all three problems. When Dulles put the "basket proposal "to Eisenhower, the President reached positively: He was `all for' the initiative and neatly for help personally. "There is no inconvenience at which Eisenhower talk," Eisenhower responded—for example, did he nearly to welcome and entertain the Prime Minister simultaneously—I would go out there.

In April 1958, frustrated by political infighting within the Congress party and tired after 11 years as Prime Minister Nehru threatened to relieve from office. The possibility of Nehru's departure from the political stage caused shock waves not only through the body-politic in India, but in Washington as well.

On hearing the news, Eisenhower instructed Dulles to send a personal word urging Nehru to stay on. The President's message apparently drafted by Dulles himself read:

> You, if anyone, Mr. Prime Minister deserve a long and restful vacation after all, these years that you have guided you country towards economic, political and social progress. However, I and countless others hope that you will not go away too far away or for long a time. It would, indeed, be a misfortune, perhaps, for all other, if at what may prove a critical formation period, your own influence was not actively present over any protected period.

For Nehru, the underlying India-Pakistan problem was the "communal conflict and hatred and violence rather than specific issues like Kashmir,"

> I see no solution till that basic conflict in the minds of the people of Pakistan and India is resolved. Great powers like the U.S. and the U.K. talk piously of goodwill and India and Pakistan making up the quarrel. But they ignore deliberately the cause and the consequences of it. And so, they do not find solutions.

"Universally," the President wrote Nehru, "You are recognised as one of the most powerful influences for peace and conciliation in the world. Your influence is particularly valuable in stemning the global rift toward cynicism, mutual suspicion, materialistic opportunism and, finally, disaster."

During much of this period, Nehru and Eisenhower were in touch about various efforts to lower international tensions through disarmament and reduced nuclear testing, issues both regarded as of utmost importance in maintaining World peace. Soviet tactics in Hungary shock the humanist in Nehru and made him more chary about the Soviets. Although the set-back to detente between the U.S. and U.S.S.R. depressed him greatly, Nehru tended to be somewhat less critical of Washington than before his talks with Eisenhower. India was, however, once more upset with the U.S. over Pakistan.

After the Baghdad Pact collapsed—following the July 1958 Coup in Iraq by the anti-Western Abdul Karim Kasim—the northern defense grouping reemerged in the form of the Central Treaty Organisation(CENTO), with Turkey, Iran, and Pakistan as regional members of the head-quarters in Ankara.

In early 1959, the U.S. concluded a bilateral defense agreement with Pakistan to buttress the security relationship. Eisenhower was frank in telling Indian M.C. Chagla that he found himself on the horns of dilemma between providing arms for an ally, Pakistan, and damaging U.S. friendship with India.

In the days before satellite imagery, U-2 mission provided unique photographic intelligence about Soviet military dispositions and capabilities. The Pakistan also permitted the U.S. to establish an electronic listening post, supposedly a U.S. air force communications facility outside Peshawar.

Because of its geographic location, the Peshawar base also enabled the U.S. to monitor electrically Soviet missile tests, the facility forming part of the chain of electronic listening posts through which the U.S. kept tabs on Soviet missiles. The fact of the Peshawar facility boosted Pakistan's value to U.S. national security interests. Although CENTO and SEATO seemed of diminishing significance, the intelligence facilities were important assets that Washington was vary of losing.

Mounting Tensions between India and China

If Pakistan's willingness provide facility for U.S. intelligence operations increased its importance to U.S.

national security mounting tensions between India and China added a new dimension to Washington's relations with New Delhi. By 1951 it was evident—even though Nehru had managed to minimize publicity—that serious differences existed over the Indo-China border. The difficulties were not just a problem of outdated maps that China had yet to correct as Chou En Lai suggested earlier.

In Ladakh, in the north of Kashmir, both India and China claimed a desolate and uninhabited 16,000 foot high plateau called the Aksai Chin. The area had no intrinsic importance for India, but for China provided a valuable link between Sinkiang province and Tibet. In 1957, the Aksai Chins significance grew after the Chinese completed a road across the plateau are permitting directly communication between the two regions.

The Indian only learned of the road through a report in the Chinese press. In the eastern portion of the frontier, the two countries' disputed the borders between India's North-East Frontier Agency (NEFA) and Tibet.

India claimed this frontier—the so called McMohan Line— was fixed by Simla Convention signed in 1914. The Chinese while implying willingness to accept the McMohan line, believed as a matter of principle India and China should formally negotiate the border delimitation rather than adopt a demarcation imposed by the British at a time when India was in British possession and China weak.

In December 1958, after tensions along the border mounted folding the Chinese capture of an Indian military patrol in the Aksai Chin, Nehru sent a detailed letter to Chou En Lai trying to smoke out the Chinese. The Prime Minister emphasised the view that "India's boundaries were fixed and well known." There was no question of "large parts of India being anything but India".

Chou's January 29, 1959 reply disagreed that the borders

were fixed, stating that "Sino-Indian boundary was never been formally delimited: Historically no treaty or agreement on the Sino-Indian boundary has ever been concluded between the Chinese Central government and the Indian government," Chinese suggested negotiations.

Two months later in March 1959, the situation became more complicated politically after Tibet revolted against the communists. When the Chinese military suppressed the uprising, the Dalai Lama, Tibet's spiritual and temporal Leader fled to India and on March 31 received political asylum. These events caused an emotional surges of anti-Chinese sentiments in India that shattered the policy of friendship Nehru had carefully nurtured.

Although Nehru tried to temperize, following internally conflicting goals—help for the Tibetans and continued friendship with China—his policy of *Hindi-Chini Bhai Bhai* was dead five years after the Nehru-Chou meetings.

For their part, the Chinese were angered by the Indian attitude toward Tibet, assuming perhaps incorrectly that Nehru was collaborating with the Chinese nationalists and the U.S. Central Intelligence Agency in providing covert assistance to the Tibetan reinstance movement. The Chinese stance on the border stiffened.

They reaffirmed their earlier maps which claimed the entire Northern Frontier Agency some 40,000 square miles—as Chinese and rejected the Indian position that the border was fixed along the McMohan Line.

A Chinese ambush of an Indian patrol killed four Indian soldiers and left five others wounded. Ten Indian soldiers were taken prisoner. This event caused an uproar in New Delhi. Under great political pressure in Parliament, Nehru released the diplomatic exchanges with China over the border dispute, making plans how serious the differences were.

The result was a renewed serge of nationalist and anti-Chinese sentiments that thereafter limited ability to manoeuvre in diplomatic dealing with Beijing. A compromise on the border dispute covering Indian desires to establish the McMohan Line along the crest of the Assam Himalayas as the border in the east for Chinese desires to control the Aksai Chin in Ladakh—might have been possible earlier. After October 1959, Indian public opinion made such a deal politically difficult, if not possible.

With trouble on its northern borders, as well as continued tension with Pakistan, India began to step up its defense build up. Responsibility for this lay in the hands of Krishna Menon, Defense Minister since 1957. Although continued his support for Menon, the latter ultimately proved a disaster, politicising and demoralizing the top ranks of the military.

Those that refused to play Menon's game, like General Thimayaya were, in effect, forced out and replaced by political General like Lt. Gen. B.N. Kaul willing to bend Menon's will. Menon minimised the significance of the troubles with China, asserting that Pakistan remained India's major security danger. Menon, to Washington's great concern, also pressed for the acquisition of Soviet Military equipment to break the British and French dominance over Indian military procurement.

As the Indian rift deepened the reaction in the West especially in the U.S. was entirely supportive of India, although the State Department took no official position on the disputed McMohan Line Border claim. Given the decade long animosity with China, Washington readily accepted the Indian version of events a view consistent with the U.S. perception of China as an aggressive bully.

To Nehru's great satisfaction, the Soviet Union adopted a neutral stance. Nehru saw Soviet military neutrality as a further verification of his non-alignment policy as well as strategically important in India's border dispute with China.

Moscow's position angered the Chinese and became an element in broader Sino-Soviet tensions then mounting between the two communist powers.

Some in Washington regarded Sino-Indian tensions as opening the way for closer U.S. relation with New Delhi, with the possibility of even making India a strategic counter-weight against China. When the NSC considered the idea in May 1959, President Eisenhower strongly disagreed.` India,' the President said, "had never announced any readiness to align itself with the West as an opponent of Communism as Japan for instance, has we could not talk of a counter-weight if the nation in question refuses to be a counter-weight."

Eisenhower commented that if the U.S. were actually to try to make India counter-weight to China the task would be so great that America would probably bankrupt itself in the process. The President argued the U.S. goal should be to "give India a chance to grow as a free and democratic country," Eisenhower, also reiterated his feelings that Indians were very wise in their attitude of non-alignment.

Mounting tension between India and China, thus, added a new dimension to Washington relations with Delhi and vice versa. For ones, the two countries shared a composition on an important security issue; both had relations with China.

"My Desire to See that Country to Myself"

In December 1959, realised this wish as he became the first U.S. President to visit independent India. Eisenhower told Lord Plowden, British Atomic Chief, he arranged his three week Europe and Middle East trip "just to get to India". Air Force one, the new Boeing 707 presidential jet, which the President used for the first time on the trip, made the extensive journey feasible, enabling Eisenhower to cover for greater distances in greater comfort than had the propeller-driven aircraft he had used for earlier travels.

On India and Pakistan problems, Eisenhower stressed "perplexed he was between his desire to provide military equipment for Pakistan and an equal wish not to cause embarassment or anxiety to India." He argued that Indian deployment of troops in Kashmir was wasteful and weakened the defense of the subcontinent.

Eisenhower, insisted that the U.S. would never permit the Pakistan to use U.S. equipment to attack India. The President informed Nehru that the Pakistanis, in any case, had limited amounts of amunition since the U.S. provided them with only one week's supply.

Nehru had proposed mutual pledges not to use forces as long as 1949. Ayub flatly rejected the suggestion. Were he to accept Ayub told Eisenhower, the people of Pakistan would say he had handed over Kashmir on a silver platter to Indians, Ayub asserted he was not against the "no war" declaration but wanted a parallel agreement on principles for solving the Kashmir dispute. Without this linkage, Ayub believed that "no war" declaration was a ploy to enable Nehru to avoid doing anything about Kashmir.

Even though Eisenhower was not able to bring India and Pakistan closer together—his visit was a tremendous success. "We are not out to get anything for each other." Nehru wrote the Chief Ministers, but to understand, and I think both of us succeeded to some extent. I believe there is a greater mutual understanding between these two countries now "U.S.-India relations had rarely been warmer".

Sidewinder Missiles for India: Eisenhower Changes His Mind

Two weeks after Eisenhower conversation, the Indians, for the first time in a number of years turned to the U.S. for military equipment. In early May, Defence Minister Krishna Menon approached Bunker about bringing 29 Fairchild C-119 transport aircraft to help in supplying the Himalayan defenses.

Bunker cabled Washington he was encouraged by the request, arguing it was "clearly in our interest to do everything possible stiffen posture vis-a-vis Chinese communists. The U.S. quickly approved the sale.

After careful consideration, the State Department Near East Bureau, then headed by G. Lewis Jones, recommended the Secretary Herter that the Indians be urged to purchase their missiles from Britain. Jones opposed selling Sidewinders to India because of the "present delicate state of our relations with Pakistan." Herter concurred and later discussed the question with President Eisenhower who reversing the position he took with Bunker—agreed to turn the Indians down.

Jones' main point was that Pakistan, as an ally, deserved better treatment that non-aligned India, Jones wrote:

> In becoming our whole hearted ally, Pakistan has undertaken real responsibilities and risks, making its territory available to us for a series of projects highly important to our national security. The hard fact remains that, if our mutual security system is to remain intact, we must show Pakistan that substantial benefits flow from a military alignment with us against the communist bloc.

Even though the U.S. refused to sell side winders to India, it remained uneasy about India's procuring increased quantities of military equipment from the Soviet Union. Only with great difficulty were the American and British in 1957 able to dissuade Nehru from by Soviet bombers instead of British Canberras.

By 1960, the combination of Krishna Menon as Defense Minister, the bargain basement rupee payment terms Moscow offered, and Nehru's perception that closer ties with Moscow were helpful against China made the situation more favourable for an expanded Soviet military supply relationship.

Understanding U.S. concerns, the Defense Department

later changed its mind, proposing that the Air Force subsidise an offer of U.S. helicopters to the Indians. Time ran out before the Eisenhower administration could make a decision. The proposal died in the transition to the Kennedy administration.

The U.S. attitude on arms aid to India was, thus, ambivalent. Washington did not want India to obtain more Soviet arms, freeing this would increase Soviet influence. At the same time, the U.S. was unwilling to sell sophisticated weaponry to India for fear of upsetting U.S. ally Pakistan.

The preferred appraisal was to direct Indians toward the British, their traditional supplier, in the hope that this would suffice to keep the Soviet out. In 1957, this approach succeeded in averting the purchase of Soviet bombers. By 1960, it no longer worked.

Final Eisenhower -Nehru Meeting, September 1960

The President discussed his desire for progress on disarmament, but was pessimistic about the prospects. He reviewed at some length U.S.- Soviet differences on verification questions, obtaining Nehru's agreement that verification was an essential part of any disarmament accord.

The two leaders also talked about Africa, where the Congo was falling into chaos after the hurried grant of independence by Belgians. The U.N. was trying, with limited success, to prevent Civil War between different factions vying for power.

Turning to India's border dispute with China, Nehru said there was unfortunately no progress toward a solution. Chou Ein Lai visited Delhi in April 1960, but to little avail. The Prime Minister said that as the two sides in these talks were disagreed on the basic facts of their border claims, official seeking to clarify these points. Nehru commented, the Chinese were better able to support forces in the Himalayan border areas than India because of the nature of the terrain and their superior road system. Eisenhower clear concern for preserving world peace—always a critical factor in Nehru's thinking was another element. The Soviet handling of the Hungarian revolt, especially the execution of Premier Imre Nagy made Nehru more critical of the Russians and, perhaps less critical of the U.S.

U.S.-Indian Relations: Increasingly Cordial

In 1956, the NSCs operations coordinating Board (OCB)—charged with monetoring implementation of U.S. policy around the world—reputed gloomily that there had been little if any improvement in Indo-American relations. Despite ambassador Coopers having established friendly relation with Nehru and somewhat better atmosphere, the OCB concluded that basic policy differences remained unresolved.

Growing troubles between India and China, added a new element to bilateral ties. India-Pakistan relations were at least improved as a result of settlement of the Indus Waters dispute.

On the Indian side, there was also satisfaction about the trend in relations even if U.S. arms for Pakistan remained a problem. U.S. economic aid was forthcoming in increasing amounts. As trouble viewed with China, the implicit support of the U.S. was a comforting factor.

Nehru after the 1959 talks with Eisenhower, he appreciated and understood our desire to keep out of military alliances, indeed he would not have it otherwise.

5

Kennedy: "Neither Kashmir nor India"

Pakistan saw Nixon as a good friend. India regarded him, unlike President Eisenhower as an irrepentent Cold War and a foe of Indian non-alignment. President caused uneasiness in Pakistan and stirred hopes in India.

As a Senator, he cosponsored the 1958 Senate Resolution calling for increased economic aid for India and criticised the Republican policy of relying on military pacts to meet the communist threat of the Third World.

Kennedy appeared considerably more sympathetic than Nixon to the aspiration of developing nations and less antagonistic toward non-alignment. The fact that Kennedy's policy adviser during the 1960 election campaign was none other than former ambassador Chester Bowles was another big plus in India and a minus in Pakistan.

The appointment of Bowles as Under Secretary of State, the naming of Phillip Talbot an Assistant Secretary of State for Near East and South Asian affairs, and the selection of John Kenneth Galbraith, a friend of Kennedy as the ambassador in New Delhi, raised Indian optimism and stirred Pakistans anxieties even more.

With Bowles experience as ambassador to India, Talbot's understanding of India dating back his days as an exchange student in 1939, and Galbraith's own knowledge from extended stays in the mid-1950s the new team gave the Kennedy administration a depth of knowledge about South Asia, and specially India, unqualified before or since.

Incoming Secretary of State Dean Rusk, while no expert on South Asia, was familiar with the territory from War-time service at the China-India-Burma theater headquarters in New Delhi.

As a Senator, Kennedy took the initiative in 1958 to sponsor the legislation urging more economic aid for India, although his personal contact with Nehru was less than sparkling. Nehru showed little interest in talking with the young Massachusettes Representative when he visited India in 1951.

Nehru's preachy neutralism put Kennedy off somewhat—it was not his style but he respected Nehru as one of great political leaders of the twentieth century and praised "the soaring idealism of Nehru" in his first State of the Union address January 30, 1961. Kennedy regarded with its vast population, economic potential, and democratic aspirations as the centerpiece of the developing world worthy of major attention by the U.S.

Well aware of the intense India-Pakistan differences, Kennedy and his aides though the U.S. could achieve friendlier with New Delhi with doing irreparable damage to relations with Pakistan. This was the administrative basic policy goal in 1961.

The Congo and Laos Crises

Among the first issues confronting the new administration was the ongoing Congo crisis, in which India played an important role as the source of the largest contingent of soldiers to implement the U.N. effort to calm the strife-ridden African nation. Kennedy modified U.S. policy to place more emphasis than Eisenhower on using UN machinery in order to ensure genuine independence for the Congo and keep the struggle out of the Cold War. Seeking actual active Indian cooperation in shaping the UN mandate, Kennedy detailed U.S. hopes for the Congo operation in a lengthy cable he sent Nehru on February 18, 1961.

Kennedy's message ended with words Nehru could himself have written, "if we and those who share overview move toward together in the support of the U.N. in the Congo, it will succeed—and with it the opportunity of every nation, even the smallest, to work out his destiny."

To meet a voting deadline at the UN, even the smallest, to workout its destiny. Although he did not agree on all points about the UN mandate, Nehru's reply was positive in tone, "I need not tell you," he cabled, "how much we welcome our cooperative with the U.S. in order to find a solution of this conflict problem of the Congo."

The Kennedy administration believed India could be helpful in Laos because of its good relations with the Soviet Union and its role as Chairman of the then Moribund International Control Commission for Laos. Kennedy sent Secretary Risk and Averell Harriman to see Nehru. "If you can take diplomatic action to halt the fighting pending political discussions, you will perform a great service," Kennedy told Nehru in a March 23 message.

In his reply, sent after Nehru had met the U.S. envoys, the Prime Minister confirmed he had urged Khuruschev to cooperate in seeking peace in Laos. Nehru's letter touched also in restrained manner on the Bay of Pigs disaster.

The Indians reacted with relative calm to the failed U.S. invasion of Cuba, reflecting the improvement in relations between Delhi and Washington.

In Laos, the India's proved willing to be helpful upto a

point, Nehru was, however, unwilling to work in harness with the U.S. against the communists in Southeast Asia.

U.S. Aid to India: Record Levels of Assistance

Even before entering the White House in January 1961, Kennedy appointed a task force to consider economic assistance to India. In line with the thrust of the Kennedy-Cooper resolution on aid to India, the task force set the goal of esuring sufficient foreign financing for India's Third Five Year Plan due to start in 1962.

To achieve this, the group proposed and the Kennedy administration agreed that the U.S. commit $ 1 billion annually for the first two years of the Third Plan on the understanding that other countries match the U.S. contribution.

The aid planners envisaged half the U.S. share or $ 500 million in development loans or grants and the remainder PL 480 food assistance. The Kennedy administration, this, called for a tripling of U.S. development lending from $135 million the Eisenhower administration provided in 1960.

To Galbraith's surprise, Nehru responded enthusiastically. By the end of 1961, the first two dozen peace corpse and volunteers reached India. The programme soon grew to several hundred volunteers whose work complimented Indian Rural Development Programmes in addition to proving a plus for the U.S. image.

If quantitatively, the Kennedy administration made good on its hope for a majority increase in US aid levels, qualitatively, Ambassador Galbraith uneasy that U.S. assistance was been spread too thin, with public relations gains not commensurate with the $ 1 billion a year Washington was providing.

U.S. officials continued worry that Soviets much less on a few highly visible public sector industrial projects, were winning more friends than the U.S. Less visible U.S. assistance was scattered around the country often in physical and human infrastructure activities like education, agriculture, health, and transportation.

Galbraith continued in first hand in Washington to win approval for two major impact projects the public sector steel mill at Bokaro and the nuclear power station at Tarapur near Bombay.

Galbraith strongly supported Bokaro as a symbol of U.S. commitment to Indian neutralization. While many democrats did not share the doubts of their predecissive about U.S. and for Bokaro, the Kennedy administration was unable to overcome opposition to the project on Capital Hill.

Galbraith had more success with the nuclear power plant to be located at Tarapur near Bombay. The size of the project $ 80 million—was for more manageable. There was no ideological objection to cooperating with the Indian Agency Commission on Nuclear power.

U.S. atomic energy specialists concluded the project was feasible given comparative fuel costs in India and technical competences of the Indian AEC. The Kennedy administration gave the green light for going ahead. All that remained was for India and the U.S. to agree on mutually satisfaction safeguards to ensure that sensitive nuclear materials were not diverted for military purposes.

It was not until May 1963—just before Galbraith left India - that the Ambassador was able to announce official approval for the project. Ironically, the Tarapur power plant-intended as a showpiece of U.S. highly technology assistance to India—became the focus for bitter controversy in the 1970s after India exploded a nuclear device.

Official Visits: Lyndon Johnson and Ayub Khan

The Vice President's trip report to Kennedy spoke of

India's being favourably inclined toward the new administration, Johnson commented:

> This is my judgement, should be exploited not with the hope of drawing of India into our atmospheric—which might be unnecessary as it would be improbable—but, cheaply with the hope of commenting under Nehru as India-US friendship which will endure beyond any transition power in India.

Perhaps, more significant than this unexceptionable was the impression of President Ayub Khan of Pakistan made on the Vice President. Like most U.S. leaders whether Democratic, a Republican, Johnson was taken with Ayub.

Johnson told Kennedy the Pakistani President was "the singularly most impressive and, in this way, responsible head of State encountered on the trip." The Vice President further recommended that the U.S. seek ways to modernize Pakistani military, asserting Ayub wants to resolve the Kashmir dispute to release Indian and Pakistan troops to deter the Chinese rather each other.

In mid-Summer 1961, President Ayub Khan himself travelled to Washington. Nervous about the shift in emphasis of U.S. South Asia policy, Ayub sent up warning signals in the Pakistan press and in interviews with American newsmen before leaving Pakistan. "Can it be," Ayub asked the Associated Press correspondent, "the U.S. is abandoning its good friends for the people who may not prove such good friends." After arriving in Washington, Ayub maintained a bold public front. Addressing a joint session of Congress, he said bluntly Americans might not like everything. Pakistan did but his country was the best friend the U.S. had in Asia.

Quite apart from the opposition of the Pakistanis and their American supporters—the unofficial Pakistan Lobby was strong in the Pentagon, the intelligence community, and among conservatives in the Congress—those forwarding a shift in South Asia policy toward India did not get much help from New Delhi.

On August 25, 1961, Nehru hurt Indians' standing with Kennedy when, in the middle of a crisis over Berlin, he called Western access to the German city a "Concession" rather than a right.

Galbraith lamented, "This has put the skunk in the air conditioner. Washington in raving." The ambassador was able to get Nehru—who seemed not to realize the import of his words to "clarify" his remarks, still the damage was done in Washington.

The anti-American tactics of Krishna Menon, who continued to represent India at the UN while in Defence Minister, also remained a chronic source of trouble.

During the summer of 1961, Menon infuriated Washington by misrepresenting American and Soviet nuclear disarmament policies—portraying the U.S. as more and the Soviet Union as less than was, in fact, the case.

When the new totalling 25 nations gathered in Belgrade for their first Heads of State meeting as a "movement" in September 1961, Nehru was initially reluctant about the idea of the summit, but in the end went along.

With the nuclear testing a major focus of attention, the results of the Belgrade meeting disappointed the U.S. administration. Washington found the communique too soft on the Soviets especially as Moscow had, in effect, thumbed its nose at the non-aligned by resuming nuclear testing just before the gathering.

The balance sheet in the fall of 1961 on Kennedy's South Asia policy seemed mixed. On the economic side, the US dramatically increased its economic assistance for India, meeting the ambitious targets the pre-inauguration task force set and helping India harvest a foreign aid crop that met its most optimistic hopes. With Kennedy as President, India saw Kennedy as a friend.

Senator Cooper, after a visit to New Delhi, told Kennedy "relations between India and the U.S. were the best I have ever known."

This did not, however, translate into broader political cooperation between the two countries. The two countries worked together in the Congo but on the most other issues, India and U.S. positions continued to reflect conflicting approaches to the Cold War. Kennedy administration officials hope the visit of Nehru to Washington in November 1961 would open the door to a better partnership between the two countries.

Official Visits: An Aging Nehru disappoints the New Frontier

On November 5, 1961 the seventy one year old Nehru arrived in New York for his fourth and his last trip to the U.S. After appearing in "Meet the Press", a television programme, he flew to Cape Cod accompanied by ambassador B.K. Nehru for private talks with Kennedy in an informal fairly setting. During lunch, the President turned the conversation to South East Asia to seek Nehru's advice on how to deal with South Vietnam. "Here is the situation we face in Vietnam," the forty seven year Kennedy said, "we have little experience in Asia. You Mr. Prime Minister, are a great Asian statesman. Tell us what to do." Ambassador Nehru recalled the Prime Minister did not really reply. Kennedy brought the discussion back to Vietnam several times in the hope of eliciting Nehru's views. The Indian leader still gave no coherent response, instead, falling into remote silence.

Things did not improve after the President the Prime Minister travelled together for the formal part of the visit.

Nehru's principal business making at the White House with the President advisers went poorly. Kennedy virtually did all the talking, laying in detail U.S. policy concerns and goals. Nehru listened, saying almost nothing and leaving the President puzzled and uneasy.

Although in a private session with Kennedy the Prime Minister inert a bit, he had little to say on the major issues confronting the superpowers: Vietnam, Berlin and disarmament. Nehru got down to specifics only on Kashmir where he reiterated his long standing willingness to settle the dispute on the basis of acceptance of the cease fix a line as the international boundary.

Kennedy, at time, had trouble keeping the conversation going. Nehru remained passive. The President said later, "It was like to grab something in your hand, only to have it turn out to be fog."

In his *Thousand Days,* Schelsinger, quoted Kennedy as describing Nehru visit as "the worst state visit I have ever had." Thirty years after the fact, B.K. Nehru agreed the trip had been terrible.

The ambassador knew Nehru was aging, but had not realized he was also tired and ailing. A younger and healthier Nehru would have enjoyed the busy schedule and crossing with New Frontiersman. Unfortunately by November 1961, Nehru was no long the man he once was.

Because Nehru kept foreign affairs as his personal, almost private domain, he failed to develop the institutional experience in the Indian Foreign Service and Ministry of External Affairs needed to maintain the activist foreign policy India pursued in the heydey of non-alignment. As Nehru began to fade, India found itself hampered in continuing the global foreign policy that Nehru successfully established in the early 1950s.

Too much depended upon Nehru's personal input, energy and prestige. The upshot was that when the U.S. foreign policy machinery was crackling with the activism and can do spirit of Kennedy New Frontier, India's foreign policy was beginning to creek. Nehru sadly stayed beyond his time.

Goa, U.S. Aid and MIGS

Expressing regret that Nehru failed to alert him to possible Goa action, Kennedy wrote:

> My major concern was and continues to be the effect of the action in our tasks, especially in terms if it impact on American opinion. Unfortunately, the hard obvious fact for our people was the resort to force—and by India. This was a shock, to the majority who had admired your country's ardent advocacy of peaceful methods, and a reinforcement to those who did not enjoy what they called "irresponsible lectures". It is not an accident that the men who are taking most advantage of the Goa matter here are the same men who are already attacking our aid programmes and our support for the U.N.

In private, Kennedy told India's ambassador he was annoyed less by India's action than by Nehru's not having said anything about Goa, when he was in the U.S. Kennedy, in fact, found an event somewhat amusing. B.K. Nehru recalled the President's saying:

> My only point is why did not do it before, 15 years before. But Mr. Ambassador, you spent the last 15 years preaching morality to us, and then you go ahead and act the way any normal country would behave and now that you have done what you should have done long ago, people are saying, the preacher has been caught coming out of the brothel. And they are clapping. And Mr. Ambassador, I want to tell you, I am clapping too.

The Sino-Indian Border Conflict

In July 10 letter, Nehru also spoke about the border trouble with China:

> We have gradually been building up position and increasing our posts in Ladakh etc. The result is that we are in a somewhat more advantageous position than were a year or two ago. The Chinese government has lately become more aggressive in tone in his statements made to us. I do not know what it signifies, and we have to be wide awake and careful.

The previous year in November 1961, India had adopted a forward policy sending patrols and establishing Indian posts behind Chinese positions in the disputed Aksai Chin plateau in the northern Ladakh. Nehru's strategy to build up India's strength in the disputed border region in order to pave the way for an eventual diplomatic settlement after two sides on moral equal military terms. Although India's tactic increased the chance for border clashes neither Washington nor New Delhi anticipated serious combat between the world's two most populous nations.

Practically no one expected the Chinese would inflict so staggering and defeat on the Indian military. According to Galbraith the U.S. Embassy had no idea how disorganised the Indians were. "We knew the terrain was difficult, he said, "but assumed the Indians knew what they were doing." Obviously they did not NSCST staffer Komer complemented, "we were fluggished when the Chinese wiped the floor with the Indians."

After July 1962, the Chinese began to stiffen their stance, threatening a forward policy of their own in Northeast Frontier Agency, if India continued to refuse to back off in the Aksai Chin. According to Allen Whiting, then the State Department senior China intelligence officer, the Chinese acted to assure victory in combat should deterrence and diplomacy fail in halting the forward policy and bringing Nehru to the Conference table.

In late summer, near the junction of India the tiny mountain Kingdom of Sikkim, and Tibet an area where the location of McMohan Line was itself in dispute—Chinese troops for the first time moved South of Indian Version of the frontier to occupy Thulga ridge, a key terrain feature.

In private, he accepted responsibility, writing Krishna Menon on October 28, "It is not much shifting about the blame. The fact remains we have been found lacking and there is an impression that we have approached these things in a somewhat amateurish way."

Giving ground to his critics—and to the enormous satisfaction of Washington—Nehru removed Menon who had become the principal scapegoat and target for criticism, from the Defense Ministry. He initially his friend to a nearly created post of Minister of Defence Production, but on November 7 dropped Menon entirely from the Cabinet when it became clear Nehru's own position was under threat under he let thin go.

India's non-alignment seemed to be a thing of the past. In the face of Indian gloring military weakness, Nehru reversed policy 180 degrees to seek military assistance from the U.S., U.K. and other Western countries. President Kennedy promptly made clear American willingness to aid India: "I want to give you support as well as sympathy" he wrote Nehru on October 28.

Nehru responded the next day, "I am deeply grateful to you what you have written and for the sympathy of the great nation whose head you are at a moment of difficulty and crisis for us." The same day, Nehru made a formal request to Galbraith for military assistance asking almost plantively that the U.S. not insist on a military alliance as a *quid pro quo.*

For the U.S. the border conflict, which coincided with and initially was overshadowed by the Cuba missile crisis, seemed to provide an unexpected opportunity to achieve the base goal of the Kennedy administration in South Asia now moving to better and closer relations with India without running a foul of Pakistan. Given a conflict of uncertain properties, the administration stood ready to do what it could to help Indian defenses against Chinese incursions.

By coming promptly to India' aid, the U.S. Government wanted to demonstrate to friendly in Asia that Washington was ready and able to assist Chinese government aggression.

If Nehru was gratified by the positive response from the West, the Soviet Union's response proved disappointing. Once fighting broke out, Moscow shifted from neutrally towards the Chinese position. Primarily concerned about Beijing's attitude towards the Cuba missile crisis, the Russians advised New Delhi to accept Chinese proposal for further talks on the border.

Moscow also informed the Indian MIG-21 deliveries were off—for the time being, at least. Most non-aligned countries similarly standoffish in their reactions. Except for Nasser of Egypt and Tito of Yugoslavia, none paved very forthcoming in backing New Delhi against Beijing.

Military aid to India immediately provoked grave difficulties in U.S. relations with Pakistan although Washington hoped that India's neighbour would suspend its hostility as India battled against the Chinese incursion. Defence against the communist threat was, after all, the supposed purpose for which the U.S. gave arms aid to Pakistan in 1954.

Mindful of Pakistan sensitivities, Kennedy wrote Ayub Khan on October 28, advising that any military aid for India's "immediate needs" and for use against China only. The President Ayub to take a broad, not practical view of the situation.

Ayub spurned the President, objecting strongly to U.S. arms shipment for India. He downplaid the seriousness of the conflict, which he described as a limited border affair rather than a broader Chinese military challenge. Ayub also complained that Washington has reneged on a promise to consult providing arms to India.

When U.S. ambassador Walter McCoroughy tried to deliver a further presidential letter to Ayub before Washington took a financial decision on military aid, the Pakistan Leader chose not to be available, going of on a hunting trip. Unwilling to wait for Ayub's return, Kennedy proceeded with a positive response to the Indian arms request.

Washington was careful, however, to send equipment that would be primarily useful in mountain warfare rather than against the Pakistanis.

As the foreign response to the frontier crisis became clearer, the popularity of the U.S. and the West soared in India, that of the Soviet Union and non-aligned countries slumped. Galbraith as typical a visit by the elderly Indian Congress Party leaders who said, they were busy considering the non-alignment policy.

The envoy's standard reply, taking a leaf from Eisenhower, was that "we might alignment with India too expensive." More astonishing, but an indicator how far things had gone, the editor of the long time pro-communist and fiery anti-American weakly Blitz advised it would be switching to a pro-American policy.

For several weeks, there was a lull on the fighting front. The Chinese held their guns without trying to advance further, India regrouped its forces in the east with an eye to defensive operations during the winter snows. Emergency American and British military aid began to arrive by air, boosting Indian morale and raising Western popularity even higher although not having any immediate impact on Indian defensive capabilities.

On November 14, the Indian launched the attacks on the eastern end of McMohan line near a place called Walong. The Chinese promptly counter-attacked, routing the Indian forces, and also launched a full scale attack against regrouped Indian troops at the Western end of the McMohan line. Although Indians had used the full to reinforce their positions in the sector to division strength, inept military leadership triggered a retreat that soon became a rout. Some Indian units fought well, but the major force, the 4th Division, crumbled under the Chinese assault. Outflanked and bypassed, the division ceased to exist as an effective military unit. Its men fled in disorder through the forests and jungles of the Assam Himalayas. In a matter of three days, as Indian defenses collapsed, Chinese troops swept south from the mountains to the edge of the plains, gaining virtual control of the entire 40,000 square miles claimed as Chinese territory.

In Ladakh, where Indian troops were better acclimatised and New Delhi let the field Commanders alone, the Indians performed credibly. Even though forced back, they were not routed.

In New Delhi a state of panic reigned on November 19, 1962. The government the Chinese would strike Calcutta. The loss of province of Assam and, perhaps, the fall of Eastern India was degraded. In this mood of crisis, the Prime Minister sent off two startling letters to President Kennedy to asking that the US intervene militarily to provide air support for the struggle against the Chinese.

Nehru asked for a dozen Squadrons of U.S. fighter air craft and air defense radar and related communications equipment to protect India's major cities, thus, freeing the Indian Force to attack Chinese forces. He also sought two squadrons of B-47 bomber to strike positions behind the front, asking that U.S. pilots fly the B-47 until Indians could be trained to replace them.

The two letters presumably drafted by Foreign Secretary M.J. Desai, were discussed with but not shown to key cabinet members. They were sent with unusual secrecy, suggesting Nehru was aware that his action would effectively undermine his cherished policy of non-alignment.

In a departure from a standard procedure, the Ministry of External received copies of the letters which apparently no senior official, other than Nehru and Desai, actually see before their despatch.

When ambassador B.K. Nehru received the message in Washington, he was embraced at being the unfortunate that had to deliver letters that ran totally against the train of Indian policy. He shown to no one in Indian embassy, keeping the messages in his personal desk. The ambassador believed Nehru was psychologically finished off by the mid-November military disaster and not himself when he signed the two letters.

As Kennedy considered a response, the U.S. Navy dispatched an air-craft carrier task force into Bay of Bengal, a move Galbraith recommended to steady Indian nerves. Ironically, the Carier was the USS *Enterprise* the same warship that became the symbol of U.S. hostility toward India when Nixon sent the Carrier towards the Bay of Bengal during the 1971 Bangladesh crises. Before Kennedy reached a decision the Chinese announced a unilateral cease-fire effective November 22 and a full back of their forces 20 kilometers north of their version of the McMohan Line in the East and their border claim in Ladakh. The Chinese relinquished control over practically all the territory their army joined in the east, but mountained their grip over the area of strategic importance to them, the Aksai Chin position of Ladakh.

In what proved a master stroke, the Chinese made clear by their action that their aim in the border conflict were limited. Rather than occupying additional territory, the Chinese underlined their ability to impose by force of arms the compromise border settlement they proposed earlier: Their acceptance of Chinese control over the Aksai Chin. Because of the crushing Indian military defeat, the Chinese achieved much more than they probably expected in launching the border offensive.

The first casualty was Jawaharlal Nehru himself. The Indian never recovered from the staggering psychological blow. Until mid-October 1962, Nehru although aging, was still a towering international political figure, the revered founder-father of the world's largest democracy the spokesman for decolonization and human rights and the founder leader of the non-alignment in spreads. Ambassador Galbraith, President Kennedy, "One other worst problem here is, that the Chinese attacked strike the country with a tired leader whose principle and ideas also have been shattered by then the events."

A second casualty was India's international reputation. Her proud army humbled in the Himalayas, India was no longer a plausible rival to China for leadership in Asia. Indian national pride suffered a deep emotional wound from the military disaster in the Himalayas.

It took many years until India could recover its national pride from the humiliating defeat in the border war. India would, henceforth, play a diminished role on the world stage.

U.S. Arms for India and Kashmir Talks

The unilateral cease-fire left was hinghow—and New Delhi—unclear whether the Chinese have marked the end of the conflict or was simply a tactical pause. On November 19, when the situation looked its bleakest, Kennedy met with Secretary of State Rusk, Secretary of Defence McNamara, CIA director McCone and Key aids Averell Harriman, Phillips Talbot, and Robert Kromer.

At the urging of McNamara, Kennedy approved sending a mission to India "to find out what the real situation was."

The President and his advisers also wanted more military support from the British Commonwealth, Kennedy decided to call in the British ambassador to press this point. Rusk thought the British should take the lead in the military mission, but the President decided to send a U.S. team while urging the British to energise the commonwealth.

Within the week, the mission headed by Averell Harriman was off to South Asia. Because of the Cease-fire the task became as much political as military. The joint state Defence Department group was charged with proposing U.S. South Asia policy for the period ahead as well as assessing India's military assistance requirements against the Chinese. The British by then more actively engaged, sent a parallel political-military team led by Commonwealth Secretary Duncan Sandys.

Flying directly from Washington, with only a one hour refuelling stop in Turkey, the team met with Prime Minister Nehru almost immediately after arriving New Delhi on November 25. As if embarrassed to find himself beholden to the U.S., Nehru took a general attitude of extreme relaxation, quite at variance with the two letters he had sent to President Kennedy.

When Harriman "with exquisite delicacy" limited at the need for a Kashmir settlement and for taking defence measures, Nehru listened and made no comments. An account of the meeting by Roger Hilsman made clear Nehru's uneasiness:

> Nehru look tired and strained. It must have difficult to greet Americans over the ruins of his long pursued policy of neutralism. And the very fact that we were determined there would be no hint or gesture of `I told you' so probably made it even more difficult. Our welcome was not warm, it was *pro forma,* it was withdrawn, it was very limited.

After shuttering between India and Pakistan Harriman and his British counterpart Duncan Sandys achieved their immediate goal: getting Nehru and Ayub to agree for discussions.

The Report Harriman submitted after his mission pointed up the dilemma the U.S. faced. The U.S. had long sought to built a close relationship with India... The present situation provides a unique opportunity to advance this aim. At the same time, there was the risk of serious adverse repercussions of processing with a major arms programme since this could lead not to a drastic weakening of Pakistan's ties with the West, but possibility to its closer association with China.

Harriman recognised that Pakistan's price for forming a joint front with India against the Communists was a Kashmir settlement `on acceptable terms.' The rub, he admitted was that terms acceptable to Pakistan were unacceptable for India.

On the ease of start of the Kashmir talks the Pakistan managed to upset the applecart, even more than Nehru had during Harriman's visit. Ayub government chose this moment to announce agreement in principle with Communist China on a border delimitation.

The announcement made the Indians livid Nehru regarded Ayub's action as a contemptuous rejection of his request that the Pakistanis not cooperate with China while India was in difficulty. Washington was dismayed that Pakistan themselves its nose at U.S. advice by counting to improve relations with China.

The Kashmir discussions dragged on through five dreary rounds of ministerial-level talks before ending in May 1963. They achieved almost nothing. Toward the end, the U.S. set-forth some areas in an effort to stir some life into the talks. After Prime Minister Nehru rejected the U.S. proposals, Ambassador Galbraith commented "I discovered we had, indeed, brought about the first agreement in some years between India and Pakistan. Both have joined in denouncing our proposals."

When Secretary of State Dean Rusk visited New Delhi on May 5, he suggested the idea of naming a Kashmir negotiator. On this occasion Nehru's response to the suggestion was not negative, initiating a lengthy but ultimately unsuccessful effort to frame the terms of reference in a manner acceptable to both the Indians and Pakistanis.

The effect of learning to Nehru was to advertise that he had become an American playing card. The Prime Minister had to compensate for his lack of strength by refusing to give on Kashmir.

Disagreeing, Phillips Talbot felt that, despite failure, the effort was worthwhile. The border war had sufficiently shaken the Himalayan scene that there was at least a possibility of solving a dispute that otherwise looked as though it could continue undefinitely to cause grave tensions in South Asia, quite apart from immensely complicating U.S. foreign policy in the region. NSC staffer Robert Kromer said he was skeptical about the chances for success was convinced by Talbot to go along with the Kashmir effort.

Neither India nor Pakistan, in fact, showed any real enthusiasm about the Kashmir talks, with pressure from Washington and London, the only reason for their agreeing to participate. After departing from South Asia, Dean Rusk pained a gloomy assessment about the prospects for an early settlement.

Ted Sovenson quoted President as saying all too accurately regarded Kashmir dispute as more important than the struggle against their communists. Reconciliation between the two foes was not in the cards.

As the Indians were hoping for a far larger arms aid programme the Kennedy-McMilan package was disappointing, Galbraith sharing Indian hopes described the talks at Bermude as "a cheese paring operation throughout," and asserted that a great opportunity to bring India much closer working association with the West had been missed.

In January 1963, he wrote Sudhir Ghosh, who was urging a Western defense guarantee that help from the U.S., Britain and others was all right, but going beyond that "will be purchased at the expense of giving up our basic policy of non-alignment. That is not merely some kind of moral issue but something which makes our people feel they have to be self-reliant and it also helps greatly in the balance of the world and our search for peace."

Several factors added Nehru's efforts. First, the fact that the Chinese maintained the cease-fire, showing no serious sign of resuming military action reduced the pressure on Nehru for a more fundamental shift in Indian policy. Secondly, once the Cuba missile crisis and the Himalayan war ended, Moscow shifted policy gears. The Soviets resumed a more neutral position on the border dispute with China, agreed to proceed with the shipment of MIG-21 to India, and showed `understanding' about Indian requests for arms from the West. Pro-Soviet leftists in India, including *Blitz*, whose switching of sides proved of short duration, reassumed ritual lambasting of the U.S. this time claiming Washington was trying to force Kashmir, concessions from weakened India.

Finally, the reluctance of the U.S. to firm up a longer term arms assistance arrangement played into Nehru's hands, undercuttings for a broader reorientation of Indian policy since it became unclear what a shift toward the U.S. would yield in security terms. Galbraith and Kromer warned Kennedy, "with further foot dragging we would have no rept no progress on Kashmir and no Indians either."

The following month in May 1963, T.T. Krishnamachari, the new Indian Minister for Defence production, came to Washington to press the Indian case with a programme with a price tag of $ 1.3 billion—over twice what even Bowles was proposing and five times as large as the Pentagon wanted. Meeting with top U.S. government figures, including President Kennedy, the Indian Cabinet received a positive response on the air defense concept, but no specific commitment on military aid funding levels.

The Pentagon, in particular, leaned strongly toward Pakistan with whom the U.S. military aid had developed many ties in the years since the arms relationship began in 1954. The future of the intelligence facilities in Peshawar was also an important factor weighing on the minds of Senior American Officials.

Since the Chinese showed no signs of resuming the conflict, Kennedy felt no great pressure to force a decision in the face of disagreements. He let the arms issue summer.

Not long after arriving in New Delhi, Bowles had to mop up two problems left over by Galbraith an agreement to instal a Voice of America transmitter and the Bokaro Steel Mill project in early 1963, eager to battle their radio broadcasting capability against the Chinese, the Indian agreed to locate a Voice of America transmitter in eastern India. The U.S. government would be able to use the facility for daily VOA broadcast at certain hours, but otherwise the Indians would control the transmitter.

In effect, the agreement would have allowed the U.S. to use the Indian territory for its propaganda broadcasts an arrangement quite alien to the spirit of non-alignment. When opposition to the accord developed to conceal the agreement on grounds that it had not been properly staffed within the Indian government. Washington was annoyed by the Indian flip-flop but could do little but fine.

In the case of the Bokaro steel mill project, it was Washington that had to back off. Despite strong support by President Kennedy for providing U.S. financial aid for the public sector steel mill, congressional opposition to the refused to go away.

The administration concluded by the 1963 that it lacked the votes to gain approval for Bokaro without a major fight. When situation became clear, the Indians helped Kennedy out by deciding to withdraw their request.

Appreciative of U.S. help against China and continuing large scale economic aid, the Indian did not want put Kennedy in a corner over Bokaro. The Soviet promptly stepped into build the mill.

A Meeting that never Took Place

In November 1963, ambassador Bowles returned to Washington. In line with Kennedy's instructions he had worked with the new Indian Defence Minister Y.B. Chavan and Defence Minister Krishnamachari to refine the Indian proposals, reducing them to a substantially more modest package of $375 million spread over five years.

6

Johnson: US Pullback from South Asia

Although Lyndon Johnson broadly supported the bipartisan policy of containment of commission and assistance to the power making of the world, he was skeptical about the favoured position Kennedy gave to India in US. South Asia policy, President Ayub Khan of Pakistan greatly impressed Johnson during his visit to Karachi in May 1961.

On the same visit he was less taken with Jawaharlal Nehru. After meeting President Johnson moved somewhat closer to Kennedy position, NSC staffer Komer, who strongly suffered putting the major emphasis on India not on Pakistan, said the most panasonic argument with Johnson related to the relative population of the two countries. The President agreed it made more sense for the US to line up with India, a country so populous rather than to chose its enemy Pakistan.

The policy argument Komer advanced was Vintage Cold War: Was India to founder or go communist, U.S. interests in Asia would suffer a major loss. "India as the largest and potentially most powerful non-communist Asian nation" Komer told the President "the fact the major prizes for which we, the Soviets, and Chrcombs are competing in Asia."

Johnson's first meeting as President with a Senior Indian in April, 1964 when he received Prime Minister Nehru's daughter, Indira Gandhi, who were travelling in the U.S., she gave the President a letter from her ailing father in which Nehru praised Johnson's efforts for a nuclear accord with the Russian assured the President India would persist in seeking better understanding with Pakistan, and expressed appreciation for U.S. economic and military assistance.

In their discussion, Johnson took friendly exception to remarks by Mrs. Gandhi to the *New York Times* that the U.S. favoured Pakistan on the Kashmir issue. With a smile the President stated "The Indian should realize that the Pakistans.... were far more unhappy about our policy toward India than India seemed to about our policy toward Pakistan." During the meeting with Indira Gandhi, Johnson did not discuss military assistance—the most important item then on the Indian-American agenda.

As the Session ended, the President asked Mrs. Gandhi to convey his `affectionate regards' to her sick father. Three months earlier, in January 1964, Nehru had suffered a debilitating stroke from which he never fully recovered. When Assistant Secretary Talbot and Ambassador Bowles called on the Prime Minister in March, they were shocked. Nehru's condition was far worse than they expected. He hardly knew who they were and had difficulty in conversing coherently. Bowles and Talbot concluded correctly that could not remain long on the scene.

Military Aid to India: Half a Loaf

The day after Johnson took office, NSC Staffer Robert Komer, tried and failed-to get the new President to consider the India arms aid proposal. We have gotten up real momentum...unless we get the new President signed on now while still carrying out the Kennedy policy, we may lose a real opportunity.

Komer urged his chief, Mc George Bundy, the NSC chief, however, chose not to put the India issue to Johnson. Instead the new President sent General Maxwell Taylor, Chairman of the Joint Chiefs of Staff, to India (and also Pakistan) to review the situation. The policy received from Secretary of State Rusk was proven by later events off the mark:

> If we can move ahead, albeit some what jerkily in each country.... these proposals for military assistance to India and Pakistan will advance our strategic objective of resisting communist pressure in the areas without placing intolerable strains on or relations with either country.

Following his trip to South Asia, General Taylor recommend a five year $ 500 million for India divided between grant-aid and low interest credits. Taylor urged that the Indians draw up their own defense plan, setting their own priorities rather than having Americans do this. After Secretary Rusk endorsed the proposal, President Johnson gave his blessing on February 8, 1969.

In New Delhi Defence Minister Y.B. Chavan worked closely with the newly established U.S. military mission to shape a comprehensive five year defence plan. The main U.N. concerns were that India not hurt its economic development programme by spending too much for defense and not seek equipment from the U.S. likely to create fresh trouble with Pakistan.

American defence specialists were, therefore, not responsive to Indian interest in obtaining three squadrons of supersonic F-104s aircraft. Although the U.S. had already given Pakistan F104s, the Pentagon argued against Indians procuring these air-craft on the grounds that supersonic fighters would be of limited utility against the Chinese and would eat up about one third of the $500 million aid package.

On May 27, Jawaharlal Nehru died in his sleep. The U.S. Air Force sped Chavan back to Washington where he immediately explained with Secretary of State Dean Rusk and ambassador Chester Bowles for the funeral ceremonies in New Delhi. Although a few days before his death, Nehru brushed off questions about a successor, his appointment of Lal Bahadur Shastri, a popular, but retiring North Indian leader, to the Cabinet, helped ensure a smooth transition of power.

Nehru led his nation for so long that life with Panditji, as he was affectionately called, seemed had to imagine. His achievements as Prime Minister were striking. He set his country firmly on the democratic path, launched an economic development programme, and charted a foreign policy course for India independent of the two contending power blocs. Even though after the 1962 War, Nehru was only a shadow at his former self, his passing marked the end of era for India.

After the U.S. refused to provide supersonics, the Soviets took up a soviet alternative. In September, 1964, Chavan signed an accord in Moscow under which the Soviets agreed to provide 45 MIG-21s and to set up factories in India to assemble another 400 MIGs making the Soviet fighter the Indian interceptor aircraft.

As Bowles warned earlier this development gave the USSR a much closer relationship with Indian military and, particularly, with Indian Air Force than they had enjoyed previously and had a major impact on Indian public opinion.

In Washington, the consequences of refusing to provide India F-104s, the Johnson administration implicitly concluded that the price it would have to pay with Pakistan—perhaps, even a final rupture in the alliance relationship was not worth the potential rewards from the Indians.

Once more U.S. ties with Pakistan set a limit on how for Washington was willing to go with India in the military supply area even if, as in the case of the F-104s, India was almost certain to turn to the Soviets as an alternative supplier of fighter aircraft.

Despite Washington's rebuff of the request for supersonics, the military assistance agreement still seemed to represent a major development establishing a new and presumably long-term chapter in the security relationship between the U.S. and India. The chapter, in fact, turned not to be very sharp; fifteen months later, during the 1965 Kashmir war, the U.S. stopped arms experts and military assistance.

India's Second Prime Minister

If Jawaharlal Nehru dominated the Indian scene like a banyan tree in the shade of which others grew with difficulty, Shastri barely five feet tall, frail-looking and already in poor health, appeared overshadowed by powerful regional Congress Party political leaders. Diminution retiring and moderate were the words the CIA used, in describing the new Prime Minister. Lal Bahadur was more at ease in his home group Indian setting and had fewer of the psychological hang ups from which English-trained Indians, like Nehru, seemed to suffer. He had never travelled outside India before he became Prime Minister and initially felt shaky in dealing with foreign policy matters.

With the 1962 war fresh in mind, Lal Bahadur Shastri's preference was to define alignment in terms of good relations with both the Soviet Union and the U.S. or as some called it bi-alignment against the threat posed by China. America's prompt help in 1962 and confined large amounts of economic and food assistance, running $ 1 billion annually impressed the Indian leadership as a sign of U.S. friendship.

Although Washington unwillingness to sell F-104s underscored limits of the security relationship, Indo-U.S. relations seemed on solid ground. They were, indeed, less troubled at the time than Washington's dealings with Pakistan.

The main target of U.S. anger, Ayub Khan, perhaps, more familiar with Johnson's unpredictable style, swallowed hard and contained his annoyance. As Komer to McGeorge Bundy, "The Paks, who probably see the blow as directred mainly at them, are lying low and letting the India's get themselves in trouble. The Indians are showing their injured pride in many ways. Shastri is nice think about the Soviets.... we have suffered a setback here.... Although in time, tempers cooled, Johnson's rude treatment of the two leaders badly strained relations with India and Pakistan just as the two countries began to edge toward a second Kashmir War.

Serious clashes broke out on April 9, 1965 in a desolate and uninhabited marsh land called the Rann became a problem in 1954 when Pakistan staked a claim to half the area, asserting it was landlocked sea.

Under International Law, thus put the boundary in the middle of the Rann than at its northern edge.

The Indians disputed the Pakistan position, insisting the Rann was a marsh, not a sea, and that the boundary should remain unchanged.

Although the cease-fire took hold India's pride suffered a fresh blow from the clash in the Rann of Kutch. It was one thing to be pushed around by China, quite another to be bested by Pakistan. The Shastri government came under angry criticism in the Indian Parliament for its handling of the affair. Part of the ire was directed at the U.S. for its failure to prevent Pakistan from using U.S. military equipment against India.

This was a sensitive issue with New Delhi since the U.S. had given at stream of assurances Washington would not permit the Pakistan's to use the arms to attack India. In the case of the Rann, Pakistan admitted using U.S. supplied equipment, but justified this on the grounds of self-defence that India began the fighting.

Not eager to enter the thicket who was the aggressor, the Johnson administration stressed the importance of stopping the fighting rather than assessing blame for the misuse of U.S. weapons. In a testy exchange with Secretary Rusk on May 8,

B.K. Nehru expressed dissatisfaction with the U.S. attitude:

> While India hopes the Kutch question will be resolved, a more important question of principles is involved. U.S. assurances to India against Pakistani misuse of arms had been the foundation of Indian defence policy. If these assurances were eroded, it would be very serious matter... as far as India was concerned the U.S. reaction had been inadequate.

The Second Kashmir War: August-September 1965

If following the Rann of Kutch episode, India in the words of William Barnd—-became `dangerously frustrated'—Pakistan became `dangerously confident.' Having ruled the country with hardly as misstep since 1958, Ayub Khan proceeded to implement operation Gibralter to seize Kashmir, supported by Foreign Minister Zulfikar Ali Bhutto and other Pakistani hawks. The bold scheme envisaged covertly infiltrating some five thousand Pakistani trained guerrillas across the cease-fire line in order to stir an uprising in Kashmir.

Badly misreading the mood in India, Pakistan apparently did not expect Shastri to counter militarily either from weakness or from fear that China would intervene. After the 1962 debacle and India's poor showing in the Rann of Kutch, an over-confident Ayub Khan had difficulty in taking India and especially its leader, "little Shastri too seriously."

The Pakistanis may have also wanted to strike in Kashmir before the military adds swing too heavily in India's favour. Although in 1965 Pakistan's armed forces could not match India's in numbers, thanks to the U.S. aid, they had gained a qualitative edge in armour and air power. The Pakistan fear that it only a question of time till India, having embarked on a defence build up after the 1962 fiasco, would erase the edge.

Infiltration of the guerillas began August 5. The Indians quickly grasped what was going on and captured many of the intruders. Sabotage caused some damage, but the raides failed to start a Kashmiri uprising. Contrary to Pakistan expectation, the Indians also responded militarily, crossing the Kashmir cease-fire line to capture key passes and terrain features that Pakistanis were using as infiltration routes. Operation Gibralter seemed doomed.

After intelligence reports indicated the likelihood of the Pakistani attack, the U.S. pressed U.N. Secretary General U Thant to urge restraint on both sides. In New Delhi, ambassador Bowles asked Indian Foreign Minister Swaran Singh or to respond calmily warning that a military thrust by India at some more favourable point will almost certainly touch off war. The Minister's reply was to protest the use by Pakistan of U.S. Patton tanks contrary to American assurances.

Bowles followed up with an urgent plea for direct U.S. pressure at earliest possible moment on both sides in support of Syes' appeal. Bowles asked authorization to tell Shastri that if the Indians agreed to a cease-fire and troops withdrawal and the Pakistani refused, the U.S. cut-off military aid to Pakistan. Washington turned Bowles down.

In Washington, ambassador Nehru echoed Foreign Minister Swaran Singh's protest about Pakistan's use of U.S. supplied equipment. The ambassador warned that unless Pakistan stopped its drive to cut off Srinagar, India would attack across the international border to the South of Kashmir.

Sides trapping Indian complaints about Pakistan's misuse of American weapons, Rusk emphasised that a cease-fire was the most important thing. Bowles made the same point in New Delhi, while reporting to Washington a crecendo of criticism in the media about Pakistan's use of American weapons against India.

On September 6—as ambassador Nehru warned the Indian army struck across the international frontier only twenty miles east of the city of Lahore, the capital of West Pakistan.

Despite the threat of all-out war between India and Pakistan, the U.S. held back from direct diplomatic intervention continuing to rely on the UN as the main vehicle to stop the fighting. Key members of the Senate Foreign Relations Committee, during September 8, Breakfast agreed with Dean Rusk that it was not wise to get out in front of the UN to carry the burden of trying to force India and Pakistan to cease hostilities.

The U.S. proceeded later the same day to embargo military exports and to suspend assistance commitments to India and Pakistan. Personally drafted by Rusk and approved by Johnson, the administration statement amend at averting even more drastic measures following a volcanic reaction by Congressmen and Senators, angry that the U.S. was fuelling both sides of the war. Washington was dismayed that India and Pakistan were halting each other, endangering their economic development programmes and shredding any slim hopes of their cooperating against the Chinese.

Like Washington, Moscow threw its support behind U.N. efforts to stop the fighting, offering its good offices for peace talks at Tashkent. After Breznev ousted Khruschev as Soviet Leader in 1964, the Russians had adjusted their South Asia policy to adopt even handed and less pro-Indian posture.

The Soviets indeed, worked with the U.S. in support of the U.N. peace effort a rare instance of the East-West cooperation during the Cold War.

The British, who had brokered cease-fire lost their influence with New Delhi after Prime Minister Harold Wilson imprudently charged India with aggression in crossing the International border. Notwithstanding U.S.-UK-Soviet support, the UN made very slow progress. Secretary General U Thant failed during September 9-14 visit to South Asia, to obtain Indian and Pakistani agreement on a cease-fire. Although Ayub Khan and Shastri tried to get Johnson to intervene directly, the President kept the focus on U Thant's peace efforts.

On the battlefield despite the fact that the Indian Army made initial gains, the front stabilized at the outskirts of Lahore about 15 miles inside the border. The Pakistan drive to cut off Kashmir bogged down, failing strategic objective.

Washington breathed a sigh of relief that an all out struggle had been averted. When the Soviet again offered to mediate, the U.S. supported this move a shortling reversal of policy after a decade of trying to build Moscows' role in South Asia. Dean Rusk explained:

> We encouraged the Russians to go ahead with the Tashkent idea, because we felt we had nothing to lose. If they succeeded in bringing about any detents at Tashkent, then there would be more peace on the subcontinent between India and Pakistan, and we would from the fact. If the Russian failed at Tashkent at least the Russians would have the experience of some of the frustration that we had for twenty years in trying to sort out things between India and Pakistan.

In January 1966, three months after the end of fighting, Ayub and Shastri met with Kosygin in the Soviet Central Asia city of Tashkent. Shuttling between the two leaders, Kosygin proved a skilful diplomat. Eventually on January 9, he obtained their agreement to withdraw to positions held before the war, to exchange promises and try to solve their disputes peacefully.

Given the enmity between India and Pakistan, the Tashkent achievement was a considerable achievement. The Conference came to a tragic end when Lal Bahadur Shastri suffered a fatal heart attack just hours after signing the accord. For the second time in a year and a half, India cremated a Prime Minister.

U.S. Policy during the 1965 war pleased neither India nor Pakistan. The Indians were angry that the U.S. failed to prevent the use of American arms despite repeatedly promises that it would do so.

Washington even handed action in stopping military and economic assistance both countries also New Delhi, for there seemed little doubt that Pakistan started the trouble by launching operation Gibralter.

The Pakistanis were even more bitter. That was higher their supposed ally not only refused to help against India but even cut off the flow of the military supplies seemed to act betrayal. U.S.-Pakistan relations plummeted. The alliance relationship appeared for all practical purposes dead.

A `Hard New Look' at Economic and PL480 Aid

During the first year and a half in the White House, President Johnson allowed the other main settlement of U.S. involvement with India—the large economic assistance and PL480 food programmes to continue largely unchanged along the lines previously established.

In September 1964, at the expiration of the four year PL480 programme approved in 1960, Johnson agreed to a new one year food accord to supply 4.5 million tons of wheat. In the spring of 1965, the Indians were back, seeking a two year PL480 programme for 10 million tons. Few expected difficulties in proceeding with the new food agreement or with the annual economic assistance request.

And then, without warning, in June 1965, the President surprised his own bureaucracy and the Indians. He called a halt to routine approval of new aid commitments for India (and also for Pakistan) and demanded a hard new look... before spent a lot more money.

In June 9 meeting, Johnson announced that he would

personally approve a new assistance for India and Pakistan until the Congress voted the fiscal year 1966 aid bill. Johnson also asked for early recommendations on the pending Indian PL480 request.

What caused the President to bring the Indians and Pakistanis up short? A number of factors appeared to explain Johnson's abrupt move. The Chief Executives sensitive political anatenna detected growing unpopularity for foreign aid with his former Congress colleagues, especially aid to South Asia which loomed large in the overall figures.

Pakistan flirtation with China made it hard to justify large scale help on political grounds. With India's economic performa lagging, those was growing feeling in Congress that New Delhi was taking half for granted "regardless of what they did or how effectively they used it."

For several years Orwill Freeman, the Secretary of Agriculture, had been voicing his unhappiness, first to Kennedy, then to Johnson, about the sluggishness of Indian efforts to boost agricultural production.

Freeman returned from a May 1964 trip to India in a gloomy frame of mind. He feared that U.S. surpluses would one day disappear, leaving India in terrible trouble unable to feed itself and unable to food from abroad.

Along with American and Indian specialists, however, Freeman was confident India could boost food production substantially if it tried seriously to do so. What then needed was higher priority on agriculture, changes in agricultural price and distribution policies, expanded better seeds, increased use of fertilizers and other agricultural inputs.

India's Third Prime Minister—Indira Gandhi

In a meanwhile, Soviet Union was growing increasingly unhappy about developments in India. The indications of improved Indian relations with the U.S. after Mrs. Gandhi's visit to Washington were unsettling. The adoption of more market oriented economic policies by Mrs. Gandhi also displeased Moscow. As the Soviet Union remained a key supporter for Indian foreign policy and was becoming an increasingly important arms suppliers, Mrs. Gandhi tried to mend fences during a visit to Moscow in July preceded by talks in Egypt and in Yugoslavia, Mrs. Gandhi pressed for an early reconvening of the Geneva Peace Conference on Vietnam.

Possibly inadvertently, possibly not, the Prime Minister made a foreign policy gesture in Moscow by agreeing to a communique on Vietnam that shifted India from an essentially neutral stance to one that echoed the Soviet line.

In contrast to earlier Indian statements that linked reconvening the German Conference and a halt to U.S. bombing of North Vietnam, on this occasion Indira emphasised the need for U.S. to take the first step. The July 16 communique also described aggressive actions of imperialist and other reactionary forces against Vietnam.

Washington was predictably unhappy about the shift in Indian stance. In July, memorandum to the President, Rostow had advised that Bowles send her a `searching personal letter' and Rusk talked Turkey with the Indian charged affairs.

At a July 21 Press Conference, Johnson bristled in response to a question about the Indians saying it would be helpful to see what North Vietnam would do.

Still shaky in her first months as Prime Minister and weakened by the devaluation debacle, Mrs. Gandhi wanted to avoid the impression India was leaning toward the U.S.—as suggested by the rousing visit in Washington and her acceptance of devaluation, criticism of U.S. policy in Vietnam was a way to pacify her critics on the left—or so it may have seemed to Indira.

Although American did not expect India to endorse U.S. policy toward Vietnam, Washington was clearly annoyed by Mrs. Gandhi's less than non-aligned remarks. Ambassador Bowles wrote that when he commented Mrs. Gandhi was not saying anything more than the Pope or the UN Secretary General, the first response he got from Washington official was, "the Pope and U Thant don't need our wheat," The U.S.-Indian political entente establish during Indira's Washington visit proved a fragile and short-lived altar.

1966: One More Drought

At the summer of 1966 progressed, it became increasingly apparent that the monsoon rain were going to fail for a second year in a row, coming on the heads of the poor 1965 monsoon and 1966 drought proved a terrible blow, with Bihar in Eastern India the worst hit area. The NSC history of the Indian Food crisis:

> For India the prospect was one more drought, one more year of acute dependence on PL 480 imports one more of submission to U.S. demands, one more year of expensive to the world as paupers. This outlook produced a sense of frustration, pessimism and fatalism.

Lyndon Johnson made things much harder by following what became known as the "Shift to month" polic-keeping the supply line so tight that foodgrains had to move directly from ships to the consumers in order to avert famine. On August 23, a recommendation from Secretaries Freeman and Rusk and aid administrator Bell urged the release of 2.5 million tons of wheat to prevent a break in the grain pipeline. Johnson refused to act, writing on to covering memo: We must hold on all the wheat we can send nothing unless we break an iron bound agreement, by not sending.

Johnson's knowledge of Indian agriculture impressed B.K. Nehru. Despite the fact the Presiden'ts refusal to authorise more food exports frustrated the envoy. In early November, the President rebuffed a plea from secretaries Freeman and Rusk to approve an additional wheat shipment.

In view of the possible need for congressional approval for another large scale Indian Food operation, Johnson also wanted to prepare the ground for sending a request forward to Capital Hill. The President, therefore, had Freeman organize a separate bipartisan congressional group (Senators Miller and McGhee and Congressmen Payage and Dole—all agriculture specialists to make its own assessment of India's needs and performance.

Both the Agriculture Department and Congressional teams found the food situation grave, concluded that the Indians were fulfilling their policy reform commitments and urged prompt action by Johnson to prevent famine in the early months of 1967.

When the American press became aware of Johnson's game of hardball, the *New York Times* and the *Washington Post* roundly criticised use of pressure tactics on an India confronted with the spectator of famine. Sing by the media criticism and with the recommendations from the teams in hawk, Johnson finally decided to release some wheat, he had ambassador Nehru, who left Washington for New York in anger chant Johnson's stonewalling tactics, call to the White House. The President personally assured the envoy he was not going to let Indians starve. Although the administration made no public announcement until the Congressional group formally submitted its report, Johnson instructed Freeman to announce the allocation of 900,000 tons of PL 480 wheat. The immediate crisis was averted.

For Indian officials trying to deal with the situation on the ground, Johnson's, tactics were tremendously frustrating and initiating.

At one point during the crisis, Mrs. Gandhi telephoned Johnson to make a personal plea that he release wheat. Her press adviser Sharda Prasad present during the conversation, remembered the Prime Minister clenching her fingers tightly on the telephone. Talking to Johnson, she was friendly and charming but when she hung up, she said angrily, "I don't ever want us ever to have a bag for food again."

One satisfied that the India's was genuine and the firm policy performance good, Johnson turned his attention to enlisting other countries in sharing the burden with the U.S. He agreed to send five million tons more in 1967 to India—as stall, agriculture and AID recommended but release the final three million tons only other donors provided a similar amount.

At Johnson's insistence, the World Bank organised a food for India consortium to food possible donors to unscore his interest, Johnson sent Under Secretary to State Eugene Rostow (brother of the NSCs Wall Rostow) on a global salt's mission. He told Rostow he wanted to raise more food for India, and also to show Congress that U.S. allies, even if critical about Vietnam policy, were willing to cooperate with him in facing other grave problems, such as the potential Indian famine.

What motivated Lyndon Johnson in implementing the `ship to month' policy? What was trying to achieve in putting the Indians through the Wringer with his handling of food aid? Most Indian observers, and some American as well, including agricultural Secretary Orwill Freeman believed he acted out of spite to punish Mrs. Gandhi for her public opposition on Vietnam. Others close to Johnson, while admitting his annoyance over India's policy denied this lay behind his tactics.

Walt Rostow and Dean Rusk stoutly maintained the President was using the leverage of food shipments to press for agricultural policy changes and then to ensure the implementation of the new policies. "The whole thing gained him not a niche politically. He offended Indian nationalism by his tactics. But he was playing a long-term game to get to feed its own people, and he succeeded Rostow asserted."

Although agriculture Minister Subramaniyam disliked Johnson's approach, he did not connect `it with Vietnam'. Subramaniyam stated, Johnson thought he was driving Indian agriculture. We need change our policy, but implementation was important.

Perhaps, he thought that unless the pressure was there the policy would not be properly implemented U.S. aid director John P. Lewis, no admirer of Johnson also did not attribute his handling of food crisis to Vietnam. Ambassador B.K. Nehru remained puzzled about what motivated Johnson, but commented that, at no time did any American official maintain India's policy on Vietnam in connection with the hold up in food shipments.

Johnson achieved his goal—Indian could feed itself—but the cost was high for Indo-American relations. As Lawrence Viet, U.S. Treasury attach in New Delhi in the early 1970, wrote "The U.S. reaped a harvest of Indian wealth which endured for more than a decade."

Although the Aid to India Consortium redeemed the pledge of $ 900 million in non-project assistance in 1966—nearly half a year after devaluation—the-consortium failed to provide prominent increased aid during the following two years.

For 1967-68 when the World Bank estimated at aid requirements at $750 million, the Consortium affected only $295 million.

To make up the difference, the Bank called for $ 1.275 billion in 1968-69. At the May 1968 Consortium meeting the donors `came up miserably short' pledging only $ 642 million—little more than half the amount the World Bank projected.

The Non-Proliferation Treaty: India says No.

Jealous of its newly waive independence, India had already proven difficult—from the U.S. stand point—in nonproliferation negotiations, opposing American efforts to impose international control as an infringement on sovereignty as far as the 1947 U.N. discussions regarding the Brauch Plan for international control of atomic energy. India and the U.S., nonetheless, cooperated in the Atoms for Peace Programme and in construction of the Tarapur nuclear power plant near Bombay.

Several months later, in early 1965, Dr. Homi Bhabha reiterated the position when he met with Under Secretary of State George Ball. Bhabha stressed that India needed to show some `peaceful' nuclear achievement to offset the prestige China had gained by testing. The Indian A.E.C. Chief asserted India, if it wished to do so, could produce a nuclear devices in 18 months.

The follow on discussion was, however, diffuse and those were no clear cut conclusions about how to influence India to close the door on the nuclear option.

In contrast to the 1963 Limited Treaty Ban Treaty, which India signed and which imposed obligations on all parties, New Delhi found the NPI a one-sided affair.

Although Indira Gandhi sent her Cabinet Secretary, L.K. Jha, to Moscow, London and Washington to explore nuclear guarantees against the Chinese threat, Jha was unable to develop a formula that satisfied all concerned.

Despite the decision to reject the NPT, Mrs. Gandhi reiterated that India was not going to develop nuclear weapons. The Prime Minister also refused to give the go-ahead for work on a peaceful nuclear explosion. A few years later, after the Bangladesh crisis, Mrs. Gandhi would change her mind and gave the India ASC the green light to proceed with a nuclear test.

At the end of 1960s, however, India maintained a position of ambivalent. Its refusal to sign the NPT kept open the nuclear option.

1967: Revised U.S. Military Supply Policy

Locke agreed that if Washington wanted to restrain Pakistan from moving even closer to China, it would ease the arms embargo, as President Ayub requested, at least permit the Pakistan to obtain spare parts for aircraft and other equipment the U.S. previously supplied.

The disagreement between the two ambassadors grew shriller. Not above sending private *ad hominem* arguments to Johnson via White House aid Marvin Watson, Locke charged Bowles favoured India over Pakistan country to the belief of President Johnson" Locke also alleged Bowles wanted to avoid the embarassment of having personal statements that the U.S. would never again arm Pakistan proven wrong.

Relations with the U.S. also suffered. The backlash against Johnsons PL 480 policy and devaluation were one cause. Another damaging factor the reaction in India to revelations of widespread funding of cultural and educational groups by the Central Intelligence Agency.

Indian intellectuals were freely offended to learn that prestigious organisations like the Asia Foundation were Secretary receiving funds from the CIA. Feeling tricked and betrayed, some Indian intellectuals led an anti-U.S. crusade, alleging academic imperialism. The Soviet and their local communist Allies and fellow travellers took full advantage of the exposures to further tarnish the U.S. image in India.

A Summing up: Indo-U.S. Relations on the Decline

The five years Lyndon Johnson served in the White House saw a major shift in relations between India and the U.S. For India, after the ignominous defeat by China in 1962, these were trying years, marked the sluggish economic performance and near famine.

Only the 1965 war, when India thwarted Pakistan's attempt to seize Kashmir by force, buyed morale. Pandit Nehru passed from the scene in May 1964. His successor Lal Bahadur Shastri was in office barely nineteen months before he died at Tashkent. Indira Gandhi, who succeeded to power in January 1966, was still struggling to consolidate her political control when Johnson's term ended in January 1969.

The U.S.-New Delhi thought, had treated India badly. Part of the problem related to Johnson's brisque Texan style, better designed for U.S. congressional arm—twisting, than dealing with touchy South Asians.

The rude councelling of the Shastri's visit in 1965 and insensitive management of, PL 480 policy left scars, whatever the President's motives.

The rupee devaluation debacle and Washington's unwillingness to meet what India saw as its legitimate defence needs additionally New Delhi's attitude towards the U.S.

Americans were also disenchanted. India seemed to be going nowhere economically. Unable to feed itself India was hardly the model of democratic development. Washington hoped other Third World countries would emulate as a rival to China. Official Washington was asking what the point was pouring hundred of millions of dollars into a country that had performed poorly and remained at odds with much of the U.S. foreign policy?

Was it worthwhile to continue to pay so much attention to South Asia, especially at a time when 500,000 American troops were fighting to save South Vietnam from a communist takeover? All the U.S. had to show for more a decade of trying to promote peace between India and Pakistan was the 1965 war. The two countries had made graphically clear that they were for more worried about each other than any external threat.

As the clock ran down on the Johnson administration, a sense of exhaustion with South Asia and its seemingly insuperable problems had taken hold even among liberal democrats favourably inclined towards India.

The glum mood of 1969 about India, John F. Kennedy became President. In the intervening eight years, because of the Vietnam War, and the revised appraisal of the subcontinents relevance to U.S. interest, New Delhi no longer seen as having major strategic importance. India, in Washington's eyes, had become just a big country full of poor people.

7

Nixon: The Tilt

When Richard Nixon replaced Lyndon Johnson in the White House, in January 1969, his main policy concern lay on winding down the unpopular war in Vietnam. He was content to continue the disengaged approach toward South Asia which Johnson began after the 1965 Indo-Pakistan war. As Henry Kissinger wrote in his memoiss when the Nixon administration took office, our policy objective on the subcontinent was, quite simply, to avoid another complication to our agenda.

This treatment presumably did nothing to lessen Nixon's preference for Pakistan, the erstwhile ally of U.S. and his dislike for India and its policy of non-alignment. "Nixon, to put it mildly; Kissinger stated," was less susceptible to Indian claims of moral leadership than some of his predecessors, indeed, he viewed what he considered their alleged obsequiousness toward India as a prime example of liberal soft-headedness." The Indian Prime Minister reciprocated Nixon's lack of enthusiasm. She told one interviewer, "I think I had excellent relations with every body (American President) except Mr. Nixon. And he had made up his mind before hand." "Mrs. Gandhi could scarcely conceal her boredom in receiving the former Vice President when he called on her in 1967.

After about twenty minutes of desultory conversation, she asked the Minister of External Affairs except speaking in Hindi, so Nixon would not understand how much longer the session would last.

In August 1969, after six months, Nixon became the second serving Chief Executive to visit India, stopping there and in Pakistan enroute from the Far East to Europe. The public welcome in New Delhi had none of the enthusiasm Eisenhower received ten years ago.

Official meetings were low key, almost perfunctory. Neither Mrs. Gandhi nor Nixon displayed much warmth. The substantive discussions, mainly on Vietnam lacked spark and animation.

Previously, Pakistan's close ties with China had caused a great tension with Washington. Now Nixon took advantage of these good relations to ask Yahya Khan to convey to the Chinese leadership his interest in an opening to China. Thus, began two years of secret diplomatic exchanges through the Pakistanis that lid to stunning Kissinger trip to Beijing in July 1971.

Mrs. Gandhi defeats the Syndicate: Shifts to the Left

When Mrs. Gandhi lost out to the syndicate over the selection of the Presidential nominee, she struck back by going the Finance Minister, her conservative rival Morarji Desai, and nationalizing India's major banks more that the left-wing of the Congress party and the communists warmly welcomed.

Lacking the votes for a clear Parliamentary majority she depended on the support of the Communist and other small parties to remain in power until the 1971 elections. In struggling against the Syndicate Mrs. Gandhi consciously shifted to the left politically, toward more socialist domestic policies, positioning herself as the champion of India's poor masses.

Although foreign policy was not a basic issue, her populist domestic shift was paralleled by strengthened relations with the Soviets—a trend hardly pleasing to the Nixon administration.

As Indira moved to the left and conservative administration took power in the U.S. new frictions arose between Washington and Delhi. Wanting to do something for his Pakistan friends, Nixon in October 1970 approved what was called the one time exception to the 1967 policy of not exporting lethal weapons systems to India and Pakistan.

Washington agreed to sell Pakistan 300 personnel carriers and some aircraft worth about $ 50 million, at the same time reaffirming the intention to continue the 1967 policy. Although Pakistan hoped for more, Islamabad was pleased to get something from the U.S. The Indian predictable were annoyed, remaining ever allergic to U.S. arms for Pakistan and suspicious of Nixon.

Vietnam became a second cause of tension after India shake of raising the level of its diplomatic mission in Hanoi to an Embassy. When Washington warned Delhi that this step would mean a cut off in U.S. aid, Mrs. Gandhi prudently deferred action. Although assistance levels were declining, India was still waiving several hundred million dollars of American aid annually. U.S. assistance remained an important source of foreign funds for Indian development that she did not want to lose for an act of political symbolism.

A third bilateral problem had an usual origin the unauthorised construction of a cultural centre in Trivandrum, the capital of South India state of Kerala. After 1954, the Indians did not permit foreign governments to establish libraries or cultural centres outside New Delhi or consular cities.

They did, however, allow the U.S. Information Service (USIS) Centre set up before 1954 in Lucknow, Patna, Hyderabad, Bangalore and Trivandrum to continue in operation.

The Soviets—perhaps, with silent assent from friends in the government of India—proceeded ,country to the rules, to start building a centres in Trivandrum, where the communists were politically strong. Unfortunately, in December, 1969, the building collapsed, killing nine workers. Because of the publicly accident generated, the Indian authorities were under pressure to take some action.

New Delhi's decision was to refuse to permit further work on the Soviet Centre in Trivandrum, but also to apply the 1954 rule to the American libraries, USIS was told to shut the five centres down.

The Soviets, who agreed to put the proposed Trivandrum centre under the ICCR, and their friends in India doubtless concluded they had not done badly from the episode. Even since revelations in the late 1960s CIA funding for some groups, Indian Leftists and pro-Soviet elements, charging the U.S. with "academic imperialism" worked hard to reduce the extent of the U.S. intellectual presence in India.

The four principles occurred in the fall of 1970 when the U.N. celebrated its 25th anniversary. Numerous heads of government, including Mrs. Gandhi and Yahya Khan attended the ceremonies in New York. Yahya and a number of other leaders accepted Nixon's invitation for dinner at the White House to commemorate the U.N. anniversary.

Perhaps, reflecting her personal feelings about Nixon—Mrs. Gandhi somewhat gracefully turned down the initially without much of an explanation.

During Yahyas' visit to Washington Nixon talked further about the opening to China. He asked the Pakistani President, then planning a trip to Beijing to tell the Chinese leaders that he regarded a Sino. American reapproachement as `essential' Nixon is also said to have told Yahya "Nobody has occupied the White House who is friendlier to Pakistan than me."

Meanwhile, the Soviets in late 1969 decided to abandon their efforts to pursue balanced relations with both India and Pakistan reverting to the precious policy of closure to India.

In March 1969, border clashes with China brought the Sino-Soviet split to the boiling point. As the China question became uppermost for the Kremlin, Moscow must have wondered about the benefits from its even-handed approach in the subcontinent.

The spirit of Tashkent proved brief, Indo-Pakistan relations soon reverting to their usual state of mutual tension and suspicion. Despite the arrival of some Soviet arms and the promise of more, the rebuffed Moscow's calls for looser ties with China.

The leftward turn to Indira's domestic policies was highly pleasing to the Russians. The Soviet Policy of balanced relations with Pakistan was, however, causing considerable strain in relations. Mrs. Gandhi and others made clear they did not like Soviet arms shipment to Pakistan; the Indians began to make noises of about a rapproachement with China. In late summer 1969, Kosyegin stopped in India enroute to and from the funeral of Ho Chi Minh.

After talks on these occasions and during a September 1969 visit to Moscow by Indian Foreign Minister Dinesh Singh—regarded at the time as pro-Soviet—the Kremlin adjusted its South-Asia policy. The Soviet gave up their efforts with Pakistan deciding against further arms agreements with Islamabad, and returned to a South-Asia policy anchored in close association with India.

Even though Indira Gandhi refused to agree to the anti-Chinese Asian Collective Security scheme, Brezhnev proposed during 1969, Indo-Soviet tensions greatly eased and relations substantially improved.

Pleased with the Kremlin's policy readjustment and decision to back off from offering additional military equipment to Pakistan, New Delhi was willing to negotiate a treaty of friendship with Moscow, similar to the agreement Moscow had with Egypt, then in its Soviet period. Negotiation proceeded quietly through the Indian Embassy in Moscow under Ambassador D.P. Dhar, an outspoken supporter of closer Indo-U.S. relations.

Although the two countries reached agreement, Mrs. Gandhi not to sign the treaty from concern that this step would cause a public stir about a change in India's non-alignment, both domestically and with the U.S. Put on the shelf, the draft re-emerged two years later as the basis for the 1971 Indo-Soviet Treaty.

Mrs. Gandhi did not, like her father, serve as Foreign Minister, but none of those who held the portfolio—M.C. Chagla, Dinesh Singh, Y.B. Chavan in the 1960s and 1970s and P.V. Narasimha Rao in the 1980s—exercised independent power. It was Mrs. Gandhi who made the decisions. The Ministers loyally implemented her wishes or ceased to be the ministers.

As the non-alignment movement (NAM) swelled to over a hundred nations even implausibly embracing such aligned States as Castro's Cuba—its periodic gatherings became like U.N. General Assembly meetings full of standard ritual speeches and the adoption of ritual resolutions invariably more critical of the U.S. than of the Soviet Union.

To occupy the bureaucracy and to develop new ideas, Kissinger commissioned a wide array of policy studies called National Security Study Memoranda or NSSM No. 109 that policy toward the subcontinent received NSC attention.

Nixon broke new ground in spelling out more clearly and publicly than previous Presidents the guidelines for U.S. foreign policy in a series of annual reports to the Congress that provided a `conceptual framework' for U.S. policy.

Looking beyond the Vietnam War and the rigidities of the Cold War, Nixon and Kissinger wanted to create a late 20th century global version of the 19th century European power balance.

A key to this was bringing China into the family of nations reversing two decades of U.S. policy to isolate Beijing. Unlike the World view prevalent in the U.S. between 1956 and 1965, India and the Third World had little importance to the Nixon/Kissinger power equation.

Reflecting the South Asia's diminished role was the blind commentary in the 1970 report—a few paragraphs out of nearly 200 pages and a low key three pages in the 1971 report. In these pages, the President made three main points:

- U.S. Strategic concerns in South Asia were limited to seeing that neither China nor the Soviet Union gained a dominant position in the subcontinent;
- The U.S. accepted Pakistan altered foreign policy and India's non-alignment. We have no desire to press on them a closer relationship than their own leads them to desire, Nixon declared and;
- The main U.S. interests in the subcontinent were to promote economic development, to respond to humanitarian concerns and to encourage India and Pakistan to put aside their differences.

But events did not allow South Asia to remain in the back waters. In 1971, the coincidence of the East Pakistan crisis and Nixon's China initiative placed the subcontinent at the centre of U.S. foreign policy concerns.

The East Pakistan Crisis

The Awamy League swept 167 of 169 seats in the east, but none in West Pakistan. An unhappy President Yahya Khan set about seeking a political settlement, a task for which he showed neither skill nor inclination.

Pledging populist economic reforms to `eradicate poverty,' Mrs. Gandhi crushed her more conservative opponents to win an unchallenged political mandate. Her Congress Party faction gained 362 of 520 seats in Parliament.

However, after demonstration of March 23, Pakistani Day got out hand with widespread booming of Pakistan flags, Yahya abruptly ended the negotiations and flew back to Islamabad. During the March 25, Pakistani military forces cracked down in the East. Yahya outyawed the Awami League, sought to arrest its leaders as traitors, and tried to disarm Bengal members of the armed forces.

The initial foreign reaction was relatively calm, largely limited to expression of hope that Pakistan despite its difficulties will return to a constitutional path. In a few weeks the mood changed after the refugee Frickle became a flood and the story of West Pakistani brutality became known.

In India, there was an insistent clamour for military action to enable the people of East Pakistan to exercise their right of self-determination. Although Mrs. Gandhi denounced Yahya, she resisted pressure for early military intervention—her generals told her they needed six months to prepare for a campaign against East Pakistan.

By May, the main outline of Indian policy were set, the goal was the undoing of Yahya's crackdown in East Pakistan although not necessarily through the emergence of Bangaladesh. On the military side, the Indians increased covet help to the Bengali of the Pakistani military who managed to escape. These became the core of Mukti Bahini or Peoples Brotherhood, a guerrilla force soon numbering in the thousands, which began to attack transportation, communications and power facilities in East Pakistan. The Indian Army also started to prepare for possible action against East Pakistan in the coming winter when dry weather could make the terrain more suitable for fighting and the snows in the Himalayas would impede Chinese help to Pakistanis.

On the political code, the Indians, together with the Bangladeshis, launched a vigorous diplomatic and public relations campaign to stir world opinion against Pakistan.

Senior Indian politicl leaders, like Jaya Parkash Narayan, and Foreign Minister Swaran Singh roamed the globe trapping support.

The foreign response was not entirely to India's liking: there was much sympathy for the human suffering of the Bengali refugees, much criticism of Pakistani brutality, but little inclination to intervene. The Soviet Union pressed Pakistan the hardest. To India's chagrin, however Moscow continued its economic assistance to Pakistan and spoke of the need for restraint in solving the crisis. Although China spoke loudly in support of its Pakistani friends, Beijing provided no tangible assistance beyond vertical encouragement.

In the U.S. the Nixon administration urged a peaceful settlement, but both in public and private acted gingerly in its dealings with Pakistan when the U.S. Consul-General in Dacca, Archer K Blood, forwarded cable protesting U.S. official silence about the human rights violations in East Pakistan, Kissinger was lived.

The message for Dacca was simple: since the U.S. had no vital interests in Pakistan, traditional concern for human rights should govern U.S. policy, resulting in condemnation of the West Pakistanis.

Blood and his colleagues in Dacca were of course, unaware of the role Pakistan was playing in the secret negotiations with China, which quite apart from Nixon's liking for Pakistan—made the President disinclined to lean on Yahya.

On April 27, a month after the crackdown in East Pakistan, Agha Hilaly, the Pakistan ambassador in Washington, delivered a key message to the White House from Chou En Lai, giving the green light for the American embassy to visit China and proposing that Pakistan serve as the channel for the arrangements.

With Nixon's most daring diplomatic manouverses now approaching realizations' the President had even less interest in upsetting Yahya, whose country had become centrally involved in the process.

The trouble was that only a handful in the U.S. government, not including the Secretary of State, knew either of the negotiations with China or of the role Pakistan was playing. Many in the government and the U.S. public interpreted Nixon's reluctance to criticise Yahya as reflecting a callous attitude toward human rights and a lack of compassion for human suffering in East Pakistan.

The force of the opinion became so strong that despite Nixon's pencilled note on a Kissinger memo, "To all bombs, Don't squeez Yahya at this time," the administration took some restrictive actions.

Although Nixon and Kissinger tried to maintain tightly centralised control, their system broke down during the South Asia crisis. The White House failed to provide sufficiently precise guidance to enable the bureaucracy to know what Nixon wanted to do. This was especially true during the spring months of 1971 when the China trip was the administration's most closely held secret.

After State asked how to deal with the Pakistani arms question, the White House failed to respond. State acted as it thought appropriate, suspending licensing military exports to Pakistan lest there he used against the people of East Pakistan under the 1970 "one time exception", Nixon had agreed to provide Pakistan some $ 50 million in equipment; sale of spare parts was also containing under the policy President Johnson announced in 1967.

Bureaucratic confusion about the arms policy, a snafu which, perhaps, only one who had worked in U.S. government could fully appreciate, made matters worse. The State

Department thought it was embargoing all arms exports to Pakistan unaware the Defence Department acted only to liar new licenses, approved earlier remained valid. Equipment already in Pakistan's custody could also be exported. According to the State Department's top Asia hand, Deputy Assistant Secretary Christopher Van Hollen neither he nor others understood this distinction.

As a result, the administration incorrectly informed visiting Indian Foreign Minister Swaran Singh that the U.S. had ended all arms shipments to Pakistan. Out of ignorance, U.S. officials misled the Indians and the sublie.

Several days after, on June 22, *The New York Times* reported that notwithstanding the embargo, several ships were about to depart from New York carrying arms for Pakistan. The news caused an uproar in India, where an incensed Swaran Singh charged U.S. authorities lied to him. In Washington, opposition democrats, led by Senator Kennedy alleged duplicity claiming that some $ 50 million in arms were being shipped to Pakistan at the time the embargo was supposedly in force.

The U.S. media had a field day lambasting the White House for saying one thing and doing the contrary. Although the administration shortly realised that the value of military equipment not covered by the embargo was only $ 5 million and not $ 50 million the larger figure struck the publics mind.

Speaking in the Parliament on June 24, Swaran Singh charged that arms to Pakistan not only amount to a condemning of these atrocities, but could be construed as an encouragement to their continuation. From this point, relations sourced badly.

Kissinger visits Beijing

Two weeks later Henry Kissinger left Washington on a supposedly routine trip to the Far East and South Asia. Only a handful of people, including the Pakistani leadership but not the Secretary of State, knew his real mission was to slip away to China during the stay in Pakistan.

After stopping for talks in Delhi, Kissinger flew to Islamabad, ostensibly for two days of discussions. A week later on July 15, Nixon astonished the world by announcing the Kissing China mission and his own upcoming trip to Beijing.

The news startled the Indians who quite apart from a U.S. China rapproachement were unified that Kissinger stop in New Delhi was part of the cover for the China talks. Here in America they were faced with a tremendous human problem, a high official stated, "We thought he had come to discuss it with U.S. and then we found were just stepping stones on the way to China."

Although the Indians expected little heed from Nixon in resolving the East Pakistan crisis, especially the arms supply ruckus, closer U.S.-Chinese relations farred the rejoined power balance at the moment when South Asia was faced possible war.

Before the Kissinger trip, the prospect of Soviet and perhaps, U.S. support against China provided Delhi with an ample security blanket. That Washington's help would no longer be forthcoming was made explicit when Kissinger called Indian ambassador L.K. Jha to Western White House in California on July 17 to inform the envoy, "we would be unable to help you against China." If there were Chinese military response to a war between India and Pakistan.

Indira spring her own surprise a few weeks late on August 9, Delhi and Moscow signed the Indo-Soviet Friendship Treaty. Supporters of closer ties with Moscow, such as Foreign Secretary J.N. Kaul, and Mrs. Gandhi's Principal Secretary P.N. Haksar, convinced the Prime Minister that it would serve India's interest to cement the links with Moscow though the

Treaty that had been negotiated but not signed, two years before.

After the Soviet signalled their willingness to proceed the two sides guided agreed on the final shape of the treaty. The key articles provided for consultation in the event of crisis and pledged that neither country would support a third party against the other.

Even though short of a formal alliance, the treaty forged a relationship sufficiently close that it was hard to assert—as India did—that New Delhi remained true to the cardinal principle of non-alignment independence from either, major power bloc. In the summer of 1971, Nehru's daughter was willing to overlook this lapse. With India facing to prospect of war with Pakistan, the important thing was to obtain political and military reinsurance against interference from China.

Despite the fact that the treaty caused modest immediate supplies in Washington, Kissinger—in an after-the-fact overstatement—described the accord in his memoirs as a `bombshell' and as an through a lighted match into a "powderkey." Although—despite the treaty the Soviet continued to press for a peaceful settlement of the crisis, Nixon regarded India as a Soviet client for the rest of the crisis. It was, in fact, not until late October that the Soviet slighted to a strongly pro-Indian stance.

After the Kissinger trip, the U.S. and China established direct communication through their embassies in Paris. Washington no longer needed the Pakistan channel to pass messages to the Chinese. U.S. South Asia policy no longer had to be hostage to the opening to China. The Nixon administration could have kept its head down—much as Kissinger claimed was the original intent—and events in the subcontinent play but according to their own logic.

The White House chose, instead to become more, rather than less, engaged. Operating from assumptions about South Asia events not shared by the U.S. government's regional specialists, Nixon and Kissinger placed the crisis in a global context, but failed to communicate this rationale to the bureaucracy.

Although Nixon urged Yahya to make political concessions in the East, he felt short of pressing the Pakistani leader to negotiate directly with Mujibur Rahman, the unquestioned Bengali political leader, American Consulate General Officials in Calcutta also met with Awami League exiles to see what sort of compromise would satisfy them.

Washington urged an expanded U.N. relief effort to help the refugees in India and improve economic condition in East Pakistan.

The White House hoped that, coupled with gradual political accommodation in the East, this approach would eventually ease the crisis. Even though "almost to a person, the officials working on South Asia were convinced the White House strategy would not work," Nixon and Kissinger persisted.

In early August, when asked at a press conference, Nixon flatly refused to put public pressure on Yahya, saying this would not be helpful in solving the crisis.

To visiting Indians like political leader Jaya Prakash Narayan support for Bengali self-determination, and confidence that in time this would be achieved. Indian officials were skeptical.

But now thoroughly suspicious of American motives they saw the flury of humanitarian activity as a smoke scream designed to allow Yahya to consolidate his grip over East Pakistan without making only the concessions that Delhi counted—the release of Mujibur Rahman and direct negotiations with the Awami League Leader. Yahya's decision in August to try Mujibur Rahman for treason hardly increased Delhi's confidence in the likely success of U.S. endeavours.

As the monsoon ended and flooded rivers of East Pakistan began to subside, the terrain became more suitable for a military solution. By September, most Indians concluded this would be likely outcome. They did not see sufficient give on the Pakistani side to permit a peaceful settlement along lines they and Bengalis to accept.

Mrs. Gandhi pressed the Soviets hard to shift their position to a more pro Indian stance and to supply additional military equipment needed to a cold weather campaign. Moscow hesitated. It was only on October 21, after Yahya spurned Soviet suggestions for political concessions, that the Russian fell fully in line with India's wishes.

Things failed to improve in the discussions between the two leaders. Kissinger called the talks the worst and most painful in which he participated Mrs. Gandhi's long time press adviser Sharda Prasad agreed. He called the White House state dinner on the most strained of the hundred or so such affair he attended.

According to Prasad, neither Nixon nor Mrs. Gandhi made much of an effort to converse with each other during the dinner. Although Mrs. Nixon tried unsuccessfully to break the tension with small talk, the atmosphere remained frosty.

In the ritual after dinner toasts, the President spoke rather aimlessly about famous statesman who sat in the chair of honour at White House State dinner and Pandit Nehru's, remarks when they first met in 1953 that indeed a generation of peace. Nixon made no mention of the East Pakistan crisis. "Mrs. Gandhi was blunter." Our people, the Prime Minister declared, commit understand how it is that we who are the victims, we who are bearing the brunt and have restrained ourselves with such fortitude, should be equated with those whose action had caused the tragedy."

The Indians regarded the hope the West Pakistani would

yield in effect admitting that their actions since March 25 were wrong an utterly unrealistic U.S. South Asia specialists shared the view that Yahia would not compromise.

If Mrs. Gandhi concluded that talking with the Americans would lead nowhere, Nixon for his part wrote in his Diary of Mrs. Gandhi's "duplications action toward as when she actually had made up her mind to attack Pakistan at the time she saw me in Washington and assured me she would not."

Kissinger informed "Mrs. Gandhi was going to war not because she feared our success." Although Mrs. Gandhi's meeting with Nixon were a failure, her public appearances in Washington were successful. An active pro-Bangladesh Lobby in Washington won the emotional support of many political activists, leading Democratic politicians and even some Republicans.

Those who criticised the Nixon administration for its handling of the Vietnam War were more than willing to fault its approach to the Bangladesh crisis, U.S. public opinion, as measured by the Louis Harris Poll, was two to one against administration policy.

The Bangladesh Crisis. The December War

In November, the tempo of military action increased. The Bangladesh freedom fighters were becoming more aggressive in their cross border forays receiving artillary support from the Indian military. Late in the month, Mrs. Gandhi authorised Indian forces to enter East Pakistan to pursue the Pakistan forces. Tensions mounted. An all out Indian military assault against the East seemed imminents.

Although there is dispute whether or not Indira fixed a Day to invade East Pakistan. Yahyya resolved the problem for New Delhi. On the night of December 3, Pakistan attacked eight Indian airfields in the Western part of the country and the next day declared war on India.

The Indians countered, attacking the east and mounting problem operations in the West to pin down Pakistani forces. On December 6, India recognized the Awami League government in exile as the government of Bangladesh.

As tension mounted during November the U.S. perceptively hardened its stance toward India, which Kissinger and Nixon claimed was inciting the conflict. On December 2, Washington announced a suspension of military sales to India (of which the most important was a $ 70 million communications system designed to improve air defense capabilities). On December 6, the U.S. froze its economic assistance to India, including $ 87.6 million worth of aid already in the pipeline.

The next day, Assistant Secretary of State Joseph Sisco declared in a press background that India bore the major responsibility for the war. Kissinger was beating the NSCs Washington Special Action Group (GSAG) for not being more responsive to Nixon's desire to tilt toward Pakistan.

Participating for the first time as a Security Council Member, China joined the U.S. in supporting the resolution, but both Britain and France, and U.S. allies in NATO, abstained in the Security vote. The U.S. and other supporters of Pakistan then shifted to the General Assembly where the call for a cease- fire won overwhelming support by a vote of 104-11 with ten absenties. Sending troups across an international border, even for a popular cause, was not an action nation-states condoned.

As badly outnumbered Pakistani forces retreated from the borders towards Dacca, that was in the east for all intents over within a week. It was only a question how long the Pakistani will hold out. On December 16, the Pakistani ended the struggle with some 93,000 soldiers surrendering. When a week earlier, they discussed giving up, Yahya urged the troops in the east to fight on apparently hoping for an intervention from the U.S. and China.

Unlike Kissinger or Yahya, India discounted the likelihood of Beijing's intervening militarily. New Delhi reached this conclusion from an on going assessment of the Chinese response since the crisis began in March—little or no increased military activity along the northern borders, a less negative public stance toward India than during the 1965 war, and the absence of payable military aid to Pakistan as opposed to srhetoric. The Indians, thus, began the fighting assuming that the Chinese would limit their support to their Pakistani friends to verbal and moral encouragement.

On the basis of talks with Chou and secret discussions in New York in December with the Chinese foreign minister, Kissinger by his own admission reached the opposite conclusion. He incorrectly expected the Chinese to intervene militarily, possibly precipitating a Soviet Military rejoinder against China.

An increased in response to the flurry of messages from Nixon—including the first use of the hot line President Kosygin sought assurances visiting Indian envoy P.N. Dhar about Indian intentions in the West. Dhar promptly gave there without finding it necessary to seek instructions from New Delhi, so sure was he that India was not interested in attacking the West Pakistan.

Based on why they heard from Mr. Dhar and from soundings in New Delhi, the Soviets passed on reassuring words about Indian intentions to Washington. These failed to satisfy Nixon.

She announced a cease-fire effective December 19, Pakistan accepted, bringing to the end the 17-day conflict. Whatever it intended mission, the *Enterprise* appeared to have played its role in ending hostilities in the West. Despite Nixon's and Kissinger's claims, U.S. actions did not seem to have a significant factor in the decision not to move against West Pakistan.

U.S. policy, however, deeply angered the Indians. In a searching letter to Nixon released to the *New York Times* on December 15, Indira Gandhi asserted that the U.S. paid:

> Lip service to the need for a political problem, but not a single worthwhile step was taken to bring this about... we deeply hurt by the innuendoe and insinuation that it we who have precipitated the crisis. We have not received, even to this day, the haved framework of a settlement which takes into account the facts as they are.

Nixon responeded a sharp but pruvale letter to Mrs. Gandhi. He rebuked Indira for having a `spurned' his efforts to find a peaceful solution to the crisis claiming he opposed the resort to force when "Statesmanship could turn the course of history away from war."

The main consequences were severe and long-lasting damage to U.S. relations with India and enhanced Soviet influence with New Delhi. In Indian eyes U.S. handling of the crisis especially sending the Enterprise toward the Bay of Bengal, providing tangible evidence of U.S. desire through India's regional hopes and aspirations. Vociferous pro-Soviet and anti-U.S. elements in India had hurted on the deployment of the *Enterprise* as a symbol of U.S. hostility for over two decades. An intended result of the crisis was to strengthen the hand of Indians who supported proceeding with nuclear testing.

After the Bangladesh Crisis: Relations at Low Ebb

The Prime Minister ordered the closing of the U.S. economic Assistance mission, where more than 1200 Americans and Indians worked. She directed the peace corpse be reduced from over 500 to 50 volunteers.

The Indian government also imposed stringent restrictions on research by American academics, paradoxically, a group that had been among the opponents of Nixon's policy in U.S.

Universities—in the 1950s and 1960s, a thriving discipline had suffered greatly ever since weakening one of the stronger voices in the U.S. for improved Indo-U.S. relations.

L.K. Jha and Kenneth Keating the two envoys during the Bangladesh crisis ended their ambassadorial assignments in 1972. Despite a distinguished Senatorial career from New York State, Keating proved himself a frosty light weight in New Delhi. Nixon, nonetheless, named him to the post of ambassador to Israel. Jha who won respect even from Henry Kissinger—as a highly intelligent and effective envoy once more became a close adviser to Mrs. Gandhi after returning to India.

She managed the Bangladesh crisis flawlessly from the Indian standpoint. Pakistan was humiliated and India gained unchallengeable regional predominance. After a dismal decade, the nation could once more hold its head high.

In early July 1972, India and Pakistan concluded a peace accord at Simla. Mrs. Gandhi agreed to return 5000 square miles of Pakistan territory, mostly dealt that India captured during the war. Bhutto who replaced Yahya as the President of a sinken Pakistan, agreed to settle all disputes into the Kashmir issue, peacefully and bilaterally.

The Simla Accord, nontheless, had to a change in the U.S. stance toward the Kashmir dispute. Previously the U.S. stood behind relevant UN resolutions including the call for a plebiscite. After 1972 Washington shifted ground, the U.S. position since Simla has been to support any settlement the Indians and Pakistanis were able to work out.

Immediately after the Simla Agreement, with the Indo-US relations still at their nadir, Nixon made a strong gesture. He sent Secretary of the Treasury John Connally to meet Mrs. Gandhi during an around the world trip. Given the hostility between Indira and Nixon and the coldness of bilateral relations, Connally was apprehensive about the talks. He was relieved when this went reasonably well.

In December 1972, Nixon made a further gesture toward India, selecting as replacement as ambassador Harvard government professor Daniel Patrick Moynihan. Although a democrat and a former Assistant Secretary of Labor in the Kennedy-Johnson years, Moynihan headed Nixon's Domestic Council and sat in the Council and sat in the Cabinet in 1969, gaining a considerable reputation for his wip and brains. During the 1971 U.N. session, as a public member of the U.S. delegation, Moynihan opposed U.S. policy toward Bangladesh crisis.

Even though Nixon regarded India, as a stoppage of the Soviet, it was big country and democracy, hence not a place the U.S. wanted to write off. Nixon stated:

> We want to join India in a mature relationship founded on equality, reciprocity and mutual interest, reflecting India's stature as a great free nation.... The U.S. respects India as a major country. We are prefered to treat with India in accordance with its new stature and responsibilities.

Mrs. Indira Gandhi stated, "The U.S. has yet to resolve the inner contradiction between the tradition of the founding fathers and of Lincoln, and the external image gives of a super power pursuing the Cold logic of power politics.

In January and February 1973, she further angered Washington by charging in public that the `savage bombing' of Vietnam would not have been tolerated if the population had been European.

After arriving, India's new ambassador J.N. Kaul whom Washington regarded as no friend of the U.S. rather confounded people by establishing good relations with Henry Kissinger, soon to became the Secretary of State.

Indians feared the U.S. would again try to use aid to influence Indian policies, economic or political. Some U.S. officials, in turn, wondered about the wisdom of giving aid if the Indian felt so badly about receiving assistance from the U.S.

The Rupee Agreement: A Two Billion Dollar Check

Another problem worrying Moynihan was the mountain of Indian rupees owned by U.S. government, repayment for millions of tons of PL 480 foodgrain programmes. Since 1954 when the U.S. government enacted PL 480, the Indians paid for food aid with rupees deposited into a special interest bearing account with Reserve Bank of India. The U.S. right to spend these deposits was limited to paying for U.S. government expenses in India. Thus a few other issues, such as loans to U.S. companies for investment in India.

Over the years, the deposit grew rapidly because of the size of PL 480 food shipments and the limited possibility for spending the rupees. Indians feared that some how the U.S. would use these huge currency claims amounting in 1971 to over $ 3 billion to destabilize the Indian economy. Even a friendly observer like Kewal Singh, then serving as Foreign Secretary and later ambassador to Washington, commented. "It was a dangerous thing for a country to have so much of its currency controlled by another power."

India Became the World's Sixth Nuclear Power

The episode strengthened the hands of proponents of India's going nuclear, as well as the voice of Indian Scientists who insisted to demonstrate their capability to detonate a nuclear device.

Mrs. Gandhi also regarded the test as a way to boost her government lagging popularity by appealing to Indian national pride at joining the nuclear club.

Since the Indian explosion was an accomplished fact, Kissinger believed public scolding would not undo the event, but only add to U.S.-Indian bilateral problems and reduce the influence Washington might have on India's future nuclear policy.

Canada was particularly annoyed because of plutonium used in the test was produced in a research reactor the Canadian had given to India. In response to criticism, Kissinger stated (though incorrectly) that unlike Canada, the U.S. had no involvement with the Indian test.

When Moynihan saw Mrs. Gandhi to present the official U.S. reaction to the test told the Prime Minister:

> India has made a huge mistake. Here you were No. 1 hegemonic power in South Asia. No body was No. 2 and call Pakistan No. 3. Now, in a decades time, some Pakistani General will call you up and say you have four nuclear weapons and we will all meet in heaven. And then what will you do?

The Prime Minister according to Moynihan, remained silent and offered no response. The lobby wanted the U.S. like Canada, to punish India by ending nuclear cooperation.

Shortly after the test, long time critic of India, Rep. Clarence Long, a Maryland Democrat and Chairman of the Foreign Aid Appropriations Sub Committee won the acceptance for a bill directing the U.S. government to vote against all loans to India in the World Bank.

The action had no practical effect since the U.S. lacked a majority in the Bank. The report from Mrs. Gandhi hurt and stung by foreign criticism of the test, was to emphasize India's need for technical development such as the nuclear programme and to suggest that the critics were trying to keep India down.

India, Mrs. Gandhi self-righteously was different from the five other nuclear powers; it was not interested in military use of nuclear energy.

Critics scoffed at the Indian explanation. By then, few specialists believed in the utility of peaceful nuclear explosions, which the non-proliferation treaty explicitly banned since it was deemed impossible to detect the difference between military and peaceful explosions. The Pokhran test would have been a violation of the NPT, but since India had not signed the treaty, the point was legally moot.

For the next eight years—until alternative fuel supply arrangements were worked out in 1982 the question of licensing exports of enriched Uranium for Tarapur became a major problem between New Delhi and Washington.

The action in mid-1974 to absorb the tiny protector of Sikkim further terminated the Indian image. The fact that the ruler of Sikkim was to a former U.S. citizen Hope Cooke meant the U.S. action received considerably more publicity than would otherwise have been the case.

Few Indian Teams Shed over Nixon's Disgrace

In August 1974, Richard Nixon resigned from Presidency rather than face impeachment charges over the Watergate scandals. India was one country where few shed tears over Nixon's disgrace.

Moscow seemed firmly established as India's friend in time agreed. It would take a long time until the legacy of Richard Nixon and the *Enterprise* would be forgotten.

8

Ford: Fragile and Thin

The new President Gerald Ford had limited experience in dealing with South Asia. As in most foreign policy matters, he took his lead from Secretary of State Kissinger.

In October 1974, Kissinger, nonetheless, took a personal step to repair the danger with India, spending three days in New Delhi. His trip signalled Washington's interest in patching thing.

Kissinger appeared unpleasant on arrival and throughout the stay in New Delhi. At a October 28, dinner, he spoke of past misunderstandings as removed and of "better, more realistic relations between the two countries in the future."

The next day, the Secretary delivered a major policy statement in a speech to the Indian Council of World Affairs. Kissinger underscored U.S. hopes for a mature relationship stressed U.S. acceptance of India as the pre-eminent power in the region, and indicated, Washington had no quarrel with India's policy of non-alignment. "The U.S. recognises India as one of the major powers of the world and conducts its policy accordingly," Kissinger declared.

These were all words the Indians had long hoped to hear from the U.S., especially from someone like Henry Kissinger, regarded New Delhi as antagonistic.

At the same time, Kissinger alluded to sensitivities over

U.S. aid, commenting, "our relationship cannot be based on dependence of one on the other." The Secretary added, Nor can our relations survive constant criticism of any by the other a reference to India's habit of smiling at U.S. policies and Mrs. Gandhi's periodic allegations of U.S. interference in Indian internal affairs.

In a press conference on October 30, Kissinger flatly denied that the CIA was interfering in Indian affairs. He stated "The U.S. is not engaged, directly or indirectly, in any attempt to influence the domestic situation in India." However, Mrs. Gandhi made it clear she still harboured resentments.

The day before the Secretary of States arrival, in an interview with the *National Herald* she complained India was regard as `marginal' by Washington and said that India was not going to beg for U.S. aid. The Prime Minister met and had lunch with Kissinger during his first day in New Delhi, but then abruptly left the capital for Kashmir in what appeared to be a calculated snub.

Appealing to Indian pride, the Secretary did not sermise about the Indian nuclear test, but stressed that the U.S. "takes seriously India's affirmation that it has no intention to develop nuclear weapons."

During the stay, Kissinger and Foreign Minister Y.B. Chavan also signed an agreement to establish an Indo-U.S. Joint Commission.

Talking about relations, Moynihan was in a melancholy mood' and said, "we have reached a kind of plateau," less notable and unstable than in the past, but also `fragile and thin.' Events would soon underscore the accuracy of Moynihan's remarks.

Arms to Pakistan: Reopening of Old Wounds

President nominated William Saxbe as the new ambassador to India. The U.S.-Pakistan arms relationship, however, once more caused problems. Pakistan's Prime Minister Bhutto had for sometime, been urging Washington to lift the embargo on sales of new weapons systems, he would have liked military aid but recognized that was in the cards.

In February 1975, Bhutto visited Washington and Kissinger obliged him with arms worth $ 100 million annually.

After President Ford gave his blessing to the policy change, the State Department announced the lifting of the arms embargo in effect since September 1965.

In Parliament, Foreign Minister Y.B. Chavan criticised the decision, charging the resumption of U.S. be that arms sales to Pakistan would unsettle the process of normalization between India and Pakistan. To underscore Indian ire Chavan cancelled the planned trip to the U.S. for the initial meeting of the new Joint Commission. Two days later, Mrs. Gandhi asserted the U.S. decision amounted to reopening old wounds.

T.N. Kaul, India's ambassador in Washington sharply denounced Kissingers action declaring it would have an adverse effect in relations. "We do not accept or agree," Kaul told newsmen "that the lifting of the arms embargo will not lead to an arms race or hinder the process of normalization."

Kissinger fired back hastilly, "The comments of the Indian Foreign Minister are restrained and states-manlike, but those of the Indian ambassador are unacceptable. "Kissinger went on to stress U.S. interest in India while claiming that an arms embargo against a friendly country like Pakistan was "morally, politically and symbolically improper."

The Indian envoy lost his valued access to Kissinger. The ambassador's usefulness in Washington came to an end.

Saxbe, who genuine liked India and Indians, quickly become pessimistic about the prospects for a better relations.

Seeking a freely as ambassador to India as he had as Senator from Ohio, or Attorney General, Saxbe started Indian officialdom by his frankness. To make sure Indians, got his message, Saxbe gave a number of interviews with the U.S. press in his first months in New Delhi a sharp contrast with Moynihan low profile approach.

In March 1975, Saxbe to the *New York Times* that the best he could hope for with India U.S. grudging respect and described U.S. interests as limited to humanitarian and cultural matters. Talking about lifting the arms embargo which he had opposed Saxbe commented to the *Washington Post* that relations did not improve whether the U.S. sold arms to Pakistan or not.

"It's hell if you do and hell if you don't" the envoy bluntly stated.

Continuing his public diplomacy, Saxbe told the *New York Times* if India is determined to make an enemy of the U.S. there is not a whole lot we can do about it. "Excepting the annoyance many U.S. officials felt about Indian criticisms but rarely voiced in public—Saxbe commented:

> When I call on Cabinet Minister, the President or Governors, they all come to talk about their sons, sons-in-law and daughters in the U.S. and how well they are doing and how well they like things. The next day I read the papers that the very same people are denouncing the U.S.

Saxbe adopted a novel style in other ways refusing to make the usual diplomatic minds of senior officials and ministers or to count the Indian media. If the Indians wanted to see him, he was available. He was not going to run after people. The point he was trying to get across that the U.S. wished India well, but Mrs. Gandhi needed to decide whether she wanted better relations with Washington or not—this was something only the Indian government could determine.

Implicit in Saxbe's approach was the fact that by the mid-1970s, India had no great strategic importance for the U.S. Although Washington through its South Asia policies, its role in international financial institutions, and the U.S. position as a major trading partner remained a major factor for New Delhi, India a much reduced shadow on U.S. interests than in the late 1950s or early 1960s.

The Emergency: The End of Indian Democracy?

By 1975, three years after Mrs. Gandhi stood at the peak of power, the Prime Minister's political position was badly eroding. Having gained an unchallengeable electorate mandate in 1971, Indira seemed unable to accomplice any of the promised reforms. Her election slogan of eradicating poverty turned out to the much more than words.

Although her shore in dealing with crisis like East Pakistan, she showed little flare for implementing a coherent domestic programme. Her main concern seemed to be the maintenance of her own political power.

A combination of harvests and the sharp rise in oil prices after 1973 Arab-Israeli war badly weekened the Indian economy. The country began to experience an unprecedented wave of domestic unrest and trade union strikes. The disparate and fractions political opposition, although badly defeated in 1971 general elections, revived as Mrs. Gandhi's popularity slumped. Gaining strength, the opposition united in support of the Janata Party, mounting mass rallies and demonstration against Indira's rule. In April 1975 Janata hopes for the 1976 general election soared after the Congress lost in state balloting in Gujarat in Western India—the home of Morarji Desai, who had become a Janata leader.

And then the Courts delivered an unexpected blow to Mrs. Gandhi. For some time a law suit by Raj Narain, her opponent in the 1971 election sought to have Mrs. Gandhi's election to Parliament set aside because of minor technical irregularities during the campaign.

Even though she had six months to win a Parliamentary seat and could continue in office as Prime Minister during this period, the court decision sapped Mrs. Gandhi's moral and political authority. An elated opposition called for mass demonstration in the hope of forcing Indira from office even before the 1976 general election, Mrs. Gandhi found herself in grave political danger once more.

At her, the President of India, proclaimed a natural emergency during the night of June 24, 1975. Imposing *de facto* martial law, the authorities arrested the principal opposition leaders along with thousands of their followers.

Press Censorship was imposed. Civil literatures were restricted. Stunned by the force Mrs. Gandhi's action, Indian democracy seemed at an end. Once so proud of its political freedoms, India became just another Third World dictatorship.

In the U.S.—the reaction was harshly negative already upset over the nuclear test, liberals turned against India, joining conservatives as biding critics of Mrs. Gandhi. The hero of Bangladesh war became of the most disliked foreign leaders for Americans.

The *New York Times* formerly a stand back of U.S. support for Indian development and a leading critics of U.S. policy in Bangladesh crisis, denounced Mrs. Gandhi's action.

Other critics were less civil, including former ambassador Moynihan, who acidly told an interviewer from *Playboy*, when India ceased to be a democracy, "our interest there plummated. I mean what does it export but communicable diseases?" Although Crude, Moynihan's basic point was valid: it was India's adherence to democracy that in the absence of other major interests—made the country of importance to the U.S.

Secretary Kissinger believed that the U.S. should not base its external relations on whether or not it liked the domestic political character of Foreign governments. He also did not want to provide Gandhi admonition to blame the U.S. for her country's domestic trouble or to have gratuitous U.S. criticism serve as an impulse for an even filtering strengthening of Indo-U.S. relations. Because of the emergency, President Ford, nonetheless decided to postpone indefinitely a trip to South Asia talked about for late 1976.

Through this period, Indo-Soviet relations remained cordial and close. However, Mrs. Gandhi gave indications of wanting to maintain a certain distance from the Soviets and to seek better relations with the U.S. despite the sears left by 1971 and the insistent U.N. media criticism of the Emergency.

Unlike his mother or grand father, Sanjay was skeptical about Indian socialism. Like many in the young generation of the Indian elite, Sanjay looked to the West particularly to the U.S. as an economic model, not to the Soviet Union and the communist bloc.

At the official level, bilateral relations between Washington and New Delhi improved somewhat. In October 1975, Foreign Minister Chavan visited Washington for the first meeting of the Joint Commission. In 1976, appeared to make a gesture toward Washington in personnel shift.

She named Foreign Secretary, Jagat Mehta's, who had long argued that friendier Indo-U.S. relations were in India's interests. To replace T.N. Kaul in Washington, she approved former Foreign Secretary Kewal Singh. In contrast to the confrontational Kaul, Kewal Singh had a polite, soft-spen style and was not regarded as pro-Soviet.

In Moynihan's book, *A Dangerous Place* the former envoy pointed out that since Mrs. Gandhi herself—as Congress Party President—received money from CIA in the late 1950, to help obist the Communist government of Kerala, it was not surprising that she thought the CIA was helping others. Moynihan concluded that apart from the help, CIA gave the Congress Party, "we had been upto very little."

Some Indians who knew Mrs. Gandhi well thought that despite the fact that she was quite capable of using the U.S. as a political scapegoat, she was genuinely worried that she might be a CIA target, especially after events in Chile. The assassination of Majibur Rahman in Bangladesh in the summer of 1975 added to the Prime Ministers' anxieties.

Tarapur: To License or Not?

In 1976, the problem of shifting enriched Uranium full for the Tarapur nuclear power plant returned to centre stage. After the nuclear test the U.S. AEC delayed a shipment in the 1974 unlike Homi Bhabha gave written assurances to U.S. AEC Chairperson Dixie Lee Ray that:

> Special Nuclear material that has been or is hereafter made available for or used or produced in the Tarapur Atomic Power Station... will be diverted exclusively to the need of his station unless our two governments, hereafter, specially agree that such material be used for other purposes. In March 1976, the NRC voted 3-1 to approve half of a pending fuel shipment or nine tons enriched uranium and to hold public hearings regarding the export of the other nine tons in late July.

Kratzer stressed the view that non-compliance with the Tarapur contract would harm U.S. interests by suggesting the U.S. was not a reliable supplier of nuclear fuel—then a major element in U.S. nuclear policy.

The opponents wanted the U.S., like Canada to end nuclear cooperation with India because of the 1974 test. They asserted that India's using heavy water supplied by the U.S. in the production of the plutanium for the test was a violation of 1956 agreement under which the heavy water was supplied.

While politically appealing, the argument was legally weak.

1969-1977: A Summing Up

The bilateral relationship sustained grievous damage during the 1970s, first from U.S. Policy during the Bangladesh crisis and from Indian actions and the 1975 proclamation of Emergency.

Psychologically, the U.S. approach during 1971 especially the *Enterprise* episode—etched the image of U.S. hostility into the Indian historical memory.

Nixon's termination of the economic assistance programme, previously a positive offset to political frictions, removed another important element of bilateral relationship. Even though the aid link brought their own problems. U.S. help was a tangible sign of American interest in supporting the economic development of the world's largest democracy.

Despite these being a few meetings for Washington to seek improved relations, U.S. interests still put a limit on how bad things would get. The U.S. felt that it could not entirely ignore India, even if, during the two-year Ford presidency there was only a modest desire to find a *modus vivendi.*

India remained the most populous democracy and a developing nation apart from China, as the White House viewed the world in the 1970s, but of some significance because of its size and leadership role in the non-alignment movement.

Even more so, India could not ignore Washington U.S. South Asia policies especially ties with Pakistan and China could directly affect Indian security. Though the strong U.S. voice in international financial institutions, the American also influenced multiplitily aid flows, of growing importance as a source of external finance for Indian development.

As much as U.S. policy during 1971 offended New Delhi, it was not in India's national interest to make hostility with Washington a permanent foreign policy feature. Despite Indira Gandhi's chronic smiling Washington, she was worry of India's becoming so closely linked to the Soviet that non-alignment would become a fiction. A firm naturalist, the Prime Minister wanted to maintain her country's freedom of manouvre in the international area. To realize the goal, India needed at the semblance of a working relationship with the U.S.

9

Carter: Unfulfilled Hopes

As Jimmy Carter led the Democrats back to White House, the prospects of Indo-U.S. relations were mixed. Carter felt difficulty. The new President pledged to make respect for human rights, a cardinal principle of U.S. foreign policy.

Carter's thinking was not far from the Liberal Congressman Donald Fraser (D. Missesrha) who declared hearings just after inauguration, that the U.S. ought to avoid "endorsing implicitly or otherwise India's suspension of civil rights." The new President's emphasis on human rights threatened to collide head on with the emergency.

During the campaign, Carter stressed his desire for a tougher policy against nuclear proliferation. Therefore, Carter ordered a major review of nuclear policy especially, whether to continue to provide enriched Uranium fuel for Tarapur?

Carter's national security advisor Zbigniew, sketched out a foreign policy agenda that gave India a higher priority than had been the case under Nixon and Ford.

The overall strategy was to deemphasize Cold War on East-West concerns and to pay more attention to North-South issues, strengthening relations with nations likely to move into positions of prominence by the end of 20th century.

Alongwith Saudi Arabia, Iran, Indonesia, Nigeria, Brazil and Venezuela, Breezuski listed India as one the "regional influentials." Carter himself was also favourably predisposed toward the Third World countries, in general, and India, in particular.

Just a week before Carter's inauguration, Indira surprised everyone by ending the Emergency, easing restrictions on democratic rights, releasing thousands from Jail and scheduling general elections in March 1977. The Prime Minister explained that with stable and the economy improved, these seemed to be no reason not to have elections.

In February, Indian President Fakhruddin Ahmad died. To represent the U.S. at the funeral, Carter designated his mother Miss Lillian.

Sending Miss Lillian was a nice way of showing the Indians that the Kissinger-Nixon era of realpolitic was over, and of signalling the new President's personal interest in better relations. The symbolism was warm and personal.

When India went to the polls in March, Mrs. Gandhi and her Congress Party suffered a stunning defeat. Running under the banner of Janata Front, the opposition won an unexpected landslide victory.

Although Janata campaigned principally against the trampling of democracy during the Emergency, coercive birth control policies promoted by Sanjay Gandhi probably stirred as much resentment among the mass of India's moral voters. In a matter of weeks, Morarji Desai, Mrs. Gandhi's long time opponent, moved from Jail to become India's fourth Prime Minister.

After only two years in power, the coalition ruined by internal rivalries and the Janata would fall apart.

Carter and Desai: Two Moral and Moralistic Leaders

Both shared genuine concern for the principles of human rights, democracy, disarmament, and the economic growth of developing countries.

In Washington, there was a quick and enthusiastic reaction to the Indian elections. Jody Powell, White House Press spokesman called them "something that should be an inspiration."

The U.S. Congress repeated the law adopted after 1974 nuclear test requiring the U.S. to vote against all World Bank loans to India.

On the Indian side, the signs were similarly positive. Over the years, Morarji Desai had gained a reputation as friendly toward the U.S. and critical of the Soviet Union.

During the campaign, Desai criticised Mrs. Gandhi's policies as too closely toward Moscow and called for genuine non-alignment in India's Foreign policy with more balanced relations with Moscow and Washington. The new Foreign Minister Atal Behari Vajpayee of Jan Sangh shared Desai's views about the need to bring better balance into India's ties with the two super powers. Desai continued in office Foreign Secretary Jagat Mehta.

Carter named former Princeton President Robert Gaheen, born in India of missionary parents.

Desai selected Nani Palkhivala, a respected Bombay Lawyer, human rights activist and outspoken opponent of the emergency. Palkhivala was an articulate booster of the free enterprise system and of close relations with the West.

On June 28, the Nuclear Regulatory Commission (NRC), under pressure from Carter administration, approved the long pending export license for nine tons of enriched uranium fuel to be exported to India.

In line with the administration desire to upgrade relations with India, Warren Christopher the Dy. Secretary of State pointedly did not follow the usual practice of coupling a visit to New Delhi with a shape in Pakistan—a practice that annoyed Indians since it suggested that the U.S. equated relations with the two countries.

In keeping with his strong personal support for disarmament, Carter also spaked consideration of an expanded arms control agenda with the Soviets in addition to SALT II talks on strategic nuclear arms limitation. One of the ideas was the total ban on nuclear testing through a Comprehensive Test Ban Treaty.

Another was to explore with the Soviet Union the possible demilitarization of the Indian Ocean position positively received by the Indians, long opposed to big power naval presence in the region.

After the British in the mid-1960s announced the withdrawal of most of their military forces east of Suez, Washington established a small naval communications facility on the British controlled atoll of Diego Garcia, about a thousand nautical miles South of the southern tip of India.

India strongly opposed this action and supported a 1971 Sri Lankan initiative in the UN for an Indian Ocean Zone of Peace. In the facility at Diego Garcia was expanded to support a larger U.S. presence near the Persian Gulf.

A second and third round of negotiations in Washington and Switzerland addressed technical questions, but did not did with broader policy issue posed by intervention by Washington or Moscow unrelated to naval deployments. Indian ocean negotiations finally collapsed following the Soviet invasion of Afghanistan in December 1979.

Carter's Visit to India

In the fall of 1977 preparations were under way for Jimmy Carter to visit India. Carter did not complete his trip to India with a stop in Pakistan.

When Jimmy Carter became the third serving President

to visit India, the welcoming crowds in New Delhi were friendly and large.

In a major speech before the Indian Parliament the President drew attention to the triumph of democratic values in the two countries, praised India's achievement since independence and proposed a broad effort to develop the economic potential of the major rivers of Eastern India, Bangladesh and Nepal.

To emphasize the importance attached to the Indo-US relationship, the President and the Prime Minister issued a "Delhi Declaration" at the conclusion of the trip instead of the usual communique.

Carter and Desai stressed common support for democracy and economic development, expressed their deep opposition to the Specter of War "and pledged that India and U.S." will do their utmost to resolve disputes with others amicably.

The Delhi declaration on a note of principle—"Ends can never justify evil means. Nations, like individuals, are morally responsible for their actions."

The Nuclear Nonproliferation Act: Trouble for Tarapur

The `Cold and very blunt' message to Desai came not in the form of a letter from Carter, but in the 1978 Nuclear Non-proliferation Act (NNPA), the legislation of the administration's nuclear policy. The U.S. Congress adopted the House of Representatives by a Unanimous 411-0 vote.

The heart of the new policy, as it related to India was that the U.S. could henceforth export sensitive nuclear materials, as enriched uranium fuel, only to countries that placed their nuclear facilities under International Atomic Energy Agency (IAEA) safeguards.

Countries like India that had previously refused to accept "full scope of safeguards" had months to conform to the requirements of the NNPA. They would otherwise be ineligible for further exports from the U.S. regardless of existing contractual arrangements.

Trouble clearly lay ahead. Unless the Indians accepted the IAEA safeguards on all their nuclear facilities, not just Tarapur, the U.S. would have to stop supplying enriched uranium fuel.

In order to get foreign assistance, the India agreed to safeguards on individual nuclear facilities, such as Tarapur and nuclear power reactors in Rajasthan funded by the Canadians but shoutly refused to accept safeguards on nuclear facilities which Indian AEC built without outside help. The Indians argued vehemently that full scope safeguards would be unjust infringement on their sovereignty.

With the India case in mind, the administration tried but failed to gain acceptance for an exemption for existing contracts from the new full scope safeguard requirement.

Paradoxically, the two democrats on the NRC roted against the expot to Tarapur and the two republican supported the President had to fill an NRC vacancy.

In India Prime Minister Desai responded sharply warning that if the U.S. blocked the enriched Uranium shipment, India would regard it and India would then be free, Morarji stated in Parliament, "to adopt any course that we like to safeguard own interest." Although aware that Carter was likely to overrule the NRC, Desai nonetheless throw down a marker that would remain the Indian position as long as India adhered to the Tarapur contract, the U.S. could not unilaterally all its terms. Legally, the Indians had a strong case, quite apart from policy considerations.

After the NRC rejected the License, the issue went to the White House, President Carter kept his promise to Desai, overturning the NRC ruling to approve the export. In a April

27 statement, Carter expressed concern that rejection of Licence would seriously undermine ongoing efforts to negotiate on safeguards with India before the NNPA's deadline of March 1980.

Carter said he wanted to use the period to find mutually acceptable way of meeting both India's need for the continued operation of the Tarapur atomic power station and our own need for full scope safeguards and the attainment of other non-proliferation objectives.

The Prime Minister visited Washington and said that if the Big powers stopped making weapons and adopted nuclear disarmaments measures, India might change its mind.

At the National Press Club, Desai was equally forthright, asking why "must India be singled out for disfavour by a friendly country like the U.S. through a unilateral modification of its contractual obligations."

Overall, despite the preoccupation with the nuclear problem, the Desai visit went well. According to the White House, the two leaders ranged the globe in their talks with few areas of disagreement. Carter and Desai looked forward to progress in disarmament, on human rights, on self-determination in South Eastern Africa, and for continued peace and stability in South Asia. The President and Prime Minister hoped that the significant improvement in bilateral relations over the past year... would be continued and deepend....

In a nice touch, Carter took Morarji on a private and unscheduled visit to the Lincoln Memorial after June 14 White House dinner. According to *The Statesman* "this gesture unprecedented by any U.S. President - speaks for itself when Indians back home ask how is the visit going."

Desai's straightforward approach had a positive impact on the Congress. On July 12, the House of Representative supported the President on Tarapur. Although opponents, like liberal Democrat Richard of New York, declared "If we do not apply the act with respect to India, we have no reason to expect anybody to think we would apply it to anybody else," the majority agreed with President voting to sustain the fuel export to Tarapur, 227-181. In line with the new policy, Louis Losenzo, Kratzors successor stated officially that the U.S. would not approve using the plant to reprocess the Tarapur spent fuel rods.

After much soul searching, John Commissioner NRC finally came in favour of issuing the license. In the explanatory statement, Ahearne said the Desai government has acted responsibly and courageously, showing a strong commitment toward world non-proliferation.

Carter said he found it "a little bit difficult" to a talk about the nuclear question with Desai when we ourselves have not restrained the spread of nuclear weapons.

For the Indians, the proliferation issue become more complicated with evidence that its long time foe Pakistan was mounting a serious covert effort to develop nuclear weapons, Former President Bhutto call for his country to develop nuclear weapons was proving more than mere rhetoric.

By early 1979, U.S. intelligence about the Pakistan nuclear programme became sufficiently hard that the Carter administration felt compelled to invoke in Symington amendment to the Foreign Assistance Act.

This provision barred providing economic assistance to countries that the U.S. believed were moving toward a nuclear weapons capability. Predictably after the U.S. suspended economic aid, U.S. relations with Pakistan never good during the Carter administration in view of the emphasis on improving ties with India sharply deteriorated.

Thin Blow the Levels of Broad Principle

The improvement in the political relationship between

the U.S. and India was real, but somewhat deceptive. According to Ambassador Gaheen, remained "thin blow the levels of broad principles and personal diplomacy." The two governments had difficulty in moving much beyond the stage of better political atmosphere. There just was not that much going on between the U.S. and India.

A hoped for expansion in the economic relationship remained largely unfulfilled. Two-way trade grew somewhat and the U.S. again became India's largest trading partner during the Carter-Desai years.

Expectations of increased U.S. investment were, however, stillborn. The Janata government, proved astonchy and naturalistic as Mrs. Gandhi in dealing with foreign investors.

Rather surprisingly giving the Janata's pro-private sector rhetoric—George Fernandes, a socialist leader, became Minister of Industries with responsibility for foreign investment. Far from easing controls, Fernandes insisted on strict enforcement of the respective Foreign Exchange Regulations Act (FERA) enacted by Mrs. Gandhi.

Under the FERA, two U.S. major Companies Coca-Cola and IBM decided to shut down their Indian operations. In the course of Coca Cola, Fernandes claimed the soft drink company was making excessively large profits—10-15 million rupees annually on initial investment of only 600,000 rupees.

Although Coca Cola was willing to restructure its Indian subsidiary to comply with FERA regulations, the U.S. company refused to relinquish control of its formula for coke syrup. When Fernandes found the offer inadequate, Coco-Cola decided to pull out. The damage to India's image in business circles caused by Coca Cola's departure was considerable.

The damage was even worse in the case of IBM. After Fernandes insisted IBM with FERA requirements the U.S. Company refused. Fernandes recalled IBM telling him,

General de Gaulle could not make us do it and we want for India either. IBM nonetheless, wanted to remain in India and proposed a compromise. IBM would split its operations having the sales and leasing operation under IBM control, but converting the service and repair division into a separate Indian registered company, in which IBM would run only 40 per cent of the share capital.

IBM also offered to find joint research projects in India to promote technology development. When the offer was not good enough for Fernandes, IBM packed up and left.

Unlike Coca-Cola, IBM's departure, just before the start of the personal computer revolution, proved a major technology loss for India. Nationalists sentiments against foreign business won the day, but India paid a price.

The twin episodes dealt a one-two punch to India's image as a good place for U.S. Investment, ambassador Goheen wrote, "The negative vibrations in the U.S. business community were immediate widespread and in some quarters lasting."

U.S. investment in India during the late 1970s, and the years since then remained small. Declining U.S. interest in India was reflected in attendence at the 1979 joint Business Council meetings, twenty eight of India's top business executives travelled to Washington; only sixteen middle level U.S. executives and 11 observers bothered to attend.

If the private engagement was disappointing, renewed U.S. economic assistance also failed to grow as much as aid supporters hoped. Instead of rising $ 300 million annual level, bilateral development assistance topped out at about $ 100 million annually.

As a result, aid funds were simply not available to increase the India bilateral programme much above the $ 100 million annual range.

Afghanistan, Mrs. Gandhi and `Peanuts'

The day after the Soviet intervention, President Carter packed up the telephone to speak with Pakistan's President Zia-ul-Haque to offer U.S. support and to revive the moribund U.S. seemingly commitment under the 1979 bilateral agreement. Pakistan ceased to be a nuclear delinquent and became a frontline state against the threat of Soviet expansionism.

The Carter administration and the Congress acted to infreeze arms sales to Pakistan. In the Senate, parallel moves were launched to get around Symington amendment bars to a resumption of military and economic aid to Pakistan.

At the U.N. the U.S. sought Security Council condemnation of the invasion of Afghanistan, only to be blocked by the Soviet veto. The U.S. position was unambiguous; "No state would be safe against a larger neighbour of the international community appears to condone the Soviet Union's intervention."

Attention shifted to the General Assembly where NATO members, virtually all Muslim States, and most of Latin America and Africa joined incessing Moscow's action.

Delivered in New York by Indian U.N. Representative Mishra in January the Statement white washed the Soviet action:

> We are against the presence of foreign troops and bases in any country. However, the Soviet government has assured our government that its troops went to Afghanistan first at the request of the Afghan government on December 26, 1979 and repeated by his successor on December 28, 1979. And, we have been further assured to do so by the Afghan government. We have no reason to doubt assurances, particularly from a friendly country like the Soviet Union with whom we have many close ties.

On returning to New Delhi, Goheen spoke frankly with

Gandhi. He stressed, what a devastating statement it had been from the American point of view and what a terrible backlash it had caused in the U.S. When the Prime Minister responded, Oh, it was not that had the ambassador Comterad, Oh, yes it really was.

In Washington, U.S. officials still angered about the Indian position on Afghanistan.

Carter declared on January 23, 1980 that the U.S. would regard any move by the Soviet Union toward the oil rich Persian Gulf as a threat to U.S. vital interests and would counter, by all means, including the use of force.

In India, Mrs. Gandhi edged her public stance away from blanket acceptance of the Soviet position. After meeting with Foreign Secretary Lord Carington on January 18, she commended to the press, "I don't think that any country is justified in entering another country."

In an interview with *Time* magazine, she said, she "disapproved" of the Soviet action in Afghanistan. To soften the public criticism however, the Prime Minister often added that the Soviets intervened only after Pakistan started arming Afghan rebels against the Kabul government.

At the end of January, President Carter sent two separate missions to South Asia, a high powered group led by his National Security Advisor Z. Brezinst and Deputy Secretary of State Warren Christopher to Pakistan and special presidential embassy Clark Clifford to India. Pakistan's cagy President Zia-ul-Haque disdainfully rejected the profered $ 400 million as peanuts.

In New Delhi, Clark Clifford sought to allay Indian concerns about renewed U.S. arms aid to Pakistan and to urge Mrs. Gandhi to use her influence in Moscow to press for a Soviet withdrawal from Afghanistan.

During Mrs. Gandhis' difficult times during the Janata period, the Americans had treated Indira politely. President Carter set the tone by sending a nice letter immediately after the March 1977 elections. Ambassador Goheen made a point of calling on Mrs. Gandhi to annoyance of Foreign Minister Vajpayee and in chatting in a friendly manner when they met at diplomatic and social gatherings.

Having shown Mrs. Gandhi respect, Goheen left Mrs. Gandhi returned the courtesy after she returned to power. Even though their discussions were often substantially difficult, Goheen never received the haughty silent treatment for which Mrs. Gandhi was well known.

Clark Clifford did not change the Prime Minister's but U.S. observer believed she appreciated his visit which showed that Washington took India seriously enough to send a envoy of stature and prestige. To Mrs. Gandhi Clifford a good listener as she carefully spelled out her main points. If the U.S. rearmed Pakistan, this would pose a threat to India limiting India's ability to press moss and placing India in a situation in which it did not want to be.

She also suggested to Clifford that the Soviets were not entirely to blame, citing interference from outside in Afghan affairs. The Indians tended to equate `intervention' and `interference,' then and later.

Reforming to U.S. arms for Pakistan, Clifford said we understand this is not a popular move with the Indian government and yet with the gravity of the threat we believe it is a helpful policy for us to follow.

Three times, the Afghan tribesmen had thwarted British efforts to dominate their country. Battling a similar attempt by the Russians in 1980, the Afghan guerillas were soon receiving covert military help from Saudi Arabia, Pakistan and others, although not initially from the U.S. Washington had, nonetheless, full sympathy and support for the Afghan cause and for the country through which most external help flowed Pakistan.

The Standard Indian Ministry of External Affairs response on arms to Pakistan made this clear—"Neither the quality nor the quantity of the arms mattered; it was the attitude that caused concern."

Given the dramatic change in the strategic environment after the Soviet invasion of Afghanistan, Carter administration officials listened to the Indians but paid little attention to their complaints about U.S. help for Pakistan.

Tarapur: Next to the Last Act

Washington recognized that Mrs. Gandhi might have some influence with the Soviets, and did not want to push her any close to Moscow. Following the logic that led to the reversal of the arms supply toward Pakistan, Carter also changed course on supplying arms to India.

Although the administration had refused permission earlier for Sweden to sell its General Electric powered Viggen fighter to India, Washington now encouraged New Delhi to consider arms purchases from U.S. companies.

In a major departure, an Indian military procurement team visited the U.S. in 1980 to explore procurement of large numbers of Tow antitank missiles and long range hourtizers, with the package, perhaps, totalling $ 300 million.

The Carter administration similarly reversed its earlier action to disapprove the use of an advanced U.S. electronic guidance system in the Jaguar aircraft India was buying from Great Britain.

In the nuclear area, despite anticipated opposition, Jimmy Carter decided to give the green light for two more enriched uranium fuel shipments for Tarapur—the last that would be legally possible under the 1978 NNPA because the transition period would have expired without India's having to agree to full safeguards.

Mrs. Gandhi like Desai was adamant on the safeguards issue, while Desai, She refused to rule out further "peaceful nuclear experiments." Inspite of this Carter accepted State Department recommendations—over Brezinks objection, that he transmit two long pending Tarapur fuel export applications to the NRC. The State Department that in light of the Afghan situation avoiding further strains with India took priority over non-proliferation objectives.

On May 16, the NRC unanimously rejected the license requests by an unprecedented 5—0 vote with the transition period over and India refusing to accept full scope. Safeguards, the NRC saw no basis for approving the licenses. After consideration President Carter decided, nonetheless, to override the NRC and to authorize the shipments. The action set the stage for a major battled on Capital Hill where the Congress could block the President's action if a majority in both houses voted against the fuel shipment.

Carter's decision came under heavy criticism with the two most prestigious U.S. newspapers—*The New York Times* and the *Washington Post* attacking the administration position editorially on June 22. *The Washington Post* called the Tarapur the ultimate test of the seriousness of U.S. non-proliferation policy. The *New York Times* argued that if the U.S. yields on safeguards to the only nation known to have carried out an explosion it can hardly expect other supplies and receivers of fuel to give the protective stipulations a high priority.

Presenting the administration case, ambassador Gerald Smith, Veteran disarmament negotiator, argued that failure to provide the fuel would loss of safeguards as Tarapur and undercut the U.S. reliability as a nuclear supplier. Smith asserted there was no question of yielding to India on safeguards since the shipments fell within the two year grace period permitted by the law.

Writing in *Washington Post* former Kennedy aide McGeorge Bundy also supported the administration, saying the Soviet Union would probably step in to supply Tarapur if the U.S. backed out.

In the Congress the tide was running against Carter, especially in the House of Representatives. With Indira back in power and refusing to condemn the Soviet action in Afghanistan, there was only modest congressional concern about maintaining good relations with New Delhi.

Mrs. Gandhi's recognition of the Palestine Liberation Organisation and the Vietnamese installed and dominated Kampuchia regime caused additional negative riffles. News at Delhi was procuring $ 1.6 billion worth of arms from Moscow did not strengthen the administration case.

In the House, which Carter supporters gave up as a lost case, Tarapur opponents won on September 18 vote by a wide 298-98 margin. In the Senate, Edmend Muskie, the respected former Senator from Mainė who had replaced Cyrus Vance strenuously lobbied his former colleagues. Although the administration lost an 8-7 vote in the Foreign Relations Committee, the President eventually out a razor thin 48-46 victory on September 24.

At the end of Seven hours of debate, two vote majority headed the plea Senator Frank Church to give the President the benefit of the doubt—but only after Secretary Muskie agreed to hold back one of two shipments. Even though President's election campaign was under way, many democrats voted against Carter, while the Republican leadership in the Senate supported the President's position.

The victory proved a Pyristic affair with the two year dead line past, and no prospect of India's accepting full scope safeguards, the Congress was not clearly not going to approve any further fuel shipments for Tarapur. In India, the U.S. won few thank through the exercise. New Delhi contended not without justification that Washington failure to supply the fuel would amount to a breach of contract relieving India of the obligation to maintain safeguards. Because the delays in fuel shipments had caused a drop in Tarapur power production, some argued the U.S. was already in breach of the contract.

In retrospect, one must question whether Carter's enormous effort to gain approval for the Tarapur shipment in 1980 was worthwhile. In the process, the administration weakend its overall nonproliferation posture without substantially helping relations with India or advancing a solution to the problem. It is hard to disagree with the editorial comment of *The Statesman* of Calcutta.

> It should have been clear long ago that there would be no accord in nuclear policy, and both countries should have accepted the consequences. By keeping the Tarapur issue alive, they succeeded merely in exacerlating feelings. Tarapur has been allowed to sour India-U.S. relations quite out of proportions of its importance.

A Disappointing Four Years

Relations between the U.S. and India at the end of Carter's term in the White House stood about where they were at the beginning. The intervening period of four years saw a period of high expectations in 1977 after the end of the Emergency and the return of democracy to India, followed by a renewed slump in 1980 after the Soviet invasion of Afghanistan and Mrs. Gandhi's return to power.

When Jimmy Carter and Morarji Desai took office, there were genuine hopes that the two countries would at long last enjoy a sustained period of positive relations. As India adopted a more balanced approach toward non-alignment and Washington took its distance from Pakistan, additional frictions lessened.

The U.S. began to pay more attention to India as a regional influential. Both countries stressed their common faith in democracy and human rights. Even though the Tarapur problem cast a long shadow, the two well disposed governments might have been able to work out an amicable divorce over this contentious issue as Mrs. Gandhi would do with the Reagan administration in 1982 had the Carter-Desai period lasted longer. Indian political developments and the Soviet intervention in Afghanistan however, ensured that India and the U.S. were again at odds in 1980.

If the relationship soured in the final year of Carter administration, the outlook after Ronald Reagan won the November election was for worsening relations. Highly critical of Carter's policies toward the Soviets, Reagan stated his primary foreign policy goal would be stem rising communist influence in Afghanistan, Africa and Central America.

The new Republican administration could be expected to address arms supply to Pakistan as a matter of top priority. Reagan was likely to be far more generous than the Democrats in providing military help to Pakistan and less concerned about India's reaction. As the Soviet Unions' most prominent non-communist friend, India could anticipate receiving even shorten shrift from the White House than during Jimmy Carter's last year as President.

10

Reagan: Gradual Warning

On January 20, 1981 Ronald Reagan took the oath of office as President of the United States. Within the hour, Iran set free in American Embassy hostages it had held for over a year, relieving Reagan from having to deal with the problem that consumed Jimmy Carter's final year in the White House.

The new administration could devote full energy to its primary foreign and national security policy goal: rebuilding U.S. military power so that the U.S. could counter the spread of Soviet influence in various parts of the world—a central America, in the horn of Africa, in Angola, in Southeast Asia and in Afghanistan.

As the Republicans assumed charge, South Asia was an area of concern because of the Soviet invasion of Afghanistan. The administration saw covert military assistance to the Afghan guerrillas, humanitarian aid to the refugees, and renewed military and economic assistance to Pakistan as the prime U.S. measures. Washington wanted to act quickly and decisively to help the Afghan resistance and to revive U.S.-Pakistan security relationship.

The Reaganite, led in the foreign policy area by Secretary of State Alexander Harg, Henry Kissinger's deputy during the Bangladesh crisis, had little interest in India and the Third World in general—except as a battle ground in the contest with the Soviet Union and its allies.

The new team had scant sympathy for India and its stance on Afghanistan. Despite the fact that the Reaganites viewed Indira Gandhi as an apologist for Moscow, they had no special aminous against her or India.

Although U.S. administration to press ahead with arms for Pakistan was the major worry. New Delhi had other concerns with the incoming administration.

The Tarapur problems remained unresolved. How would the Reagan administration deal with this dispute? Even if the Republican attitude on non-proliferation was less fervent than that of the Democrats, the White House had little incentive to expend political capital with the Congress for India's benefit. In terms of Law there was, in any case no basis to continue exports of enriched uranium fuel. The new administration attitude toward international financial institutions was another cause for anxiety. India was increasingly dependent on the World Bank and the International Monetary Fund for external financial support. If the Reagan administration insisted on tougher loan terms and stricter conditionality and opposed Capital increases, India could suffer.

Indira Gandhi wanted to reduce her country's dependence on Soviet arms supplies as a way to avoid over dependence on Moscow and to have access to better technology. Despite the fact that the Soviets remained, by far, the largest arms supplier, offering payment terms the West could not match, India had already began to diversify military equipment procurement. New acquired Jaguar bombers for U.K. submarins from West Germany, the Mirage air craft and other equipment from France. For the first time since 1965, the Indians were talking about the possibility of arms purchases from the U.S.

Realizing the limits of Soviet technology, the Indians hoped for greater access to the more advanced technologies of the West especially the U.S. not only in the defense sector but across the economic spectrum.

Better ties might also, the India's hoped, influence Washington to continue a positive attitude towards India in international financial institutions and to take greater account of India's views in U.S. dealings with Pakistan.

Indian interest in the friendlier ties with the U.S. was influenced by the proving Indian immigrant community. Although Mrs. Gandhi's generation had strong educational and emotional ties with U.K., the younger generation of the elite was flocking to the U.S. for higher education by the thousands. So may stayed on that by 1980. The immigrant community had swelled to a million.

The immigrants, typically professionals with advanced degrees, had the highest per capita income of any ethnic group in the U.S. Helped by their fluency in English, the Indian immigrants fit in with relative ease; the fact that many immigrants were members of the elite magnified the impact—and the attraction—of the U.S.

Arranged to convey the impression of a chance encounter, the Session took in the Capital Hill office of Senator Paul Luxait, a close friend of the President elect. The gist of Indira's message was that she wanted friendly relations with the U.S. and had no anti-American feelings.

Although B.K. Nehru was not sure how much impact the words had on Reagan, the fact that Indira chose to send such message understood the seriousness of her desire not to return the frosty hostility of the Nixon years.

Arms to Pakistan: No longer "Peanuts"

The Pakistanis, in effect, made the F-16 fighter the most advanced U.S. aircraft previously supplied only to NATO allies, Egypt and Israel. Totalling $2.5 billion, the aid programme a multi-year commitment.

The Pakistanis, in effect made the F-16, the test of U.S. seriousness, the Zia-ul-Haq insisted that Washington pay to offset buying bitterness in the 1960s, and 1970s. Islamabad pressed hard to receive these state of the art aircraft superior to anything India possessed and capable of repelling possible Soviet or Afghan air incursions.

The administration argued that by providing Pakistan greater confidence about its security U.S. arms assistance would make it easier for that country to forego nuclear weapons.

Bolstering Pakistan against the Soviet threat drew wide support. The aid was seen as good in itself and as a reasonable *quid pro quo* for Pakistan serving as the Channel for covert aid to the Afghan Mujahiddin, an enormously popular cause. The man effect of Indian complaints was to damage New Delhi's credibility. As a senior State Department official put it:

> The Soviet army is standing on the marchlands of India and they are screening about F-16s not the Soviets in Afghanistan. People on the India desk could explain how India looked at things, the historic perspective of Pakistan but people higher up who made policy had much greater difficulty in understanding India's response.

Second, the Reagan administration avoided the trap Eisenhower fell into of offering assurances that the arms provided Pakistan would not be used against India, the administration opposed no guarantee Pakistan would refrain from deploying the weapons against its neighbour.

Even though the Indian grumbled, the new U.S. instance had the virtue of candor. The experience of the 1960, showed that guarantee was meaningless, and prompted recriminations in the event of India-Pakistan conflict.

Third, the Pakistan attitude in the 1980s differed substantially from that of 1950s. In return for U.S. arms in 1954,

Pakistan became a U.S. ally and court follower joining two mutual security packs and bringing its foreign policy into line with U.S. anti-communist stance. As Pakistan's primary concerns in the 1950s, were not the communists, but the Indians, Washington and Karachi had different and ultimately conflicting motivations in entering the alliance relationship.

In 1981, the U.S. Pakistan arrangement responded to the situation in Afghanistan and a shared perception of the Soviet Threat. The relation was more realistic, close to a marriage of convenience than an alliance. Pakistan did not change its foreign policy, remaining a non-aligned state. Bilateral tensions continued over Islamabad's quest for a nuclear capability, even though the Reagan administration obtained Congressional approval to ease restrictions on aid to Pakistan in the event of countering the Soviets in Afghanistan.

A decade later, while serving in Kabul, Griffin irked the Soviets by briefings Western Journalists on developments in Afghanistan during visits to New Delhi to see his family. After the diplomat was assigned to India, the Soviets mounted a successful disinformation campaign to discredit Griffin as a spy.

Accepting Soviet fabrications despite categorical U.S. denials the government of India refused to issue him a visa. Mrs. Gandhi herself told the press India denied the visa because Griffin was an intelligence officer. Angry that Mrs. Gandhi believed the Soviets rather than the U.S. the State Department retaliated, refusing entry for the diplomat India wished to assign as its political counsellor in Washington.

No episode by itself was earthshaking, but cumulatively disinformation by the Soviets and their friends added to U.S. problems in India in particular strengthening suspicious that the CIA was interfering in Indian internal affairs.

The most serious substantive dispute arose over India's

application for $ 5.8 billion loan from the International Monetary Fund (IMF), the largest ever sought by a member country. After U.S. Treasury Secretary Donald Reagan spoke against the loan at the World Ban-IMF meetings, U.S. Executive Director Richard Erli criticised the proposal as not justified by India's financial situation.

In the end—after President Reagan and Mrs. Gandhi met at Cancun, Mexico—the U.S. softened its position to abstain —rather than to vote against the loan. The fact that no other major economic power joined the U.S. created an impresion that the U.S. position was as much politically as economically motivated. As the *Economist* wrote, it is difficult to believe that the U.S. administration would have dealt in this way with one of its friend.

Cancun and Tarapur: Back From the Brink

France would replace the U.S. as the fuel supplier—a far more preferable substitute politically to Washington than the Soviets, who were the most likely alternative. Although some details remained to be moved out, the dispute that caused rancour for nearly a decade seemed near solution.

Indira Gandhi had, in fact, been eager for an invitation ever since returning to office in 1980. Except for a one day stop to see a friend in late Placid, New York, in 1973, she had not been to the U.S. for eleven years, since the ill-facked November 1971 meeting with Nixon during the Bangladesh crisis.

Indian rhetoric regard U.S. arms to Pakistan also began to later off. In addition to wanting to create a positive atmosphere for the U.S. visit the Indians recognised that their protests were not going to alter U.S. policy toward Pakistan. Although their meeting remained unchanged, according to then Foreign Minister P.V. Narasimha Rao, India tried "to be more persuasive and less rhetorical" in addressing the arms question.

Indira Gandhi Charms Washington

The Prime Minister Indira Gandhi arrived in Washington on July 30. To meet her at Andrews Air Force Base was George Schulz, the new Secretary of State, who had just replaced Alexander Harg after the latters stormy resignation. Mrs. Gandhi was welcomed by a smiling and relaxed Ronald Reagan, a marked contrast with Nixon's fense reception eleven years ago.

Reagan spoke of his hope "to broaden and deepen the dialogue we began at Cancun and of renewed recognition of the mutual importance of strong, constructive ties between India and U.S." In replying, Mrs. Gandhi described her journey as an adventure in search of understanding and friendship... to find a common area, how so ever small, on which to build and enhance cooperation."

First, the two leaders announced the Tarapur settlement rather akin to a no fault divorce. Under this France was to replace the U.S. as the enriched fuel supplier and India would continue the safeguards on the plant.

Second, Reagan and Mrs. Gandhi launched an initiative for science and technology cooperation.

Third, they named 1958 as "the year of India," during a mammoth Indian art and cultural exhibition would tour the U.S.

An unexpected source of support for selling arms to India, came from a conservative Republican Senator Orren Hatch of Upah, speaking on the Senate floor, Hatch raised eye brows by asserting that a historic shift was underway in Indo-U.S. relations brought about by the `Strategic vision' of the Reagan administration urging the President to play the `India Card,' military equipment sale `India dares to request.'

Underlying Hatch's enthusiasm was the hope that the

U.S. could gradually wean New Delhi away from Moscow by reducing Indian dependence on Soviet weaponry. The approach was rather unrealistic given the closeness of India's foreign policy and defense links with the Soviet Union which the U.S. had neither the funds nor desire to displace.

Support from a night-wing Republican Senator for an opening to India, nonetheless provided a politically helpful host to the new ambassador Barnes' non-ideological approach of trying to construct an Indo-U.S. relationship of sufficient substance that it could stand on its own.

Opposition focussed on Security issues, specifically on New Delhi's ability and willingness to prevent U.S.-supplied equipment from falling into the hands of India's Soviet friends. This worry applied with equal force to exports of non-military items, especially civilian electronic and computer technology, that might have military applications—so-called dual use items.

After the unilateral cut off during the 1965 war and U.S. reluctance to carry out the Tarapur contract, the Indians were sensitive to the terms of U.S. government contracts. They did not like U.S. insistence on the right to break an agreement at any time, New Delhi wanted assurances Washington would not arbitrarily cut off supplies. The Indians also disliked a standard provision that barred foreign governments from claiming refunds of prior payments in the event of a unilateral U.S. cutoff.

Without an agreement that would satisfy U.S. export control requirements, neither technology transfer, nor military procurement would be feasible to any substantial extent. The conclusion of an MoU, thus, became a key to expanding cooperation in these areas between U.S. and India.

Schulz and Bush Visits: An Improvement in Relations

Despite the fact that the discussions between Schulz and

Mrs. Gandhi featured long pauses when neither spoke, the two appeared to get along personally. Their talks maintained the dialogue begin during Indira's 1982 visit to Washington.

The World Bank its soft money affiliate, the International Development Authority (IDA) and the Asian Development Bank had all come direct and indirect pressure from Washington in ways that affected India. The U.S. supported the membership of China in the IDA and a related drop in India's traditional 40 per cent share of low interest IDA loans.

Finally the U.S. opposed India's borrowing from the Asian Development Bank, a financial institution whose resources India had not until the tapped although it was not a member of the Asian Bank.

Mrs. Gandhi could not object to U.S. to Pakistan, "but they are being armed to an extent that is well beyond their need" and the `guns one pointed toward us and not Afghanistan.' She alleged reduced U.S. funding for an international lending agencies seemed to be done in such a way that it hits India.

The State Department review of voting records in the UN for 1983 providing striking conformation that India and the U.S. continued to have major differences. India opposed the U.S. position on all ten UN questions that Washington judged important in 1983. By contrast, on the same ten issues. Pakistan voted with the U.S. five times, Bangladesh four times and Sri Lanka three times. Overall, India sided with the U.S. on about 20 per cent of votes, and with the Soviets on 80 per cent.

For its part, New Delhi was reluctant to concede anything in the wake of a review procedure by U.S. officials that could be construed as of an infringement on India's sovereignty. The Indians maintained they had ample experience and a good record in protecting foreign equipment from unfriendly hands. The U.S. side, in particular the Defence Department, doubted the Indian Control system was leak proof.

Rajiv Gandhi Replaces His Mother

On October 31, 1984 Indira Gandhi died assassinated by two Sikh bodyguards in relations for her having ordered the Indian Army in June 1984 to storm the Golden Temple of Amritsar, the holy shrine of the Sikh religion. Sikh militants who were agitating for an independent homeland, had occupied the temple in June as unrested movement in the Punjab. The bloody army assault caused many casualties, severely damaged the temple complex, and aliented the Sikh community still further from the Gandhi government.

Mrs. Gandhi violent death shocked the world; President Reagan who signed the condolence book at the Indian Embassy sent Secretary Schulz along with former U.S. ambassadors John Sherman Cooper, J. Kenneth Galbraith, Daniel Patrick Moynihan and Robert Goheen to participate in the funeral ceremonies. In a mourning meeting with Mrs. Gandhi's son and India's new Prime Minister Rajiv Gandhi each envoy, at Schulz request, spoke of their personal dealings with Indira.

Even though Mrs. Gandhi's associates insisted that she had no bias against the U.S. India made no headway the years about her suspicious and dislike of U.S. policy toward India and U.S. policy, in general. She never seemed to shed the negative attitude about the U.S. developed in her student days in Britain in the 1930s, and, to some extent, passed on from her father.

This attitude was strengthened by her view of U.S. policy as unfriendly toward India, a perception that emerged from her unhappy personal experience during the Johnson and Nixon administration. A pragmatic politician and above all, an Indian nationalist, she was still prepared to seek better relations in her last years with Washington when she concluded this was in India's interest.

Whatever Mrs. Gandhi personally thought of the U.S., her impact on U.S. attitudes toward India was, on the whole, quite negative. In the late Krishna Menon became the symbol of Indian antagonism to the U.S. Mrs. Gandhi assumed this role during most of her years as Prime Minister. Her often cold manner, his occasional cutting sarcasm and her frequent criticisms abenated many Americans. Quite apart from her mannerisms, Indira succeeded in offending liberals and former Indian supporters through her decision to explode a nuclear device in 1974 and her imposition of the emergency in 1975. She disenchanted Conservatives by aligning India closely with the Soviet Union, a policy symbolised by her willingness to condemn the Soviet invasions of Czechoslovakia in 1968 and Afghanistan in 1980.

Although she lacked in eloquence or vision of her father, she still articulated aspiration for a better life for hundred of millions of Indians and other in the Third World. At the time of her death, Indira had been India's Prime Minister for fifteen years. In 1964 it was hard to think of India without Nehru; in 1984 it seemed equally had to think that his daughter was no longer ruling India.

As Prime Minister Rajiv got off to an impressive start, initially representing a general change as well as a new look in Indian politics. His coming to power appeared to herold the arrival of a modern Indian leadership. One that marked the passing of a British trained and oriented elite, often with a strong anti-American strain. Reflecting the prevailing views of the younger urban elite, Rajiv leaned towards the private sector and had a healthy skepticism about the Socialist economic dogma adopted by the Congress party.

Capitalizing on the sympathy vote and his image as representing a new younger generation, he won a record 415 seats in Parliament in the general elections in January 1985—and a bigger victory than either his mother or grand father had ever achieved.

The immediate challenge was to overcome the obstacles to technology transfer from the U.S. to India by finishing up the negotiations for the technology MOU.

In keeping with the policy of creating indigenous defense production capabilities rather than relying on imported equipment, India hoped to produce the LCA as its Air Force mainstay in the 1990s Ikle also discussed was to speed up U.S. processing of Indian applications for exports of defense related equipment, at the same time stressing Washington concerns that India's system of internal controls needed strengthening to prevent diversion of items to the Soviets.

Although, this type of cooperation was standard in Indian military supply arrangements with the Soviets and West European countries, collaboration on the LCA would be a first with the U.S. after the limited and brief defense production arrangements twenty years earlier following the 1962 India-China war.

Looking to the 21st century, Ikle said he envisaged possible security cooperation in which together with the U.S. could contribute to world stability. "And that I think," Ikle shaped effusively "is an exciting possibility and, perhaps, a new chapter in the U.S.-India relations."

The New Prime Minister impresses Washington

The handsome young Prime Minister differed from the preachy, arrogant Indian stereotype. He was quite, seemed to listen to what American leaders had to say, spoke softly, but directly, and had a touch of humor.

One of the world's most advanced computers superior to anything the Soviet Union pressed the Cray XHP-24 which India sought had the capability of being used for nuclear weapon and ballistic missile development, for deciphering crytographic codes, and for a host of theoretical tasks and military applications that had little to do with India's stated objective of aiding agriculture through enhanced tracking of global weather patterns. Since the U.S. had not sold a computer as powerful as the Cray XMF-24 outside the circle of close allies, its export to India was a difficult decision, raising security questions about the Soviets and concerns about the computers possible use for nuclear weapons and missile guidance development. The Crazy provided a genuine test of the Reagan administration seriousness apart improving relations.

In the end, the Indians expressed interests in the procuring the General Electric 404 engine as the initial power plant for their next generation fighter. Used in F-18, the GE 404 was one of the most advanced U.S. aircraft engines. Early approval in principle by the Pentagon and the White House for its sale to India was a tangible sign of the more forthcoming U.S. stance on security cooperation with India.

In the New York Rajiv also seemed to take a more pro-Soviet line than during his visit to Washington in June. A hurried trip to Moscow on the way back to India raised eyeblows in Washington.

As Rajiv's comments made clear, underlying policy of differences between India and U.S. remained even if there were improvements in style in form since Rajiv succeeded his mother as Prime Minister.

A few days later, in neghbouring Pakistan, the Secretary of Defense managed to set relations back when he unexpectedly announced that the U.S. was in favour of providing Pakistan with the Boeing 707 Advanced Warning and Control System (AWACS) as part of a new multi year military and economic aid package that was being discussed with Pakistan.

Despite an informal understanding with the Indians to avoid springing surprises on each other, Weinberger said nothing about the AWACS during his stay in New Delhi.

Launching a vigorous counter attack, New Delhi argued that the AWACS would be of little use against the Soviets, were not needed against the Afghans, but would be enormously helpful against India.

In Washington, Indian ambassador P.K. Kaul former Cabinet Secretary and successor to Shankar Bajpai protested the AWACS in meeting with Weinberger and senior State Department officials.

Adding to the chorus, visiting Indian Foreign Secretary A.P. Venkateswarn warned Washington in January 1987 that providing AWACS would triger a very destabilising arms race in South Asia, requiring heavy Indian expenditures to make Pakistan's new capability.

The Democratic Congressman Stephen Solor of New York who was establishing himself as an expert on Asia, opposed the AWACS because he did not believe Pakistan was sufficiently responsive to U.S. desires it sought its nuclear weapons programme.

In the face of Congress doubts, the administration wavered about the AWACS, exploring a less expensive and less capable early warning aircraft to meet the genuine air security concerns faced by Afghan counter attacks inside Pakistan territory. Islamabad, however, rebuffed U.S. efforts to substitute a more modest system such as the E-2C insisting on the AWACS.

With the Soviets bogged down in a genuine war of natural liberation in Afghanistan, the Reagan Administration had a strong policy incentive to pay Pakistan's price as part of the new multi-year aid package.

Devastations about Soviet technology espionage in the U.S. heightened anxiety about sending sensitive technology to India. If they can steal it from Silican Valley, they can steal it from Bangalore, a Pentagon official told the *Wall Street Journal.*

In March 1987, the Reagan administration after much delay finally decided on a compromise solution: it would approve the sale to India of a Crazy model XMP-14 computer which had less capability than the Cray XMR-24 India wanted. U.S. specialists asserted the Cray XMP-14 could do sophisticated Weather research work but lacked the tracking capabilities that aroused NSA concerns. That disappointed the Indians.

Foreign Secretary Venkateswaran urged Prime Minister Gandhi to accept, arguing it was in India's interest to buy the XMP-14 in order to gain entry into the U.S. high technology world. Rejecting the offer, Venkateswaran warned, would freez India of high technology cooperation with the U.S. In the end, Rajiv accepted this reasoning and approved the purchase of the XMP-14.

After Broofield Congressmen's criticism Indian Foreign Policy support for the Kabul regime, for the Sandmistay in Nigeria and for the Vietnamese Kampuchean, the member voted 18-14 in favour of reduction. Even if the vote was not great consequence—given the aid programme small size-episode was an eye opener regarding continuing resentment about India on Capital Hill.

Knowing how difficult a battle in Washington against the cuts would be, ambassador John F. Dean decided not to contest the reductions. Dean doubted in terms of better relations with India would be worth the bureaucratic struggle.

Rajiv Gandhi adopted a tougher stance, demonstrating Indian displeasure by abrupting cancelling a visit by External Affairs Minister N.D. Tiwari a week before he was due in U.S.

Rajiv Gandhi: The Glow Weans Off

Reverting to his mother's style of fightly centralized control, Rajiv frequently shuffled ministers at the Central and the State level, more with an eye to maintaining personal political power than improving efficiency or rewarding achievement.

About the same time Indian troops intervened in Sri Lanka, worrisome developments regarding Pakistani efforts to develop nuclear weapons surfaced.

In late July 1987, a Canadian national of Pakistan was trying to export certain prohibited material to Pakistan for nuclear programme.

The incident underscored fears that Pakistan despite their protestations to the contrary, were pressing ahead with their covert effort to develop a nuclear capability. The news also played into the hands of those critical of providing the AWACS to Pakistan—a proposal already under fire as a destablizing system.

By establishing a line that Pakistan could not cross if it were to receive U.S. aid, the amendment in effect gave Pakistan a choice; either hold off crossing the bomb threshold or forgo U.S. aid. Although President Reagan continued to provide the certification, U.S. officials were uncomfortable cross between mounting evidence about the Pakistan nuclear programme and the desire to maintain the pressure on the Soviets in Afghanistan.

According to the White House, the President and Rajiv also agreed to expand defense cooperation proceeding along the lines that already established in waiting together on aspects of Light Combat Aircraft, and in other areas.

During his stay in India, the Secretary of Defense Carlucci announced further agreement for cooperation in developing the Light Combat Aircraft approving the use of the LCA of a highly advanced gyroscope, something the Pentagon had previously been unwilling to permit.

Rajiv also continued trying to mend relations with China, especially after Gorbachev initiated an effort to reduce the frictions between Moscow and Beijing.

In December 1988, Rajiv became the first Indian Prime Minister to visit China since his grandfather travelled there in 1956. Although the long standing dispute over the Himalayan borders remained unresolved, the two Asian giant pledged to work harder to improve relations so as to negotiate a border settlement and to ensure that in the meantime the situation along the disputed frontier remained calm.

1981-1989: A Gradual Warning

The Reagan administration initially wrote off as politically opposed and economically irrelevant to U.S. interests. In South Asia, the Reagan team had its eyes in reaming Pakistan and promoting resistance against the Soviets in Afghanistan; to the extent India mattered, it was primarily as a function of New Delhi's continuing leadership role in the nonaligned world.

Washington eased barriers to technology transfer and approved some advanced technology cooperation with India's defense industry. Although the bilateral rhetoric became more positive, adding milestone to the better atmosphere was not easy. During Reagan's eight years in office high level dialogue freely increased. The Vice President, Secretary of State, two Secretaries of Defense and three other Cabinet members visited India, Indira and Rajiv paid Reagan three visits to Washington. Mutual understanding increased at the top levels of government.

By 1988, both the U.S. and India seemed more realistic about what they could not expect from each other. Even though the bilateral framework remained fragile and progress toward substantive cooperation was uneven, there were smiles not frowns in New Delhi when Vice President George Bush, a friend of Rajiv Gandhi, defeated the Democrats in the November 1988 elections.

11

Bush: End of the Cold War

President Bush was familiar with the issues in South Asia from his eight years as Vice President as well as from the earlier service at the United Nations and his tenure as Director of CIA.

Most others in his administration, however, had limited previous exposure to India and the subcontinent. Although Washington had at first no need to undertake initiatives in South Asia, the dramatic shifts in Soviet Policy greatly affected the U.S. stance toward the region.

The departure of Soviet troops drastically reduced Washington's interest in the guerilla conflict between the Kabul regime and its Islamic opponents. Although the U.S. continued to funnel arms aid through Pakistan to the Mujahidin to parallel continuing Soviet Aid to Afghanistan government forces, Pakistan ceased to be a `frontline' state.

In congressional testimony in 1989, the Bush administration altered its justification for military aid, especially for providing Pakistan with additional FA-16. Defence and State Department witness no longer urged these aircraft as a way to boost Pakistan's self-confidence in the transition to democracy and doubtless the strongest argument in order not to lose out to French competition.

The President decided he would not certify that Pakistan did not possess a nuclear weapon, and, as a consequence in keeping with the Pressler amendment—stopped military and economic assistance. Press reports attributed the decision to Islamabad's refusing to roll back its Uranium enrichment programme—a key element in its covert effort to develop a weapons capability.

Whatever the reason, Bush's action caused much satisfaction in India. Uneasy to Pakistan nuclear aspirations, New Delhi had believed the U.S. was applying insufficient pressure against Islamabad to stop the move toward weapons. In addition to the nuclear dimension, the Indian were pleased that the flow of U.S. arms aid to Pakistan had for the time being at least ended.

1989: Rajiv Gandhi loses the Indian Election

The Central government's heavy handed management of Sikhs separatist unrest failed to calm the Punjab where terrorist intimidation rather than law and order became the norm. As the crisis in the Punjab and unrest in Assam in eastern India were not sufficient trouble, Rajiv began to face major turbulance in Kashmir.

Although chronically poor economic conditions stored discontent, pro-Pakistan or pro-independence element appeared to be an unthreating minority. Afer the Sheikh died in 1982, however, the situation gradually began to unravel. The blatant rigging of state elections by Abdullah's son, the then Chief Minister, and allegations of widespread corruption sparked serious discord in Kashmir.

One of the most outspoken and persistent critics was Republic Wally Herger of California whose district Yuba city, the home of many sikh imigrants, moulding Didar Singh Bains, an outspoken supporter of Khalistan—the name of the Sikh homeland and the largest peach grower in the United States.

With the assistance programme already reduced to just over $ 20 million annually, the measure had many symbolic importance. That it nearly carried underscored India's bringing public relations difficulties in the U.S. Congress despite the gradual warning in official relations that had occurred since 1982.

Despite the fact that India's ambassador P.K. Kaul, the former Cabinet Secretary, whom Rajiv sent as successor to K. Shankar Bajpai proposed that India hire a labbyist familiar with the byways of political Washington, was an appreciate way to spend governments money.

India's rival Pakistan had no such reluctances in seeking support for its cause in Washington, during most of the 1980s, Pakistan was represented by Denis Neil, regarded as one of the most skilled Washington labbyists.

With the Soviet Union disengaging itself around the globe from former battlegrounds with the U.S.—Angola, Ethiopia, and Nicaragua, as well as Eastern Europe and Afghanistan—the Cold War wound down. The goal of trying to wean India away from the Soviet Union, thus, had a much reduced strategic relevance in Washington.

In the absence of a push from the political level, the Pentagon traditional reluctance to expand high technology sales to India again became apparent. Even though the MOU was supposed to facilitate technology transfer, the export review process began to drag once more.

Congressional concerns focusing on India's space programme added to the problem. The fact that in April 1989, India was on the verge of launching an intermediate range rocket, the Agni, prompted senator Jeff Bingaman, a Democrat from New Mexico, to call the development "profoundly disturbing to the countries of the region and, indeed to the world community and to urge the U.S. government to end cooperation with their space programme."

The Licensing for export of $ 12 million Combined

Acceleration Climate Test System (CAVTS), a sophisticated rocket testing device that stimulated the heat and vibration of reentry into the earth's atmosphere, became an issue.

Although Washington initially leaned toward approval, after India successfully tested in Agni in June, the Bush administration reversed field. The U.S. refused to approve the export on the grounds that CAVTS could aid in developing a nuclear missile system.

The export of Second Super Computer, discussed during Rajiv Gandhi's 1987 visit, also encountered serious delays. When India for a Cray XMP-22, U.S. export review authorities argued the pros and cons of selling a super computer to India.

Defense, ACDA, and Energy expressed unhappiness about proceeding because the Cray XMP-22 could help develop a nuclear weapons capability, state and commerce urged approval of the License for the $ 50 million sale. It was only in December 1990 that the President Bush finally ruled in principle in favour of the export license.

Opponents of the sale gained some satisfaction, however when Bush required the computers use in Nuclear weapons development.

V.P. Singh Forms a Minority Government

Rajiv became the leader of the opposition in Parliament. Cross-border firing, chronic in Kashmir became more intense. India-Pakistan tensions rose to the highest level in years. In New Delhi, Prime Minister V.P. Singh warned the country to prepare itself for possible war with Pakistan.

Gates and Kelly also made clear that Washington, no longer backed a U.N. plebiscite as the preferred way to solve Kashmir dispute, but supported bilateral India-Pakistan talks in accord with the 1972 Simla agreement between the two countries; U.S. Kashmir valley, thus, corresponded with

India's own strongly held preference to bilateral negotiations and was at odds with Pakistan's traditional desire to involve outsiders in setting the dispute.

The U.S. had, in fact, favoured this approach ever since the 1972 Simla Accord. Because the Kashmir dispute remained quiet until the 1990 flore up, the shift in the U.S. position had attracted little attention.

The Super 301 Dispute: A New Source of Friction

The volume of Indo-U.S. trade grew gradually during the 1980s to reach $ 5.8 billion in 1989, with India showing a $690 million trade surplus with the U.S. in that year. One time, the U.S. had emerged as India's most important trading partner absorbing about 18 per cent of India's exports and 11 per cent of imports. India, in contrast was a major commercial partner for the U.S. accounting for less than 1 per cent of total U.S. trade.

In 1989, when the Bush White House issued the first Super 301 watch list, Japan, India and Brazil were cited as trade offenders with three complaints about India.

The first concerned Indian policy toward foreign investment which, in the U.S. view, effectively excluded foreign companies by limiting their equity participation to 40 per cent.

Although the Indians vehemently denied the accusation the extremely small size of foreign investment lent credibility to the charge. In 1989, overall investment from abroad was just $ 200 million, that of the U.S. only $ 37 million a miniscule amount for an economy as large as India's.

In view of the fact that India nationalised the entire industry including domestic and foreign Insurance Companies, the basis for a complaint of discriminatory treatment was hard to justify. It appeared as if Washington raised the problem mainly as a stop to U.S. insurance companies.

The third and the most contentious dispute related to the so-called intellectual property, specifically the length and character of certain types of patent protection, especially for pharmaceuticals in the Indian market.

The Indian government countered that its drug patent policy had important social implications, enabling India's vast, poor population to have access to medicines at far lower prices than U.S. and other foreign pharmaceutical companies charged.

The U.S. action to put India on the Super 301 list caused a stormy reaction to New Delhi. According to the Congressional Research Office, Washington move "offended India's deep seated sense of economic naturalism and long held views that its status as a developing country entitled it to a favourable treatment by the industrialized world." The fact that India, with its low *per capita* income and almost *de minimis* $ 690 million trade surplus, further licensed New Delhi.

Upset by Indian tactics, U.S. trade negotiator Corla Hills took a tough line in a speech to the Indo-U.S. Joint Business Council in Washington in mid-April 1990. Calling Indian economic policy shortsighted and flowed, Hills warned that the V. S. would not hesitate to retaliate against India if Super 301 issues remained unresolved.

On April, Hills removed Japan and Brazil from Super 301 watch list, leaving only India. As New Delhi flatly refused to talk about the issues an unnomed U.S. trade official asked, How can you not name India and maintain the credibility of our law? New Delhi responded angrily.

Rejecting trade talks, Arun Nehru, Commerce Minister in the V.P. Singh government, told Parliament that was not going to be "intimidated or policed by anybody on the issue of sovereignty or economic independence."

In a display bipartisanship, Rajiv Gandhi's former Defence Minister, Dinesh Singh, investigated against the sheer arrogance of power of the U.S. Because of the 1988 Act called for formal relation unless circumstances changed, serious bilateral trouble seemed imminent.

Abid Hussain, the new India's ambassador tried to prevent the Super 301 controversy from boiling over. Hussain convinced the U.S. trade officials that the talks in the framework of the multilateral Uruguay Round of GATT negotiation provided a basis for postframing Super 301 penalties. The White House declared relation inappropriate at this time given the ongoing negotiations on Services and investments in the Uruguay Round of global trade talks. Hussain found Corla Hills understanding but believed some Americans needed to realize that "India is a place where if you try to push in the door, the tendency is to push right back." The whole decision cooled off the Super 301 dispute even though the underlying issues remained unresolved.

1990-91: Indian Politics in Turmoil—Persian Gulf War

India found itself in domestic political discarry throughout the Persian Gulf crisis. After the trouble began Iraqi's seizure of Kuwait in August 1990, the V.P. Singh government's first concern was the fate of about 200,000 Indian national trapped in Kuwait and Iraq.

Traditionally India and Iraqi had friendly relations. Baghdad was a major supplier of petroleum, backed India on Kashmir—unlike most Arab States and like India had close ties with the Soviet Union.

Foreign Minister I.K. Gujral made an early visit to Iraq to seek favourable treatment for early evacuation of Indian nationals. Gujral effusively embraced Saddam Hussain provoking controversy in India and abroad.

The fact that the Soviet Union was working in harness with the U.S. in the post-Cold War crisis doubtless eased India's decision which also reflected the improvement of relations with Washington.

After India joined the U.N. Security Council in January 1991 as one of the rotating, non-permanent members, New Delhi joined an important voice in deliberation on the Persian Gulf crisis. India's weak government also found itself like all Security Council members under great pressure from Bush administration to join the consensus for keeping Saddam's Iraq out in the cold.

In a show of handball diplomacy over the Security Council votes, Secretary Baker announced Cessation of U.S. aid to Yemen, after that country—alongwith Cuba—supported Iraq and voted against U.S. to Washington annoyance, India seemed to be leaning toward Yemen and Cuba in initial 1971 vote to oppose preposed reparations.

1991 General Elections—Assassination of Rajiv Gandhi

India's tenth general election since independence and the Second in two years, focussed entirely on domestic issues.

Although both V.P. Singh and Chandra Shekhar as Prime Ministers India's intention to renew the Indo-Soviet Treaty, the relations with Moscow in either economic or security terms was of increasingly questionable relevance.

New Delhi was much at Sea in adjusting to the new realities in the wake of the collapse of the familiar Soviet counterweight. Regionally India remained the dominant power, but relations with Pakistan continued to be tense and nerves prayed over the belief that Islamabad was fanning the flames of unrest in Punjab and Kashmir.

At the same time, the possibility that armed showdown with Pakistan—something discussed more than a nuclear confrontation lent a new and for greater danger to the India-Pakistan rivalry.

The successful conduct of the Gulf crisis was further source for satisfaction, even if Saddam remained in power.

Despite the U.S. global success and Indian economic policy shift toward market forces, the Bush administration showed little inclination for closer bilateral engagement even though Washington wished India well in dealing with its enormous domestic problems.

In contrast to the heavy traffic during Ronald Reagan's second term, not a single U.S. Cabinet level officer visited India in the first two years of the Bush Presidency. Vice President Dan Qyale represented the U.S. at the funeral of Rajiv Gandhi in May 1991, although that hardly counted as an official visit for substantive talks. The only issue that continued to get high level attention in Washington was the threat of nuclear confrontation between India and Pakistan.

A half century of diplomatic relations between the U.S. and India concluded in the summer of 1991, the end point of the history. In New Delhi, there was a desire for better relations with the U.S. after the end of cold war. The Indian authorities seemed, however, unsure how to go about this and more broadly how to define India's foreign policy after the collapse of the Soviet Union. In the U.S. there was a similar lack of clarity about U.S. policy toward South Asia and toward India.

Washington seemed unsure how it wanted to relate to India in the changed global environment and where India fit into President Bush's New World Order. Bilateral ties between Washington and New Delhi were thus superficially friendly, but considerable uncertain by just below the surface.

12

Concluding Thoughts

In 1941, India and the U.S. initiated diplomatic relations when India's Agent General Sir Girja Shankar Bajpai and U.S. Commissioner Thomas Wilson presented their letters of introduction to President Roosevelt and Viceroy Lord Linlithgow, India was already engaged in World War II at the behest of the Viceroy and without the consent of the Indian people.

The U.S. would be at war before the year was over. By the end of the decade India would become free, but in the process lose a quarter of its population to the newly created state of Pakistan, with which it would fight three wars.

After the defeat of the Axis powers, the allied war time coalition would crumble and the U.S. would find itself engaged in a global struggle with the Soviet Union that lasted forty five years.

In this environment, a half-century of relations between India and U.S. have been uneven on occasion friendly, sometimes hostile, but, more often, just estranged. Given their different historical, social and economic experiences, India and U.S. were almost certainly destined to adopt conflicting policies on many issues.

Their differences, however, might not have been as jagged in the absence of more profound sources of friction. Why have there two nations both democracies, so often found themselves at odds with each other in the international arena? What his behind their difficulties in getting along politically?

This history suggests that the root cause can be found in the clash over national security issues of major importance to each country. For India, the principal stumbling bloc has been the U.S.-Pakistan relationship. In arming and aligning itself with Pakistan, the entity of the participation of British India, the U.S. linked arms with the country which independent India considered its principal security threat.

For the U.S. the decisive problem has been India's attitude toward the Soviet Union. In establishing the policy of non-alignment under Nehru, India annoyed the U.S. by refusing to agree with America's perception of the Soviet threat.

Under Mrs. Gandhi, India went much further, establishing close security and political ties with Moscow, making common cause with the nation which the U.S. regarded as the major threat to its security and to global peace and stability.

Until the mid-1960s, Indo-U.S. policy differences were, to some extent, offset the percepting of India's strategic importance as a democratic alternative to communist China, and by large scale commitment of U.S. resources to support India's economic development.

Since then, the fact that the U.S. and India have shared few important security interests has contributed, in a passive manner to the sense of mutual estrangement. The two countries have had little in common other than their adherence to political democracy.

Certain factors, however limited how for Washington and New Delhi have been willing to let their relationship deteriorate. For India the U.S. has had great economic importance for two decades, from 1951 until 1971 as the major donor of bilateral aid and, more recently, as a result of U.S. influence over the decisive of international financial institutions.

The U.S. has become India's largest trading partner and an important source of investment and technology even though conversely, India has played only a minor role in U.S. external commerce. Politically, also, especially after the signing of the friendship and cooperation Treaty with Moscow in 1971, India at least the Semblence of a working relationship with the U.S. to lend credibility to its policy of non-alignment and to avoid being ragged as a Soviet Camp follower.

Until the collapse of communism in the Soviet Union, half of the people under democrat rule were Indians. Its geographical location astride the strategic oil soil supply routes of the Indian ocean and along the Southern ruin of China has reinforced India's own sense of national importance as heir of one of the World's great civilizations growing military power has also made India a factor to be reckoned with as the prominent force not only in South Asia but the Indian ocean region at large.

As the fifty years reviewed in this history of Indo-U.S. relations concluded in 1991, the global strategic environment undervent a fundamental change. Gorbachev's reforms and the accelerating disintegration of the Soviet Union and its version of communism brought to an end the Cold War which had decisively shaped U.S. and Indian policies. The U.S. engaged as the sole superpower, its ideology of democratic victories over Marxist communism.

U.S. relations with India slowly improved during the 1980s but a legation of suspicion and mistrust remained. Although Washington insisted New Delhi well in tackling its enormous domestic problem, the U.S. showed little disposition to rethink its relationship with India. Washington seemed uncertain—some would uninterested in —how to fit India into the post-cold war policy framework.

It was almost as if the U.S. did not know what to make of India. The continued poverty of the majority of the country's vast population contrasted with the rising affluence of the burgeoning middle classes. Unrest and terrorism in Punjab and Kashmir and Hindu-Muslim communal tensions contrasted with the resilience and strength of Indian democratic institutions.

India's growing military power, the worlds fourth largest army, the beginnings of blue water navy and the presumption of a nuclear weapons capability contrasted with the economy that continued to progress for more slowly than most other Asian countries and remained hobbled by bloated and inefficient public sector industries.

The rapid growth of the Indian immigrant community in the U.S. almost three times the 1980 count—reinforced the view. An alternate approach reflected in the anti-U.S. sentiment during the Gulf War, was for India to remain anti-gonistic to the U.S. Washington was seen as continuing to be infriendly, trying to `keep India down,' and unwilling to respect India's position as the preeminent power in South Asia or as spokesman for the worlds poorest nations.

Whether the two countries will take advantage of this opportunity remains uncertain. The history of past estrangement has left its scars. Public opinion, of particular importance in the case of democracies such as India and the U.S. poses an obstacle to improvement in relations. The same is true for the often negative attitude among the foreign policy and national security establishments.

Were those concerned with foreign policy and national security affairs in Washington and New Delhi to accept that their opposite numbers are not *per se* anti-American or anti-Indian and that pursuing respective national interests can bring the two countries closer together on many issues, a constructive rather than an estranged relationship may prove attainable.

Indian and the U.S. now have a shared interest in stability in the Indian Ocean region and a viable balance of power in Asia. India is large enough, and economically and militarily of sufficient importance, that the Indo-U.S. relationship could have strategic importance in its own right.

India's apprehension about a military threat from Pakistan may be irrational and ill-official, they are the nonetheless, real for Indians.

Unless the Indian government vigorously carries through with its economic reforms, genuinely modifying India's economic policies to open the country to the rest of the world and to give greater scope for market forces, U.S. business is unlikely to show much greater in India than it has in the past. New Delhi also needs to understand that investment and other commercial decisions are in the hands of the U.S. private sector, with the governments role at best a moderate one.

Related to this, is the future of non-alignment after the end of Cold War move a slogan than a guide to policy. The prospects of improved relations would dim should New Delhi redefine non-alignment in North-South terms positioning itself as a leader of the Third World in a strident struggle against the U.S. and the industrialized West.

The quasi-nuclearization of the subcontinent could, indeed mark as important a change in South Asia on the end of the Cold War. A nuclear Pakistan has, in effect, achieved the strategic parity with India, something it could never have hoped for with conventional weapons.

How effectively and calmly Washington and New Delhi deal with this difficult and dangerous problem is certain to have a major impact on the future course of the U.S.-Indian relationship.

The two countries found themselves on opposite sides of major foreign and security policy issues despite their common adherence to the democratic system. With the Cold War over, Indo-U.S. relations could become more positive. It is uncertain, however, that the two governments take advantage of this opportunity.

Eventhough past problems are for the moment out of sight, they are not out of mind. New Delhi and Washington need to study and absorb the lessons of the past five decades if India and the U.S. are to forge a more constructive relationship in the years ahead.

Bibliography

Official Records and Document Collections

Mensergh, Nicholas ed. *The Trans of Power* 1942-1947, London:

His Majesties Statutory Office 1970-1983.

Selected Works of Jawaharlal Nehru, New Delhi: Orient Longman, 1972-1982 (vol. 1-14).

Selected Works of Jawaharlal Nehru, Second Series, New Delhi.

Jawaharlal Nehru Memorial Fund, 1984-1991 (vol. I-II).

U.S. Department of State, Foreign Relations of the United States, Washington: Government Printing Office.

U.S. Presidential files at the Harry S. Truman Library, Independence, Missouri, the Dwright D. Endowment Library, Boston, Massachusettes; and the Lyndon Bains Johnson Library, Austin Texas.

Note on U.S. official documents: In researching this Book only unclassified or declassified U.S. government documents available through a variety of sources, including requests through the Freedom of Information Act. For the years 1960, documents were primarily found in the *Foreign Relations of the United States series*. For the following decades most came from the collections at Kennedy and Johnson Libraries. Some documents were also located through the *Declassified documents catalogue* (Woodbridge, CT: Research Publications

1977-1991) available in the State Department Library. This service lists and provides copies of national security documents declassified under the Freedom of Information Act. Finally, a few documents cited in the text were referred to or quoted in memoirs and other studies that touched on the Indo-U.S. relations.

Memoirs

Acheson, Dean. *Present at the Creation.* New York: W.W. Norton, 1969.

Azad, Maulana Abul Kalam. *India Wins Freedom,* New York: Longmans, Green and Co., 1960.

Azad, Maulana Abul Kalam, *Promises to Keep. My Years in Public Life,* 1941-1959. New York: Harper & Row 1971.

Brizezinski, Zbigneew. *Power and Principle,* New York: Farrar, Strans & Guroux, 1983.

Chagla, M.C. *Poses in December: An Autobiography,* Bombay, Bhartiya Vidya Bhawan, 1973.

Chakravarty, B.N. *India Speaks to America,* New York: The John Day Company, 1966.

Churchill, Winston S. *The Hinge of Fate,* Boston: Houghton Mifflin Company: 1950.

Darvi, Brig. J.P. *Himalayan Blunder: The Curtain Roses to the Sino-Indian War of 1962,* Bombay: Thacker and Company, 1969.

Dutt, Subimal. *With Nehru in the Foreign Office,* Calcutta: Minerva; 1972.

Eisenhower, Dwright D. *The White House Years, Waging Peace 1956-61* Gorden City, NY: Doubleday, 1965.

Freeman Orville L. *World Without Hunger.* New York Praegar, 1968.

Galbraith, John Kenneth. *A Life in our Times. Memoirs,* New York: Bellantine, 1981.

_________ *Ambassador's Journal* Boston: Haughton and Mifflin Company 1969.

Gandhi, Indira. *My Truth.* New Delhi: Vision, 1981.

Gundevia, Y.D. *Outside the Archvies,* Hyderabad, Sangam Books, 1984.

Harriman W. Averell and Elie Abd. *Special Envoy to Churchill and Stalin,* 1941-1946. New York: Random House, 1975.

Hull, Cordell. *Memoirs,* New York: Macmillian 1948.

Jha, C.S. *From Banding to Tashkent: Glimpses of Indian Foreign Policy.* Madras, Sangam 1983.

Johnson, Lyndon Bains. *The Vantage Point, Perspectives of the Presidency,* 1963-1969, New York: Holt Rinchart, and Winston, 1971.

Johnson, U. Alexis, with J.O. McAllister. *The Right Hand of Power,* Eaglewood Cliffs N.J. Prentice-Hall, 1984.

Kaul, W. General, B.N. *The Untold Story,* Bombay: Allied Publishers, 1967.

Kaul, T.N. *Reminescenses Discreet and Indiscreet.* New Delhi: Lancers 1982.

_________ *The Kissinger Years: Indo-American Relations,* New Delhi: Arnold Heinmann, 1980.

Khan, Mohammad Ayub. *Friends not Masters,* London: Oxford University Press, 1967.

Kissinger, Henry A. *The White House Years.* Boston: Little, Brown and Company, 1979.

McGhee, George, *Envoy to the Middle East,* New York: Harper & Row, 1983.

Moynihan, Daniel Patrick. *A Dangerous Place*. Boston: Little, Brown & Company 1978.

Mullik, B.N. *My years with Nehru: The Chinese Betrayal*, Bombay. Allied Publishers, 1971.

Nehru, Jawaharlal. *A Bunch of Old Letters* Bombay. Asia Publishing House, 1958.

_________ *Discovery of India*, London: Meridian Books, 1956.

_________ *Independence and After*: New York: John Day Company, 1950.

_________ *Visit to America*, New York: The John Day Company, 1950.

Nixon, Richard, R.N. *The Memoirs of Richard Nixon*. New York: Grosset & Dunlop 1978.

Pandit, Vijaya Laxmi. *The Scope of Happiness. A Personal Memoir*, New York: Crown, 1979.

Phillips, William. *Ventures in Diplomacy*, Boston: Beacon Press, 1952.

Rusk Dean. *As I saw it*, New York: M.W. Norton & Company, 1990.

Subramaniam, C. *The Strategy for Indian Agriculture*, New Delhi, Vikas 1979.

Truman, Harry S. *Memoirs* vol. 2, *Years of Trial and Hope*. Garden City: Doubleday & Company, 1956.

Zumalt, Elmo R. *On Watch: A Memoir*. New York: Qudrangle, *New York Times Book Co.* 1976.

Secondary Works

Ambrose, Stephen E. *Eisenhower, The President*, New York: Simon and Schuster; 1984.

________ Nixon, *The Education of a Politician*, 1913-1962, New York: Simon and Schuster, 1987.

________ Nixon, *The Triumph of a Politician*, 1962-1972, New York: Simon and Schuster, 1989.

Anderson, Jack with George Clifford. *The Anderson Paters*, New York: Random House, 1973.

Bandyopadyaya, Jayant. *The Making of India's Foreign Policy*, New Delhi: Allied 1970.

Borands, William J. *India, Pakistan and the Great Powers*, New York: Praegar, 1974.

Bhagat G. *American in India* 1784-1860. New York: New Look University Press. 1970.

Bhatia, Krishnan, *Indira*, New York: Praegar 1974.

Blechman and Kaplan. *Force without War*, Washington D.C. The Brooking Institution, 1978.

Bradnock, Robert. *Indian Foreign Policy since 1911*, London: Royal Institute of International Affairs. 1990.

Brandon, Henry. *The Retreat of American Power*, Garden City: Doubleday & Company, 1973.

Brands, H.W. *India and the United States. The Cold Peace*, Boston, Twayne Publishers, 1990.

________ *The Specter of Neutralism, The United States and the Emergence of the Third World War*. New York. Columbia University Press, 1989.

Brecher, Michael, *India and World Politics: Krishna Menons' View of the World*. London: Oxford University Press, 1968.

________ *Nehru, A Political Biography*, London: Oxford University Press, 1959.

Brines, Russel. *The Indo-Pakistani Conflict*. London: Pall Mall Press, 1968.

Burn James McGregger, *Roosevelt: The Soldier of Freedom*. New York: Harcourt Brace Jovanovich, 1970.

Caroe, Olaf, *Welles of Power*, London; Macmillian & Co. 1951.

Carvas Mary, *Indira Gandhi, In the Crucible of Leadership*, Boston: Beacon Press, 1979.

Chopra, Pran, *Indians Second Liberation*, Cambridge: The MIT Press, 1974.

Chowdhry, G.W. *India, Pakistan, Bangladesh and the Major Powers*, New York. The Free Press, 1975.

_________*The Lashdays of United Pakistan.*

Cohen, Stephen P. ed. *The Security of South Asia*, Urbana: University of Illinois Press, 1987.

Cohen, Stephen, P. and Richard L. Clark. *India: Emergent Power*? New York: Crane, Russak & Company, 1978.

Crocker, Walter R. *Nehru: A Contemporary's Estimate*, New York: Oxford University Press, 1966.

Crunden, Robert M. ed. *Traffic of Ideas Between India and America*, New Delhi. Chanakya, 1985.

Dagli, Vadilal, ed. *Two Decades of Indo-US Relations*. Bombay: Vora & Company.

Damodaran, A.K. and U.S. Bajpai eds. *Indian Foreign Policy: The Indira Gandhi years*, New Delhi: Radiant, 1990.

Das Durga, *India From Curzon to Nehru & After*, London, Collins 1969.

Denaon, David D.H. *Devaluation Under Pressure*, Cambridge M.A. MIT Press, 1986.

Donaldson, Robert H. *Soviet Policy Toward India: Ideology and Strategy*, Cambridge: Harvard University Press, 1974.

Eldridge, P.F. *The Polices of Foreign Aid in India*, New York: Spoken Books, 1969.

Embree, Ainslec, *Anti-American in South Asia, In Anti-American in the Third World*, Alvin Rubmitein and Donald Smith eds. 137-150. New York: Praeger, 1985.

Evans, Humphrey. *Thimayya of India: A soldiers Life*, New York: Herteant, Brace and Company 1960.

Ferrell, Robert H. ed. *The Eisenhower Diaries*, New York, WW, Norton and Company, 1981.

Fisher, Margaret W., Leo Rose, and Robert Huttenback *Himalayan Background: Sino-Indian Rivalry in Ladakh*. New York: Praegar 1963.

Ganguly Sumit. *The Origins of War in South Asia*, Boulder & Co. Westview Press, 1986.

Ganguli, Sivaji. *U.S. Policy Toward South Asia*, Boulder: Westview Press, 1990.

Garthoff, Raymond L. *Detente and Confrontation: American-Soviet Relations from Nixon to Reagan*, Washington: The Brookings Institution 1985.

Gopal, Sarvepalli. *Jawaharlal Nehru, volume one 1889-1947* London. Jonathan Cape, 1975.

_________ *Jawaharlal Nehru, Volume Two 1947-1956* London; Jonathan Cape, 1984.

Gould, Herold A. and Sumit Ganguly, eds. *The Hope and Reality, U.S.-Indian Relations for Roosevelt to Bush*. Boulder: Westview, 1992.

Gupta, Bhabani Sen. *Rajiv Gandhi: A Political Study*, New Delhi: Konark, 1989.

Gupta Sisir, *Kashmir, A Study in India-Pakistan Relations,* Bombay, Asia Publishing House, 1967.

Haendal Dan. The Process of Priority Formulation: U.S. Foreign Policy in the Indo-Pakistan War of 1971. Boulder: Westview Press, 1977.

Hare, Paul. *A Diplomatic Chronicle, Middle East and South Asia: Biography of Ambassador A. Hare.* 1924-1966. Lanham, MD: University Press of America, 1992.

Harrison, Selig S. *The Widening Gulf: Asian Naturalism and American Policy,* New York: Free Press, 1978.

Harrison, Selig S. ed. *India and the United States,* New York: Macmillan, 1961.

Harison, Selig S. and K. Subramaniyam eds. *Superpower Rivalry in the Indian ocean. Indian and American Respective,* New York: Oxford University Press, 1989.

Heinsath, Charles H. and Surjit Mansingh. *A Diplomatic History of Modern India,* New Delhi; Allied 1971.

Hersh, Seymour. *The Price of Power: Kissinger in the Nixon White House,* New York: Summit Books, 1983.

Hess, Gary R. *America Encounters India* 1941-1947. Baltimore: John Hopkins University Press, 1971.

Hoffman, Steven A. *India and China Crisis,* Berkeley: University of California Press 1990.

Hope, A. Guy. *America and Swaraj,* Washington: Public Affairs Press, 1968.

Horn, Robert C. *Soviet-Indian Relations,* New York: Praegar, 1982.

Isacs, Herald. *Scratches in our Mind,* White Plans: M.E. Sharpe, 1980.

Jackson, Richard L. *The Non-Aligned, the U.N. and Superpowers,* New York: Praegar, 1983.

Jackson, Robert. *South Asian Crisis: India, Pakistan and Bangladesh,* New York: Praegar, 1975.

Jauhari, R.C. *American Diplomacy and Independence for India,* Bombay: Vora & Co. 1970.

Jenson, Joan M. *Passage from India: Asian Indian Immigrants in North America,* New Haven: Yale University Press, 1988.

Jones, Rodney W. *Nuclear Proliferation: Islam, the Bomb and South Asia,* Georgetown University, 1981.

Kalb, Marvin and Bernard Kalib, *Kissinger,* Boston: Little, Brown and Company, 1978.

Kamath, M.V. *The United States and India,* Washington: Embassy of India, 1976.

Kapur Ashok. *India's Nuclear Option: Atomic Policy and Decision-making.* New York: Praegar, 1976.

Karunakaran, K.P. *India in World Affairs 1947-50,* London: Oxford University Press, 1958.

Kaufman, Butan I. *Trade and Aid. Eisenhower Foreign Economic Policy,* 1953-1961. Baltimore: John Hopkins, 1982.

Karvic, Lorne J. *India's Quest for Security,* Berkeley: University of California Press, 1967.

Khera, S.S. *India's Defense Problem,* New Delhi: Orient Longman, 1968.

Korbel, J. *Danger in Kashmir,* Princeton: Princeton University Press, 1954.

Krishnan, T.V. Kunhi. *The Unfriendly Friends: India and America,* New Delhi. Inter Culture Assoriates, 1974.

Lamb, Alistar *The China-India Border: The Origins of the Disputed Boundaries*. London: Oxford University Press, 1969.

_________ *The Kashmir Problem*, New York: Praegar, 1966.

_________ *The Sino-Indian Borders in Ladakh*: Columbia: University of South Carolina Press, 1975.

Lewis John P. *Essays in Indian Political Economy*: Princeton University Press.

Limaye, Satu. *U.S.-India Relations: The Pursuit of Accommodation*, Boulder Co. Westview Press, 1992.

Louis, W. Roger. *Imperialism at Bay. The United States and the Decolonisation of the British Empire 1941-1945*, New York: Oxford University Press, 1978.

McMohan, Robert J. *Choosing sides in South Asia. In Kennedy's quest for Victory*, ed. Thomas & Patterson, New York: Heath, 1989.

Malhotra, *Inder. Indira Gandhi: A Personal and Political Biography*, London: Hodder & Stroughton, 1989.

Mansingh, Surjit. *Indians Search for Power, Indira Gandhi Foreign Policy* 1966-1982. New Delhi, Sage Publication, 1984.

Masani, Zareer: *Indira Gandhi: A Biography*, London: Hamsh Hamilton, 1975.

Maxwell, Neville. *India-China War*, New York: Anchor Books, 1972.

Mellor, John W. ed. *A Rising Middle Power*, Bolder: Westview Press, 1979.

Menon, V.P. *The Transfer of Power in India*, Princeton: Princeton University Press, 1957.

Mervil, Dennis J. *Bread and Ballet: The United and India's*

Reid, Escott. *Envoy to Nehru,* New Delhi. Oxford University Press, 1981.

Roosevelt, Elliot. *As He saw Int.* New York: Duel, Sloan, and Pearce, 1946.

Rose, Leo E., and Richard Sisson. *War and Secession, Pakistan, India and the creation of Bangladesh,* Berkeley University of California Press, 1990.

Rosinger, Lawrence K. *Indian and the United States Political and Economic Relations,* New York: The MacMillan Company, 1950.

Rostow, Walt. W. *Eisenhower, Kennedy and Foreign Aid.* Austin: University of Texas Press, 1985.

Rubinstein, Alvin ed. *The Great Gane: Rivalry in the Persian Gulf and South Asia*: Praegar 1983.

Rudolph, Lloyd! Susanner Rudolph et al. *The Regional Imperative. Atlantic Highlands*: Humanities Press, 1980.

Sar Desai, D.R. *Indian Foreign Policy in Cambodia, Laos and Vietnam, 1947-1964.* Berkeley University of California Press, 1968.

Schaffer, Howard B. *New Dealer in the Cold War: The role of F. Chestrn Bowles in K.S. Foreign Policy.* Washington, D.C. Institute for the Study of Diplomacy.

Schlesinger, Arthur M., Jr. *A thousand Days, John F. Kennedy in the White House,* Boston. Houghton Mifflin Company 1968.

Sen Gupta, Bahabani, *Rajiv Gandhi, A Political Study,* New Delhi, Konark, 1989.

Seton, Marie. *Panditji: A Portrait of Jawaharlal Nehru,* New York Taplinor, 1967.

Sherwood, Robert S. Roosevelt and Hopkins. New York: Harper & Brothers, 1950.

Singh S. Nihal. *The Yogi and the Bear, Story of Indo-Soviet Relations*, New Delhi: Allied Publishers, 1986.

Singh, Diwakar Prasad. *American Attitude Towards the Indian Nationalist Movement*, New Delhi. Munshiram Manohar Lal, 1974.

Sovension, Theodore C. *Kennedy*, New York: Harper & Row, 1965.

Spector, Leonard with Jacqueline Smith. *Nuclear Ambitions, The Spread of Nuclear Weapons*, 1989-90. Boulder Co. Westview Press, 1990.

Stein, Arthur B. *Indian and the Soviet Union: The Nehru Era*, Chicago: University of Chicago Press, 1969.

Talbot, Phillips and S.L. Boplan. *India and America*, New York: Harper & Brothers, 1958.

Tiwari S.C. *Indo-U.S. Relations*, 1947-1976. New Delhi. Radiant, 1977.

Tharoer, Shashi. *Reasons of State*, New Delhi, Vikas Publishing House, 1982.

Thomas, Raja G.C. *Indian Security Policy*, Princeton: Princeton University Press, 1986.

__________The Defense of India, Meerut: Macmillan, 1978.

Thorne, Christopher. *Allies of a Kind. The United States, Britain and the War against Japan 1941-1945*. London: Hamsh Hamilton, 1978.

Van Eckelen, W.F. *Indian Foreign Policy and the Border Dispute with China*, The Hague: Martinus Nijhoff, 1967.

Keit, Larence. *India's Second Revolution: The Dimensions of Development*, New York: Council on Foreign Relations, 1976.

Venkataraman, M.S. *The American Role in Pakistan* 1947-1958. New Delhi, Radiant Publishers, 1982.

Venkataman, M.S. and B.K. Shrivastava. *Quit India: The American Response to the 1942 struggle,* New Delhi: Vikas Publishing House, 1979.

________*Roosevelt, Churchill and Gandhi,* New Delhi: Radiant Publishers, 1983.

Ventzberger, Yaacov, Y.I. *Misperception in Foreign Policy making, The Sino-Indian Conflict 1959-1962.* Boulder Westview Press, 1984.

Weintranb, Sidney, ed. *Economic Coercion and U.S. Foreign Policy: Implications of Case Studies from the Johnson Administration,* Boulder: Westview Press, 1982.

Whitting, Allan S. *The Chinese Calculous of Deference,* Ann Arbor: University of Michigan Press, 1975.

Wolpert, Stanby. *Roots of Confrontation in South Asia: Afghanistan, Pakistan, India and the Superpowers,* New York: Oxford University Press, 1982.

Woodman, Dorothy. *Himalayan Frontiers,* London, Cresset Press, 1969.

Wright, Denis. *India-Pakistan Relations* (1962-1969), New Delhi: Sterling Publishers, 1989.

Yager, Joseph, ed. *Nonproliferation and U.S. Foreign Policy,* Washington: The Brookings Institution 1980.

Ziring, Lawrence, ed. *The Subcontinent in World Politics: India, its neighbours and the Great Powers.* New York: Praegar, 1982.

Journal Articles

Banerjee, Jyotimay, "Moscow's Indian Alliance," *Problems of*

Communism, 36 (January-February 1987): pp. 1-12.

Banerjee, Sanjay. "*Explaining the American `Tilt' in the 1971 Bangladesh Crisis. A Late Dependency approach.*" International Studies Quarterly 31 (June 1987): pp. 201-206.

Barnds, William J. "*India and America at Odds.*" *International Affairs*, no. 3 (July 1973: pp. 371-384.

_________"Indian Concepts of Asian Security." *Asian Forum*, 8 (Automn 1976) pp. 85-96.

_________"The Indian Subcontinent: New and Old Political Imperatives "The World Today, No. 1 (January 1973): pp. 24-33.

Brecher, Michaell. Nehru's Foreign Policy and the China-India Conflict Revisited *Pacific Affairs*, 50 (Spring 1977): pp. 99-106.

_________*Non-Alignment Under Stress*: *The West and the China-India Border War" Pacific Affairs* 52, No. 4 (Winter 1979-1980) pp. 612-630.

Chadda, Maya, "*India and the United States: Why Detente, Won't Happen.*" Asian Survey 26 (October 1986), pp. 118-136.

Chellaney, Brahma. "*South Asia's Passage to Nuclear Power.*" *International Security* 16 (Summer 1991). pp. 43-72.

Chopra, Pran, "India's Foreign Policy" *The Round Table*, No. 275 (July 1979): pp. 227-231.

Clausen, Peter *A. Non-Proliferation Illusion: Tarapur in Retrospect Orbis* (Fall 1983): pp. 741-760.

Clymer, Kenton J. "Franklin D. Roosevelt, Louis Johnson, India and Anti Colonialism: Another Look." *Pacific Historical Review* 57 (August 1988) pp. 261-284.

________Jawaharlal Nehru and the United States: *The Pre-independence Years." Diplomatic History* 14 (Spring 1990), pp. 143-162.

________"The Education of William Phillips: Self Determination and American Policy Toward India, 1942-45," *Diplomatic History,* 8 (Writer 1984) pp. 13-36.

Cohen, Stephen P. "*Balancing Interests: The U.S. and the Subcontinent*", *The National Interest* (Fall 1987): pp. 74-84.

________"South Asia After Afghanistan", *Problems of Communism* 34 (January-February, 1985): pp. 18-31.

________"*U.S. Weapons and South Asia: A Policy Analysis*". *Pacific Affairs* 49 (Spring 1976): pp. 49-69.

________ed. "India and America Toward a Realistic Relationship" *Asian Affairs* 15 (Winter 1988-89).

Cronin, Richard P. "*Prospectives for Proliferation in South Asia.*" *The Middle East Journal.* No. 4. Autumn 1983: pp. 594-616.

Gandhi, Indira, "India and the World," *Foreign Affairs* 51 (October 1972), pp. 65-77.

Ganguly, Sumit, Avoiding war in Kashmir, *Foreign Affairs* 69, No. 5 (Winter 1990-91) pp. 57-73.

Goheen, Robert F. Problems of Proliferation: U.S. Policy and the Third World," World Politics (January 1982), pp. 44-215.

Haas, Richard N." South Asia, Too Late to Remove the Bomb?" *Orbis* 321 (Winter 1988) pp. 107-118.

Harrison, Selig, S. "Pakistan and the United States," *New Public* 10 (August 1959).

________"South Asia and the United States: A Chance for a Fresh start". *Current History* (March 1992): pp. 97-105.

Hess Gory. "Accommodation and Accord: the United States, India and the Third World" *Diplomatic History* 16 (Winter 1992): pp. 1-23.

________"Global Expansion and Regional Balances: The Emerging Scholarship on United States Relations with India and Pakistan". *Pacific Historical Review* 56 (May 1987) pp. 259-295.

Horn, Robert C, "Afghanistan and the Soviet-Indian influence Relationship." *Asian Survey* 23 (March 1983): pp. 244-26.

Jaipal Rikhi, "Indian Nuclear Explosion" *International Security,* (Spring 1977): pp. 44-51.

Kapur, Ashok. "Nuclear Proliferation: South Asian Perspectives." *Pacific Affairs* 57 (Summer 1984): pp. 304-311.

Kapur, Harish. "India's Foreign Policy under Rajiv Gandhi." *The Round Table* No. 304 (October 1987): pp. 469-480.

Keenleyside, T.A. Prelude to Power: The meaning of non-alignment Before Indian Independence." *Pacific Affairs* 53 (Fall 1980) pp. 461-483.

Kennedy John F. "*A Democrat looks at Foreign Policy,*" Foreign Affairs 36 (October 1957).

Kochanek, Stanley A: "Indians Changing Role in the United Nations," *Pacific Affairs* 53 No. 1 (Spring 1980): pp. 48-68.

Kreisberg, Paul. "The United States, South Asia and American Interests." *Journal of International Affairs* 43 (Summer Fall 1989): pp. 83-96.

Economic Development 1947-1961. Chapel Hill: University of North Corolina Press, 1990.

Misra, K.P. ed. *Janata's Foreign Policy*, New Delhi. Vikas, 1979.

Move Robin J. *Churchill, Cripps and India*, Oxford: Cranden Press, 1979.

_________ *Endjames of Empire*, New Delhi: Oxford University Press, 1988.

Moraes, Don. *Indira Gandhi*, New York: Little, Broom and Company, 1980.

Moshaver, Ziha, *Nuclear Weapons Proleferation in the Indian subcontinent*, New York St. Main Press, 1951.

Nanda B.R. ed. *India's Foreign Policy in the Nehru Years*, New Delhi. Vikas Publishing House, 1976.

Nayar, Baldev Raj. *American Geopolitics and India*, New Delhi.

Nayar Kuldip. *India: The Critical Years*. New Delhi. Vikas Publications, 1971.

Recorlberg, Robert Food Trade and Foreign Policy: India, the Soviet Union and the United States, Ithoca: Cornel University Press, 1985.

Palmer, Norman D. *South Asia and United States Policy*. Boston: Houghton Mifflin, 1968.

Pandey, B.N. *Nehru*. London: MacMillan, 1976.

Pillai, K. Raman. India's Foreign Policy. Meerut: Meenakshi Prakashan, 1969.

Prasad, Bimal ed. *India's Foreign Policy. Studies in Continuity and Change*. New Delhi. Vikas, 1979.

Rajan, M.S. *India in World Affairs*, 1954-6, New Delhi. Asia Publishing House, 1964.

Long, Clarence. "*Nuclear Proliferation: Can Congress Act in June*?" International Security (Spring 1977): pp. 52-76.

McMohan Robert "Food As Diplomatic Weapon: The India Wheat Loan of 1951" *Pacific Historical Review* (August 1987): pp. 349-377.

________*United States Cold War Strategy om South Asia: Making a Military Commitment to Pakistan, 1974-1954*". Journal of American History 75 (December 1988): pp. 815-822.

________"*The Evolution of American Geopolitical Strategy and India 1947-1963*". Papers presented at India International Center, Indo-U.S. Relations Conference, 7-10 January 1991.

Merrill Denis. "*Indo-American Relations, 1947-1950: A missed opportunity in Asia.*" *Diplomatic History*, 11 (Summer 1987): pp. 203-226.

Mukherjee Dilip. "U.S. weapons for India," *Asian Survey* 27 (June 1987): pp. 595-614.

Nayar, Baldev Raj, "*Treat India Seriously*" *Foreign Policy*, No. 18 (Spring 1975).

Nehru Jawaharlal: "Changing India" *Foreign Affairs* 41 (April 1963): pp. 453-65.

________"India's Demand and England's Answer," Atlantic, 165 (April 1940): pp. 449-55.

________"Unity of India". Foreign Affairs, 16 January 1938, pp. 231-43.

Noorani, A.G. "Foreign Policy of the Janta Party Government," *Asian Affairs* 5 (March/April 1978): pp. 216-228.

________"India's Foreign Policy". *Asian Affairs* (March/April 1979): pp. 231-42.

_________"Indo-U.S. Nuclear Relations," *Asian Survey* 21 (April 1981): pp. 399-416.

Power, Paul. "The Indo-American Nuclear Controversy," *Asian Survey* 19, (June 1979): 547-96.

Ram, N. "India's Nuclear Policy: A Case Study in Flaws and Futility of non-proliferation" 2-4 April 182 Annual meeting of the Association of Asian Studies, Chicago."

Rao, R.V. Chandra Sekhara: "*Searching for a Mature Relationship The Round Table* No. 263 (July 1976): pp. 249-60.

Seth, S.P. "*The Indo-Pak Nuclear Duet and the United States*" Asian Survey 28 (July 1988). pp. 711-28.

Singh S. Nihal. "Can the U.S. and India Be Real Friends?" *Asian Survey* 23 (September 1983) pp. 1011-24.

Stegler, Kurt "Communism and Colonial Evolution: John Foster Dulle's, Vision of India and Pakistan "*Journal of South Asian and Middle Eastern Studies* 15 (Winter 1991): pp. 68-69.

Tanham, George, "Indian Strategic Culture." *The Washington Quarterly* (Winter 1952): pp. 12-41.

Thorton, Thomas Perry. "American Interest in India under Corter and Reagan", *SAIS Review* 5 (Winter-Spring 1985): pp. 179-199.

_________"The New Phase in U.S.-Pakistan Relations". *Foreign Affairs* 68, No. 3 (Summer 1989): pp. 142-159.

_________"The United States and India: The Political Relationship," Paper delivered at the U.S.-India Bilateral Forum, New Delhi. February, 1988.

Thomas, Raju G.C. "*Prospects for Indc-U.S. Security Ties.*" Orbis 27 (Summer 1983): pp. 371-92.

________"Strategic Relationship in South Asia: Differences in the Indian and American Perspectives". *Asian Survey* 21 (July 1981): 689-709.

________"U.S. Transfers of `Duel Use' Technologies to India," *Asian Survey* 30 (Septermber 1990): pp. 825-45.

Thurston, Raymond L. "United States Relations with the Government of India," *Middle East Journal* 1, no. 3; pp. 292-306.

Van Hollen, Christopper. "The Tilt Revisited: Nixon-Kissinger Geopolitics and South Asia." *Asian Survey* 20 (April 1980): pp. 339-61.

Van Pragh, David. "India After the Elections," *Asian Affairs* 7 (March/April 1980): pp. 218-32.

Winsing, Robert G. "Arms Race in South Asia: Implications for the United States", *Asian Survey* 25 (March 1985), pp. 265-91.

Index

D

E

F

N

Q

R

V

❑❑❑